ENCYCLOPEDIA OF THE
Animal World

Vol 11   Hoopoe—Kittiwake

Bay Books Sydney

A hoopoe with its crest lowered.

HOOPOE *Upupa epops,* a pink-buff and black-and-white striped bird in its own family, Upupidae, widely distributed in warmer parts of the Old World (see also Wood hoopoe). Throughout their range, the four races of the hoopoe, which differ only in slight variations of size and shade, cannot be mistaken for any other bird. Because they are handsome and striking and frequent gardens, lawns and parks near human habitation and are not particularly shy, they are well-known and liked. They feature widely in folklore and mythology, receive mention in the Old Testament and formed an Egyptian hieroglyph. Hoopoes are 10–12 in (25–30 cm) long, with a body about the size and proportions of a dove. They have a slender decurved bill set on a small head, but the most diagnostic feature is a large fan-shaped crest, rich buff with a black tip, which can be sleeked down on the crown or raised fore and aft. The crest, which is generally depressed, is erected when the bird is at all

excited and alone suffices to identify the hoopoe, but the rest of the plumage renders it equally unmistakable. Head, neck, back and breast are pinkish-buff, richer above and paler below, and the wings and tail are broadly barred black and white. This feature is particularly striking when the bird flies, for the flight on rounded wings is slow and undulating, with the irregular flicking action of a butterfly, and this seems to enhance the pied-pattern of the wings and tail.

Hoopoes are not sociable, except sometimes during migration, and the sexes are similar. For their small size, their gait is stately, and they walk over lawns, gardens and arable land probing in search of the insects, larvae, spiders and worms which comprise their diet. Occasionally small vertebrates, such as young lizards, are taken too. Although they spend much time on the ground, hoopoes roost in trees, and often nest in tree-holes.

In several languages including English

this bird's vernacular names are onomatopoeic, imitating its far-carrying but soft, dove-like, trisyllabic call 'poo-hoo-hoo'. The systematic name is derived from Pliny's Latin *upupa* and Aristophanes' Greek *epops*, both onomatopoeic.

The breeding range of hoopoes embraces all of Europe except Scandinavia, Finland and Britain, although they have nested sporadically in most of these countries and have occurred as drifted migrants as far off-course as Iceland. From Europe they range across Asia to the Pacific, but are summer visitors only to these latitudes, wintering in Africa and southern Asia. In addition there are breeding populations of hoopoes throughout Africa, occurring everywhere except desert, highland and forest, and in India. They too are migratory: *U. e. senegalensis* of the northern tropics of Africa migrates north and south within the savannahs in time with the European hoopoes; and *U. e. africanus* of southern Africa and *U. e. ceylonensis* of Ceylon and southern India are also migratory.

The nest is always a natural cavity—in a tree, wall, the ground or a termite hill—and is seldom lined. Four to six or more immaculate pale blue or brown eggs are laid. The nest becomes foul as it is not cleaned in any way. FAMILY: Upupidae, ORDER: Coraciiformes, CLASS: Aves.   C.H.F.

HOPPER, a term applied to various groups of invertebrate animals, notably certain crustaceans and insects. Members of the crustacean order Amphipoda which live a semi-terrestrial existence on the shore between watermarks are often known as sandhoppers or Beach fleas. Among insects, the young active stages, or nymphs, of grasshoppers and locusts are frequently referred to as 'hoppers'. The Hemiptera, or true bugs, includes three families of jumping insects, namely the Frog hoppers, Tree hoppers and Leaf hoppers. The term is used in a general way to identify these groups of arthropods, all of which progress by a leaping form of locomotion. See Amphipoda, locusts, Frog hoppers, Leaf hoppers, Tree hoppers. PHYLUM: Arthropoda.

HORMONES, chemical messengers secreted directly into the blood stream by the *endocrine or ductless glands. They play an important role in regulating many physiological processes, including the mechanisms by which the animal adapts to environmental change, energy exchanges, growth and reproduction.

The function of hormones. The action of any particular hormone may often be described in terms of its effects both on metabolic processes and on structure, and thus the classification of hormones according to their roles is to some extent arbitrary. It is con-

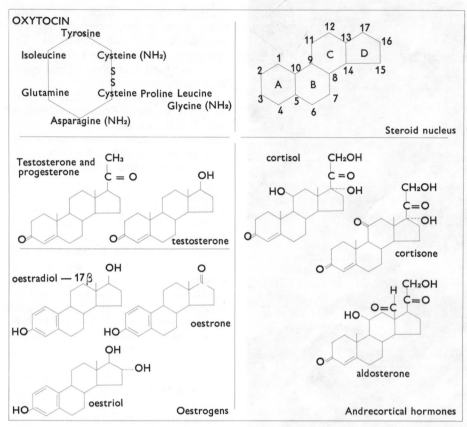

The chemical structure of some hormones.

venient to review the acuvity of hormones under four main categories: growth and metamorphosis, reproduction, metabolism and ionic balance.

Hormones in growth and metamorphosis. The post-natal growth of the bones and soft tissues of mammals is dependent on the growth hormone somatotrophin, of the pituitary. An excess of hormone during adolescence causes gigantism: an excess after the onset of maturity causes overgrowth and distortion of the skull and hands, a condition known as acromegaly. This disorder was described and shown to be associated with enlargement of the pituitary by Professor Pierre Marie in 1886, many years before the discovery of pituitary hormones.

Many developmental and post-embryonic changes require thyroid hormone. If the thyroid of infantile rats is inhibited by the use of goitre inducing substances, such as thiouracil, the growth and differentiation of the central nervous system and the development of reflexes is delayed. In man, the birth of deformed and idiotic children known as cretins is associated with hypothyroidism (diminished activity of the thyroid) of the mother. The condition was at one time common in limestone districts where the diet and water were deficient in the iodine necessary for production of thyroid hormone, and was described in the Salzburg region as early as 1603 by Paracelsus, who even pointed out that it was associated with goitre.

The role of thyroid in mammalian development has a striking counterpart in amphibians. By feeding thyroid hormone to frog tadpoles or simply by putting thyroxine into their water, they can be made to metamorphose into very small frogs long before the normal time; conversely, tadpoles with their thyroids removed do not metamorphose but continue growing to an abnormal size. Each of the various changes of metamorphosis: loss of horny teeth, growth of limbs, shortening of gut and reabsorption of tail, seems to be directly brought about by thyroid hormone. Indeed, isolated tails can be made to regress in culture, a process which seems analogous to a snake swallowing its own tail. Thyroxine can also affect metamorphosis of some, not all, Amphibia which, like the Mexican axolotl, normally remain and breed in the larval state.

Insects undergo a transformation or metamorphosis between larva and adult. Some forms (Hemimetabola) show a graded metamorphosis, with a succession of juvenile forms rather like the adult; others (Holometabola) have juvenile forms completely different from the adult. Moulting is initiated by a hormone of the neurosecretory cells of the brain, which in turn stimulates the thoracic glands to produce a moulting hormone called ecdysone. However, the degree of metamorphosis which occurs at each moult is regulated by another hormone, neotenin, secreted by the corpora allata.

Thus, if neotenin is present, a larval moult is the result; if the amout of neotenin is decreased, a pupa is formed and if neotenin is absent, an adult is produced. The secretion of the corpora allata may itself also be controlled by neurosecretory hormones from the brain.

Moulting in crustaceans is also hormonally controlled. But in most of these animals it seems that the eyestalks produce a hormone which inhibits rather than stimulates moulting. In polychaete worms a neurosecretion from the brain is necessary to permit the regeneration of posterior segments, for in headless worms regeneration does not occur when the tail is cut off, although it does so in worms which have kept their heads.

Hormones and reproduction. Animals are not capable of breeding throughout the whole span of their lives. The reproductive period is always preceded by a stage when the sexual organs are not fully developed and may, as in man, be succeeded by a stage during which the organs are degenerate. Even during the reproductive period most, but not all, mammals have definite breeding seasons. Moreover, during this breeding season individual females will only accept the male at certain times, when she is said to be in heat, or oestrus. In the absence of mating and fertilization, oestrus often recurs at intervals.

The length of the sexual cycle varies from mammal to mammal; it is, for example, about 28 days in man, 4–5 days in the rat or mouse, and 13–20 days in the Guinea pig. The domestic dog has a much longer cycle with periods of heat about every 5–8 months.

The sexual cycle involves a number of changes in the reproductive system. In humans, the most noticeable is the periodic breakdown and discharge of the uterine lining known as menstruation. But there are also detectable changes in the epithelium of the vagina, and both the uterine and vaginal changes are linked by hormonal mechanisms to a cycle of maturation and discharge of eggs from the ovaries. In each ovary, ova are formed in a spherical sac or follicle, and numbers of small follicles can be seen lying just below the germinal epithelium which surrounds the ovary. Groups of these follicles mature cyclically; in so doing the follicle ultimately enlarges rapidly due to the formation of a fluid-filled cavity or antrum. As a result, the ovum remains surrounded by a ball of cells known as the discus proligerus, and the follicle lined by a group of cells known as the membrana granulosa. The ovum – or rather the oocyte, since the final maturation division of the nucleus has not yet occurred – is released from the ovary by rupture of the follicle, and passes into the oviduct. In humans, ovulation most often occurs about 12–14 days after the start of the previous menstruation and it is at this stage that fertilization can occur. After ovulation the granulosa tissue hypertrophies to form a structure known as the corpus luteum.

As the follicle is growing, the uterine wall thickens and, as the ovum passes down the oviduct to the uterus, the uterine wall becomes vascular and glandular. These changes in the uterus are respectively brought about by two ovarian hormones: oestradiol which reaches the peak of production around ovulation time and progesterone which is secreted by the corpus luteum. Cyclic changes in the vaginal epithelium are also induced by oestradiol, and the shedding of cornified cells from the vaginal wall, a process easily detected in rodents or man by making a smear of the vaginal contents, is a useful biological test for oestrogens and, indeed, it made possible their isolation and chemical identification.

For the fertilized ovum to be implanted, progesterone is necessary. This was classically demonstrated by Ludwig Graenkel, who removed the corpora lutea from pregnant rabbits so that the pregnancies failed. However, the corpus luteum is not necessarily essential for the whole of pregnancy. In man, although the amounts of pregnanediol – a metabolite of progesterone – rise progressively during pregnancy, the concentrations of progesterone in the ovary reach a peak at three months and then decline. At this time the embryo becomes dependent on the placenta for progesterone instead of on the corpus luteum. The placenta also is responsible for producing large quantities of oestrogens.

The activity of the ovary both during the sexual cycle and during pregnancy, is dependent on gonadotrophins from the pituitary or from the placenta. The development of the ovarian follicle is induced by follicle stimulating hormone (FSH), ovulation and formation of the corpus luteum by luteinising hormone (LH). In some species, the rat for example, functional maintenance of the corpus luteum requires prolactin (or luteotrophin, LTH).

The placenta, also, produces a gonadotrophin in humans and probably in a number of other mammalian species. Human chorionic gonadotrophin (HGG) is a luteinizing hormone, and it reaches a peak of production at the third month of pregnancy. It appears, therefore, that it acts on the maternal corpus luteum during the phase before the placenta takes over the progesterone secreting function. Another gonadotrophin, known as PMS, appears in the serum of pregnant mares and is known to be secreted by cup-like areas of the uterus wall. Associated with its production is the formation of multiple secondary corpora lutea

within the maternal ovary.

The secretion of pituitary gonadotrophins is controlled by hypothalamic releasing factors, which are themselves subject to feedback control by steroid hormones. Ovulation, and hence conception, can thus be prevented if LH secretion is suppressed by the use of progesterone or its analogues. Contraceptive pills usually also contain oestrogens, which make lower doses of steroid effective.

The reproductive activity of invertebrate animals also is regulated by hormones. In most insects, for example, the corpora allata are essential for development of the ova, and in some insects the neurosecretory cells of the brain also play a part. In polychaete worms, sexual maturation is normally prevented by a hormone produced by the neurosecretory cells of the brain. Formation of sex cells is initiated by a fall in concentration of this juvenile hormone, though, oddly enough, it is not completed unless a small amount of hormone is present.

Hormones in metabolism. A number of hormones play a part in the control of metabolism. The importance of the pancreatic hormone, insulin, was emphasized in 1921 when Banting and Best first used it to treat the disease diabetes mellitus. This condition is caused by a failure of the insulin secreting tissue – the islets of Langerhans – of the pancreas. The result is that the normal utilization of glucose or its storage in the form of glycogen is prevented. Instead, fats and proteins are metabolized as sources of energy, and the incomplete oxidation of fat leads to the production of ketones which are excreted. The level of sugar in the blood and urine is greatly raised.

In addition to insulin, the pancreas produces another hormone, glucagon, which appears to promote the breakdown of glycogen. Carbohydrate metabolism is also affected by adrenocortical hormones such as cortisol and cortisone, which promote the formation of carbohydrates from protein. Adrenalin promotes the breakdown of glycogen to glucose in the liver, thus raising the blood sugar. Finally the thyroid hormone has an overall effect on the basal metabolic rate – the production of energy – by the body, though its points of action are not completely understood.

Hormones and Ionic Balance. In order to survive in changing external environments animals have evolved so-called homeostatic mechanisms to maintain constant internal conditions. Of particular importance is the maintenance of ionic balance in the body fluids, a process which is controlled by hormones.

Sodium, chloride and bicarbonate ions are important constituents of the blood tissue fluids, whereas cells are rich in potassium. Normally sodium and chloride are

selectively retained by the kidney at the same time as unwanted metabolites are excreted. When mammals are adrenalectomized, that is, they have their adrenals removed, they become unable to retain sodium, even if the intake of salt is increased. In consequence, there is a fall in the concentration of sodium, chloride and bicarbonate ions in the blood with a consequent increase in acidity, and at the same time potassium leaks out of cells. The administration of mineralocorticoids, such as aldosterone, restores the ionic balance and reduces the acidity of the blood. Another major factor in the regulation of ionic balance is the secretion of a neurohypophysial factor, vasopressin or antidiuretic hormone (ADH), which prevents fluid loss by the kidney. The exact interrelationships between hypothalamic, pituitary and adrenal factors which regulate ionic balance are complicated and incompletely understood.

The mode of action of hormones. It is uncertain how hormones produce their action at a cellular level in their target organs. There is evidence that hormones may become attached to proteins, lipids or nucleic acids, but usually no criteria by which their primary action can be established.

Many hormones can be shown to become attached to proteins. For example, cortisol not only becomes bound to blood proteins but is also taken up in tissue, particularly in the liver. If such a protein formed part of a membrane, an attachment of a steroid could alter permeability. An effect on the permeability of cell membranes could certainly result by the attachment of steroid hormones to the orientated lipid layers which make them up. Thus it has been proposed that the activity of steroid hormones depends on which side groups are exposed when the nucleus of the steroid becomes embedded.

The view that hormones can act in the cell by switching on or off the instructions which emanate from the deoxyribonucleic acid (*DNA) of the chromosomes is an attractive theory. It has, for example, been shown that in their action on uterine cells, oestrogens increase both ribonucleic acid (RNA) and protein synthesis and that this can be prevented by actinomycin, which is known to be a specific block to the formation of messenger ribonucleic acid (RNA). Striking evidence that hormones may affect the chromosomal DNA comes from insects. Midge larvae have very large banded chromosomes (so-called polytene chromosomes). The deeply staining bands are considered to be the regions which are most rich in DNA. Many of the bands appear 'puffed' or expanded, and these puffs are the sites of synthesis of RNA – a visible sign of gene activity. Injection of moulting hormone – ecdysone – into the mid-larval stages of a

midge induces a sequence of puffing in the giant chromosomes within about 30 minutes. This has been cited as evidence that the ecdysone acts directly on the genes. But the action could, of course, be equally well explained if the hormone altered the permeability of the cell or of its organelles to allow movement of other materials which might alter gene action.

Chemical nature of hormones. Hormones fall into a number of chemical categories, but the most important are polypeptides and steroids. Polypeptide hormones are produced by the hypothalamo-hypophysial system (=pituitary), the pancreas, and the parathyroids of vertebrates, and probably also by the neurosecretory systems of crustaceans and insects. Steroids are produced by the adrenal cortex and the sex organs of vertebrates, though their synthesis may well be completed in other tissues. A steroid, ecdysone is produced by the insect thoracic glands.

The simplest active polypeptides are those, such as oxytocin, which are stored by and released from the posterior pituitary. Oxytocin, which is found in all vertebrates from fish to mammals, consists of eight amino acids. Five of these are in a ring – of which a single acid cystine itself comprises two molecules of cysteine joined by two sulphur bonds, and three are in a side chain. In mammals, oxytocin causes contraction of the smooth muscles of the uterus and also causes milk ejection, being rapidly released from the pituitary in response to suckling. Among several other neurohypophysial octapeptide hormones is vasopressin, which raises blood pressure.

The melanocyte-stimulating hormones (MSH) of the intermediate lobe of the pituitary have rather larger molecules. From the pig, for example, two such substances, α–MSH and β–MSH, have been isolated having respectively 13 and 18 amino acid units. The adrenocorticotrophic hormone (ACTH) has 39 units. The hypothalamic releasing factors are probably also polypeptides of small or moderate size. For example, it seems probable that there are two corticotrophin releasing factors; one is an analogue of α–MSH and the other of vasopressin. Of the larger polypeptides, growth hormone is best characterized. Ox growth hormone is composed of 416 amino units and has a molecular weight of about 45,000. Lactogenic hormone (LTH) has a molecular weight of about 30,000 and thyrotrophic hormone (TSH) of less than 10,000. TSH contains carbohydrates as well as amino acids it is thus known as a glycoprotein. The gonadotrophic hormones (FSH and LH) are also glycoproteins of large molecular weight.

Steroids are a class of compounds having a nucleus of 17 carbon atoms arrayed in four rings, three six membered and one five membered, fused together so that some of the carbons are shared. There are several major types of hormonal steroids.

Testosterone (male hormone) and progesterone (pregnancy hormone) each have two methyl groups, containing carbons 18 and 19, in the angles between the rings. Progesterone also has two additional carbons (20 and 21) attached to carbon 17.

Naturally occurring oestrogens lack the methyl group at carbon 19 and have a hydroxyl (–OH) group at position 3. These include oestradiol–173, the hormone produced by the ovary of mammals, and oestrone and oestriol, excreted during pregnancy.

Adrenocortical steroids such as cortisol, cortisone and aldosterone all have 21 carbon atoms. Other important steroid hormones are ecdysone of insects and a similar substance, crustecdysone, which controls moulting of Crustacea.

The hormones of the thyroid and the adrenal medulla do not fall into the above categories. The molecule of thyroxine, or tetraiodiothyronin, contains four atoms of iodine; it is synthesized from the amino acid tyrosine and is a relatively simple compound. The hormones of the adrenal medulla, adrenalin and noradrenalin, are amino derivatives of catechol.   J.E.

HORMONES AND BEHAVIOUR. The influence of hormones on behaviour is undeniable, but the way they act is often debatable and, especially in man, it is frequently difficult to disengage their role from that of other determinants. With these reservations, it is possible to say that hormones exercise profound effects on sexual, parental and social behaviour.

Whereas in fishes and amphibians the mating behaviour of the female is a passive response, this is not so in birds and mammals. In mammals especially, the female usually exhibits so-called oestrous behaviour, which includes some form of presentation to the male, male-like mounting of other animals and in some species, such as the rat, increased running activity. Oestrus behaviour is abolished by removal of the ovaries. The response can be restored by giving an oestrogenic hormone in combin-

The Black hornbill, of Malaya, Sumatra and Borneo.

A Yellow-billed hornbill *Lophoceros flavirostris* in the Kruger Park, South Africa.

ation with a small amount of progesterone. When ovariectomized female Rhesus monkeys are given oestradiol subcutaneously they make more sexual invitations and the males respond. But if the oestrogen is given intravaginally, the males are aroused while the females remain unreceptive. Thus it seems that male arousal is produced by a sex-attracting substance or *pheromone produced by the female vagina, whereas female receptiveness requires a systemic action of oestrogen on the nervous system.

Male hormones are necessary for the sexual behaviour of the male. In male mammals, sexual performance is reduced after castration and can be restored by giving testosterone. The effect of castration is not, however, immediate; in many animals limited copulatory activity continues for a period. It seems possible that the male hormone brings about a relatively enduring state in the nervous system; once sensitized it remains excitable after the stimulus is withdrawn.

Parental behaviour involves the interactions of several hormones. In birds for example, the principal physiological instigator of nest-building is an oestrogenic hormone. Ovulation, as in mammals, is under the control of gonadotrophic hormones from the pituitary, and the actual laying of the eggs involves activity of the posterior pituitary. Incubation behaviour—broodiness—seems to depend upon the production of prolactin by the pituitary. However, non-laying hens and male birds do not incubate when injected with prolactin, so clearly the effect of prolactin depends on the presence of a female gonadal hormone or hormones.

In view of the close relation between the reproductive state and social behaviour in birds and mammals, it is not surprising that social behaviour is affected by sex hormones. Agonistic behaviour, comprising the aggressive and submissive acts that are concerned with the establishment of social hierarchies and the occupation of territory, is influenced in this way. In most vertebrates, males are more aggressive than females. Such aggressiveness, which increases at maturation and during the breeding season, can be reduced by castration and increased by administration of male hormone. Experiments on Swordtail fishes and on chickens, have recorded that advancement of rank can be brought about by treatment with androgen, but results from mammals have not led to consistent conclusions.

The steroids of the reproductive organs are not the only hormones concerned with aggressive behaviour. The adrenal cortex also plays a part. Fear and rage are associated with an increased output of the medullary hormones, adrenalin and noradrenalin, but it is not clear how far the hormones cause the emotional state and how far their secretion results from it. It is generally agreed that adrenocortical hormones, also, are concerned with fitting the animal for fight or flight. Finally it should be mentioned that the thyroid gland also influences emotional states and behaviour. In man, an excess of thyroid causes agitation and a deficiency results in torpor.   F.J.G.E.

HORNBILLS, an Old World family of birds

with large, brightly-coloured bills. The hoopoes are the closest relatives of hornbills and the two groups have sometimes been classified together in the suborder Upupae. The hornbills are divided into two subfamilies: the Bucoracinae, which includes the two mainly terrestrial African Ground hornbills (*Bucorvus*) and the Bucerotinae of rather more than 40 mainly arboreal species. Hornbills are not closely related to the superficially similar toucans (Ramphastidae) of the New World.

Hornbills are characterized by a relatively large bill which is usually surmounted by a large decorative casque from which their name is derived. Both bill and casque are often brightly coloured while the bill itself may be ridged and grooved. The casque is sometimes enormous and reaches its extreme development in males of the Black-casqued hornbill *Ceratogymna atrata* of West Africa, the Great hornbill *Buceros bicornis* of India and much of Southeast Asia and the Rhinoceros hornbill *B. rhinoceros* of Malaya, Sumatra, Java and Borneo. The general effect is of being unwieldy and top-heavy, although the casque is very light, being composed of a thin outer covering of horn which is filled with a sponge-like cellular tissue. An exception to this rule is the Helmeted hornbill *Rhinoplax vigil* of Malaya, Sumatra and Borneo. It has a solid casque, with the consistency of ivory, red on the outside but golden inside. After being specially processed this is known as hornbill ivory, or *ho-ting* to the Chinese who, in ancient times, valued it more than jade or ivory.

Many hornbills have brightly coloured patches of bare skin on the throat and around

Southern ground hornbill *Bucorvus cafer.*

the eyes. The most common colours are blue, red and yellow and the colours may differ between the sexes. In addition, the Black-casqued hornbill and the Yellow-casqued hornbill *Ceratogymna elata,* both of West Africa, have bright, cobalt blue neck wattles. Another rather bizarre peculiarity of hornbills is their eyelashes which are long, thick, black and curly and quite as attractive as the false variety worn by some women. Most species also have a distinct and rather hairy crest. The plumage of hornbills tends to be boldly patterned in black or brown and white. The sexes are usually similar in general appearance, although the casque is often bigger and more brightly coloured in the male.

Hornbills vary greatly in size ranging from the 15 in (38 cm) long Red-billed dwarf hornbill *Tockus camurus* of West African forests to the turkey-sized Ground hornbills of African savannahs and the 4 ft (1·3 m) Great hornbill of Asian forests. Most species have rather thick tarsi while the toes are broad-soled, the three that point forwards being partially united to form a pad. The two Ground hornbills have much longer and thicker tarsi, clearly an adaptation to their terrestrial habits. The flight of the larger species is rather slow and laboured, consisting of a series of wing beats followed by a glide. In the smaller species flight is light and swooping, the tail appearing disproportionately long and cumbersome. The larger species are remarkable for the great rushing noise their wings make. This noise is said to be caused, or at least accentuated, by the lack of feathers covering the bases of the flight feathers which allows air to rush between them.

Hornbills are distributed almost throughout the Old World tropics: 25 species occur in Africa, although there is none in Madagascar, while the remaining 20 species occur across southern Asia from India through Burma, Thailand, Indo-China, Malaya, the Greater and Lesser Sunda Islands and Celebes to the Philippines and New Guinea, but not Australia. They occupy a variety of habitats ranging from rain-forest to grassland with scattered trees. The presence of at least some trees is essential as hornbills are dependent upon hollow trees for nest sites, although the Ground hornbills occasionally make use of holes in cliffs. It is probable that the range of some species is restricted by the absence of sufficiently large hollow trees in areas that would otherwise be ecologically suitable.

The breeding behaviour of hornbills is even more remarkable than their appearance because the females of all species except the Ground hornbills are walled into the nest chamber during incubation, presumably as a defence against predators, and are fed by the males. The wall, which blocks the entrance to the nest hole, is built by the female with her own droppings which are viscid at first but harden on exposure to air. In some species the male assists by bringing pellets of clay mixed with saliva. When the wall is completed there remains only a narrow slit just large enough to allow the male to feed the female. The female of Von der Decken's hornbill *Tockus deckeni,* and presumably the females of other *Tockus* species, breaks out of the nest hole when the young are two to three weeks old and about half-grown, and thereafter helps the male to feed them. It is particularly remarkable that the young replaster the hole after the female has departed. The young, usually two to four, are fed on insects which are brought one or two at a time. Presumably the male is unable to find sufficient food to feed the female as well as several young once the latter are half-grown. On the other hand, the females of many other species, for example the Silvery-cheeked hornbill *Bycanistes brevis,* remain in the nest until the young fledge. This hornbill feeds its young on fruit and the male is obviously capable of bringing sufficient to feed the female as well as the one or two young for the whole of the fledging period. However, the fledging period is longer in *Bycanistes* species than in *Tockus* species and this may be related to the fact that fruit is a less satisfactory food than insects for growing young.

The female hornbill's long sojourn in the nest raises problems of nest sanitation. This has been solved by her defaecating at high velocity through the narrow entrance slit. It is not clear at what age the young become capable of this performance. Fruit stones are cast out of the nest hole and scavenging insects take care of any remaining refuse. While in the nest the female usually, though not invariably, undergoes a complete moult and may indeed become temporarily flightless although this is no disadvantage in her prison. Only the Ground hornbills, which do not wall up the nest cavity, follow the more normal procedure of moulting after breeding.

Hornbills are extremely catholic in their feeding habits. Most species consume fruit when it is available but otherwise eat almost any animal which they can overpower. Even small birds and bats are readily taken, while poisonous animals make up a high proportion of the animal diet of at least a number of the Asian species. A number of hornbills, such as the White-crested hornbill *Tropicranus albocristatus* which lives below the continuous canopy of rain-forest where fruit is scarce, eat little else but insects. Indeed, the White-crested hornbill regularly catches insects in flight.

Hornbills are exceedingly dextrous in the way they manipulate objects with the bill. Combined with the length of the bill this is of great importance in dealing with small poisonous animals. Snakes, centipedes and scorpions are caught and held in the very tip of the bill, and repeatedly squeezed along their whole length as they are manipulated backwards and forwards. As each end of the animal is reached, be it head or tail, it is given a particularly vigorous squeeze, the process being repeated many times, depending on the size and hardness of the animal. The value of this behaviour is clear; it ensures that the dangerous part of the animal – the head of the snake or centipede, or the tail of the scorpion – is completely crushed. Free-flying tame Rhinoceros hornbills, Wreathed hornbills *Aceros undulatus* and Black hornbills *Anthracoceros malayanus* treated any long flexible object, such as a piece of rope, in precisely the same way and also spent much time playing with twigs and leaves, tossing them up in the air, catching them and passing them backwards and forwards in their bills. Such 'play' has also been observed in the wild in several species and can probably be regarded as practice for a feeding pattern that demands skill and precision. This ability to manipulate delicately is also related to their fruit-eating behaviour and hornbills are quite capable of peeling the unpalatable outer skin from a fruit using no more than their bills.

Hornbills are noisy and conspicuous birds and produce a great variety of whistling, cackling, grunting and roaring noises. They frequently form flocks and a number of species are known to form communal roosts of up to a 100 or more individuals during the non-breeding season. In tropical forests the habit of forming communal roosts seems to be confined to fruit-eating species. Hornbills congregate at these roosts from a large area and the following morning disperse in flocks to wherever fruit was found on the previous day. Probably communal roosting is a means of increasing the efficiency of exploitation of a food supply that tends to be patchily distributed but is very abundant where it does occur.

An important role is played in mythology and augury by hornbills wherever they occur. Two species that are particularly important in this respect are the White-thighed hornbill *Bycanistes albotibialis* of West Africa and the Rhinoceros hornbill of Borneo. They are also

regularly eaten in various places and their feathers are valued for headdresses and other decorative purposes. In the Sudan, hunters tie the stuffed heads of Ground hornbills to their heads when stalking game, the apparent presence of so wary a bird being reassuring to their quarry. FAMILY: Bucerotidae, ORDER: Coraciiformes, CLASS: Aves.
M.P.L.F.

HORNED FROGS, very distinct and bizarre frogs of the genus *Ceratophrys,* found in most of South America, east of the Andes, from Colombia to Argentina. Once seen, they are easily remembered and identified. They resemble toads (Bufonidae) and are very stocky, almost round when sitting with their legs tucked in. The legs, particularly the forelegs, are short and powerful. The most characteristic feature, however, is the large head with a blunt snout and very wide jaws. In most other tailless amphibians the head is dorso-ventrally compressed, leaving only a narrow space between the eye and the margin of the jaw. This space usually equals the diameter of the eye and is frequently much less in big-eyed frogs. In Horned frogs the head arches high. Although the eye is moderate in relation to the overall size, the distance between the eye and the jaw may equal two and a half to three times the diameter of the eye. It is this and the horizontal pupil that gives these frogs their peculiar facial expression and their unique appearance. The 'horns', for which the Horned frogs are named, are not present in all members of the genus nor are they found only within it. Similar structures are found in other species in unrelated families, usually in fairly large species. In some Horned frogs these soft extensions of the upper eyelid are well developed, pointed, and may even curve slightly from their own weight. In other species they are rounder, little more than a heavy brow, while in some they may be absent altogether. Horns or no horns, however, there is no mistaking a Horned frog.

The function of the horns and their advantage to the bearer is a matter for speculation. They are soft, therefore useless for defence. They may shade the eye or camouflage it by breaking the circular outline, or afford some protection from injury to the eyeball. They may be purely decorative and enhance the bearer's appearance to the opposite sex, although this is doubtful, or they may make the individual look larger and more formidable to an aggressor, including other Horned frogs. Horned frogs are cannibalistic so discouraging predation by a fellow Horned frog may have definite survival value.

Different species of Horned frogs vary greatly in adult size. The smallest are little larger than a bottle cap; the largest would

Male of Von der Decken's hornbill, of Africa. The female's bill is all-black.
A Horned frog *Ceratophrys dorsata*, of South America, looking more like a toad.

nicely fill a large soup bowl. They have a toad-like warty skin. Many species have a bold pattern of blotches or bars and some are vividly coloured. There are anatomical features that are apparent only when the skeleton is examined. Some species have a bony shield under the skin which protects the head and back. They also have teeth in the upper jaw.

Horned frogs live well in captivity. Because of their colourful patterns and peculiar expression, they are impressive and the larger species in particular are desirable amphibian exhibits. Usually they sit partially buried in the earth in their terrarium. Unlike many other frogs, they are unlikely to damage their noses by leaping against the walls. They are unafraid; instead, when annoyed, they may attack and bite ferociously and can inflict a painful wound with their long teeth. This aggressiveness is well known in their native lands and inspires the belief that the bite is venomous. This is not so, however, and after some time in captivity they become tame and can be handled safely. They feed readily on frogs and mice which they easily subdue and stuff into their capacious mouths with their stout forelimbs.

Reproduction takes place in the typical frog manner, with the male grasping the female from behind with his forelegs. Several hundred eggs in a clear jelly-like mass are deposited. FAMILY: Leptodactylidae, ORDER: Anura, CLASS: Amphibia.   E.L.J.

HORNED POUTS, a family of freshwater North American catfishes. Included in this family are the madtoms which have a long adipose fin, sometimes confluent with the tail. Members of this family are found from Canada to Mexico, some species preferring the slow warm waters of the Southern States while others inhabit the cold trout streams of the north.

One of the best known species is the Channel catfish *Ictalurus punctatus,* originally from the St Lawrence basin but now introduced into almost every American state, and at least four of the Hawaiian islands. This fish is generally pale grey with a few distinct dark spots on the sides, although the general colour may vary with the kind of water in which the fish is living. The Channel catfish reaches over 50 lb (22·7 kg) in weight and makes good eating. The results of marking experiments have shown that in spite of their appearance, these are not really sluggish fishes and in one case an individual travelled 46 miles (74 km) in 45 days. These fishes migrate upstream or into the feeder streams of lakes during May and June in search of breeding places in undercut banks or in hollows. The male cleans the site and the female lays 2–3,000 eggs which stick together in a yellow, jelly-like clump. The male then guards the eggs and constantly aerates them until they hatch. Thereafter his duties are those of a sheep-dog, keeping the shoal of young together until they are old enough to fend for themselves. The Channel catfish is fished commercially and artificial rearing is practised to increase stocks.

The Flathead catfish *Pylodictis olivaris* inhabits sluggish waters chiefly in the central and southern parts of the United States. The wide flat head, coupled with the underslung jaw, make this species easily to identify. It occasionally reaches 100 lb (45 kg) in weight.

The largest member of the family is the Blue catfish *Ictalurus furcatus* which ranges from South Dakota and Iowa to Mexico. Superficially it resembles the Channel catfish but it lacks the spots on the flanks and the body is much bluer. In the last century a fish weighing 150 lb (68 kg) was recorded from the Mississippi at St Louis. The record weight by fair angling is 102 lb (46·2 kg), a fish from Kentucky Lake.

The White catfish *I. catus* is found in the east and central parts of the United States but has been introduced into other waters. It grows to only 12 lb (5·4 kg) and unlike the previous species is also found in estuaries. The Brown, Black and Yellow bullheads *I. nebulosus, I. melas* and *I. natalis* rarely exceed 1 ft (30 cm) in length. They are all amenable to life in aquaria and the Brown bullhead has for some time been imported into England as the Cold-water catfish. FAMILY: Ictaluridae, ORDER: Cypriniformes, CLASS: Pisces.

HORNED TOAD, the confusing common name of the iguanid lizard genus *Phryno-soma,* which is preferably known as the Horned lizard. Horned 'toads', which are very widespread in North America and Mexico, have short, flattened bodies armed with spines.

Typical species are small, about 3–4 in (7·5–10 cm), with a very short tail and have long hard spines on the head. The general appearance is somewhat toad-like. They have the odd habit of squirting thin jets of blood from the eyes, which is believed to constitute a passive defence mechanism. This behaviour is, however, sporadic and some people who know these reptiles well have never seen it happen. FAMILY: Iguanidae, ORDER: Squamata, CLASS: Reptilia.

HORNED TOAD AND OTHER BLOOD SQUIRTERS. The ejection of blood from the eyes of Horned toads is something of a mystery as not every individual performs and its function is a matter of speculation. This habit is not unique to Horned toads, being also found in the Dwarf boas *Tropidophis* of the West Indies and in a north African Bush cricket *Eugaster guyoni.* The Dwarf boas squirt or dribble blood from their mouths and as little is known about the function of the habit as it is in Horned toads. The Bush cricket squirts blood from pores at the bases of the front and middle legs. Apparently it squirts blood at its enemies and has a range of 2 ft (60 cm).

Also called a Horned frog, *Megophrys nasuta* lives in India and belongs to the family Pelobatidae.

The Horned toad, really a lizard of the genus *Phrynosoma*.

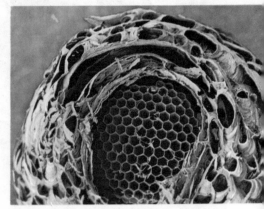

Nest of the hornet *Vespa crabro*.

HORNETS, wasps that construct a large, globular nest of papery material. Originally the name was given to the European *Vespa crabro* which has been introduced to America, but it has been applied to many large wasps, such as the American *Dolichovespula*. Unlike many of the commoner wasps, which nest underground, the hornets build their home in trees or in human dwellings attached to rafters or the underside of the eaves. The nest is constructed of a series of horizontal combs, each comb lying parallel to its neighbours above and below it, and connected by a central spindle made of toughened paper; the whole structure is enclosed in a paper shell. Each comb consists of a cluster of cells in which the young are reared, and the entrance to each cell is closed by a wafer-thin paper seal. When the adult stage is reached, it bites through this delicate envelope and emerges. The papery material used in the construction of the nest is manufactured from woody plant material chewed by the hornets and mixed with saliva until it is transformed into a soft pulp. The outer paper shell which envelops the nest serves to protect the combs and their occupants from the weather.

In some countries, notably the warmer parts of the Americas, hornets are treated with a considerable amount of fear and respect on account of their painful stings and their habit of congregating around human dwellings. The popular remedy for removing hornets by burning down their nests is not always successful. FAMILY: Vespidae, ORDER: Hymenoptera, CLASS: Insecta, PHYLUM: Arthropoda. J.A.W.

HORN SHARKS, also known as Bullhead sharks, primitive fishes found in warm and temperate seas throughout the world except in the Atlantic and Mediterrenean. The head is large and rather blunt and there are two dorsal fins, each preceded by a spine; tissue surrounding the spines secretes a venom capable of causing considerable pain. The suspension of the jaws shows an arrangement intermediate between that found in most sharks and that found in the Cow sharks, the upper jaw fitting into a deep groove in the cranium and thus hinting at the condition found in the chimaeras and lungfishes where the upper jaw is completely fused with the head. An equally important, but more easily seen, characteristic of the Horn sharks is the curious arrangement of the teeth, with sharp cutting teeth in the front of the jaws and blunt molar-like teeth towards the edges. This pattern is virtually unique amongst living sharks but is found in the fossil hybodonts of the Jurassic period. The two best known species are the Port Jackson shark *Heterodontus phillippi* and the Pacific Horn shark *H. californicus,* the first from Australia and the second from the Pacific coast of North America. These fishes feed on molluscs and crustaceans and reach about 4 ft (1·2 m) in length. The Horn sharks are oviparous, laying eggs in cases that are decorated with curious spiral flanges quite unlike those of any other group. About ten species of Horn sharks are known. FAMILY: Heterodontidae, ORDER: Pleurotremata, CLASS: Chondrichthyes,

HORSE *Equus przewalskii.* Wild horses occurred, in prehistoric times, over most of the Eurasiatic continent and, as can be judged from the huge piles of bones near the dwellings of Stone Age cave men, in immense numbers. They survived until historic times in eastern Europe and in Siberia and Mongolia but are now on the verge of extinction. Wild horses have been exter-

Horn shark or Port Jackson shark showing arrangement of teeth in jaw and characteristic egg case.

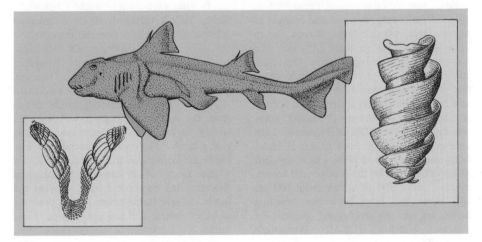

The Eastern wild horse or Przewalski's horse with characteristic upstanding mane.

minated by man because they damaged the crops and were competitors with the domestic stock for food and water.

Three subspecies are recognized: the Steppe tarpan *E. p. gmelini,* the Forest tarpan *E. p. silvaticus,* and the Eastern wild horse or Przewalski horse *E. p. przewalskii.* The domestic horse originates from these three wild horses and its scientific name is *E. przewalskii caballus.* It is, however, usually referred to as *E. caballus.*

The Steppe tarpan lived in the open steppe country of south-eastern Europe. They were grey animals with black manes and tails and with a dark line along their backs. They were finally exterminated in the 19th century.

The Forest tarpan was an animal of the wooded areas of western, central and eastern Europe, and only in the east did it survive the Middle Ages. Some small populations still existed, at the beginning of the last century, in the forests of Bialowieza and eastern Prussia. Forest tarpans were taller than the Steppe tarpan; they had a shoulder height of about 48 in (1·20 m).

The Przewalski horse inhabited the steppes and semideserts of southern Siberia, Mongolia and western China. In the wild they also are now probably extinct, although occasional resightings have been reported during the last few years from the Gobi desert on the Mongolian-Chinese frontier. It

is, however, doubtful that these animals are pure-blooded wild horses, as these are known to abduct domestic horse mares and to interbreed with them. Przewalski horses vary in colour from yellow-brown to reddish-brown and grey. Their legs are dark brown or black, the muzzle is whitish, and a brown line down the back is prominent in their summer coats. Mane and tail are black or dark brown; the mane is erect and bordered by lighter hair. The shoulder height is from 48 to 58 in (1·20 to 1·46 m) about the size of a pony.

The Przewalski horse was first described by Poliakow in 1881 and its discovery was quite unexpected by scientists. From 1899 to 1903 54 foals were captured and brought to a game farm, Askania Nova, Russia, and to various zoological gardens. All the wild horses still in captivity derive from this stock, with the exception of a few individuals that were caught later. Due to the efforts of interested scientists an international society for the conservation of the Przewalski horse was formed in 1958. One of its members, the eminent zoologist Dr Erna Mohr, of Hamburg, compiled a stud book which contains all important data on the captive wild horses, totalling about 300, of which about 100 are still alive. The most important breeding herds are in the zoological gardens of Prague, Catskill (USA), Whipsnade

(London), and Munich. The species has thus been saved from complete extinction and it can be hoped that it will be re-established in the wild.

Only a few observations have been made on the biology and behaviour of freeliving wild horses. They are reported to have lived in groups of 10 to 15, led and protected by a stallion. Stallions were seen fighting for mares. Colts were chased away from the group by the group stallion and they stayed solitary or joined up to form bachelor groups. Since the wild horse formed the stock from which the domestic horse is derived it can be assumed that their behaviour is identical.

Wild horses were domesticated in prehistoric times and probably all three subspecies were used to obtain this versatile companion of man, the domestic horse, which has been used as draught, riding, meat and milk animal. Domestication was started in Asia about 2,500 BC. Horses are first recorded by the Greeks, Babylonians, and Chinese around 2,000 BC. A thousand years later they were already used throughout most of Europe, Asia and northern Africa. Horses were, until modern times, and in contrast to all other domestic animals, a decisive factor in human history. At first they were used to pull war chariots, later, as stronger horses were bred, as riding horses. The empires of the Arabs and Mongolians were conquered by their cavalry, and horses were of primary importance in the wars of the Middle Ages. Later they were mainly used for transport and for farm and ranch work as they still are in many countries today, although their number is declining due to increasing mechanization. There is, however, no danger of the horse becoming completely replaced by machines. Horses are indispensable for specialized jobs, e.g. cattle ranching, and they are and will be widely used for entertainment and sports.

Horses are bred in many different races. They can be grouped as ponies, e.g. Exmoor, Dartmoor, Welsh, Shetland, New Forest, Iceland, Mongolian; heavy draught horses, e.g. Belgian, Percheron (France), Clydesdale, Shire, Suffolk (Britain), Rhine-Wesphalian (Germany); and light (weight) draught and riding horses, e.g. Barbs, Arabs, thoroughbreds, Lippizan, Trakenhnen, American Standardbred, Hunter, Hackney, Hanover. Barbs and Arabs originate from a northern African stock. The thoroughbreds derive from the Arabs and both have been used widely in breeding the light draught and riding horses. The ponies, especially the Icelands, are considered to be descendants of a Celtic stock of prehistoric British and Scandinavian domestic horses, whereas the heavy draught horses come from a breeding stock of central and western Europe. Feral horses are a mixture of various races. Most

of them are the descendants of escaped stock horses, and they are living in North and South America and in Australia. It is of particular interest that feral horses are doing well in North and South America where their ancestors died out only a few thousand years ago.

The behaviour of the domestic horse has been studied mainly in the New Forest, England, where a population of over 2,500 ponies leads a semi-wild existence. Unfortunately this population is controlled by man and most of the colts are caught and castrated and/or sold, so that the number of adult stallions is minimal compared with a natural population. The results gained from studying this population are, however, most valuable as they are the only conclusive ones obtained from the domestic horses. It can be assumed that they are valid for the species as a whole. Fighting, grooming and sexual behaviour are in general the same as in the other Equidae. The ponies associate in small groups of one to six mares and their offspring. The associations between adult mares are stable and last for years, whereas sub-adult animals leave their groups and join others. Stallions associate with a particular group of mares, but they also copulate with other mares if there is no other stallion. It is, however, known from undisturbed feral horse populations that one stallion is associated with each group of mares. A stable rank order exists in which the stallion is dominant. Each group occupies a defined home range, but home ranges of different groups overlap. This type of social organization with coherent, non-territorial families is practically identical with that of the two zebra species, the Plains and the Mountain zebra (*E. quagga* and *E. zebra*). FAMILY: Equidae, ORDER: Perissodactyla, CLASS: Mammalia.   H.K.

HORSE, DOMESTIC, the many breeds of which can be divided into two groups: light horses mainly used for riding and drawing light vehicles and heavy or draught horses used to draw heavily loaded carts or to do work on farms.

Among the riding horses the Arab is thought by many people to be the most beautiful of all. It has a very distinctive appearance, with a short back, small head, large eyes and sensitive nostrils, and slender legs with small rounded hoofs. It moves easily and gracefully with the tail carried high. The Arab has been crossed with other breeds to produce a very fast horse for racing with great powers of endurance. The swiftest of all these is the British Thoroughbred. In the American West the quarter horses, being one quarter thoroughbred, are widely used by cattlemen for rounding up. Among other light horses are the Hackney, an old local breed from the eastern counties

Disappearing rural scenes: a herd of domesticated horses in a field in Holland (above) and mare with foal.

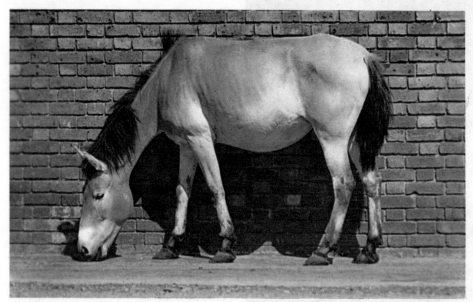

A hybrid between the last truly wild horse, Przewalski's horse and a domesticated horse as shown by the falling mane.

Shetland ponies, the smallest of the ponies.

of England, once much used as a coach-horse, and the American Standard Breed, the famous American trotting and pacing horse bred mainly for speed and now almost entirely confined to the race tracks.

The most important heavy draught horses are the Shire, Clydesdale, Suffolk, Belgian and Percheron, all of which have been exported to North America and other parts of the world. The Shire is a large horse said to be descended from the English war horses of the Middle Ages. The finest are over 17 hands high (a hand being 4 in (10 cm)) and weigh more than a ton. It has been used mainly for farm work and can pull a load of 5 tons. In spite of its enormous size it is a most docile horse. The Clydesdale, bred in Scotland since the 18th century, is the same height as the Shire but less massive and more active. It has a lot of white on its legs and sometimes on the underside of its body. Like the Shire it has a large amount of silky hair on its heels called 'feather'. It also has been used mainly on farms and for dray work in cities. The Suffolk, sometimes called the Suffolk Punch, originally came from the English county of Suffolk. It is always chestnut coloured with very short legs and a short strong neck. It stands $16\frac{1}{2}$ hands and is a good hardy farm horse, being very economical to keep as it works well on the minimum of food. The Belgian is a direct descendant of the old Flemish heavy horse and is an excellent horse for dray work. Finally, the Percheron which is a French breed which originally came from the area of Perché in northern France. This is one of the most

The walk is a pace of two-time (two hoof beats): 1. the off hind foot is lifted while the near front foot is in mid-step; 2. the off hind foot touches the ground as the near front foot is lifted; the near hind foot is lifted as the off front foot is in mid-step and so on.

The trot is a pace of two-time in which each diagonal pair of legs (near front and off hind and off front and near hind) touch the ground together. The speed of a trot is about 200 m a minute.

The gallop is a pace of four-time with four hoof beats in the sequence: near hind foot, off hind foot, near front, off front (or leading leg) or off hind, near hind, off front, near front (leading leg).

popular heavy draught horses being about the same size as the Suffolk but is always grey or black.

There is not much difference in appearance between horses and ponies except in their size, the small size of the ponies being due to the poor condition of their habitat, mainly the Mongolian and Manchurian deserts and Norwegian, Welsh and Scottish mountains. In most countries 15 hands is the limit for a full-grown pony. All true breeds of pony wherever they are found must be hardy, sure-footed and able to live on small amounts of poor food. They are usually more intelligent than horses apart from those of the Arab breed. Probably the best known and most important ponies of Europe are those found in the mountain and moorland regions of England, Scotland and Wales. There are nine distinct breeds including the Shetland, less than 9 hands and once much used as a pit pony, and the Welsh Mountain, less than 12 hands, a very old stock, said to be the most beautiful of the mountain and moorland group.

It is doubtful whether there are any true breeds of pony outside Europe, Asia and Africa. The 'cow' pony of the western parts of the United States and the Criollo of South America, although called ponies, are really horses.   M.B.

HORSE, FOSSILS. The fossil record of the horse family is so well documented that it provides one of the classic examples of evolutionary progress. The earliest animal which can be placed in the family was *Hyracotherium* from the early Eocene of both North America and Europe (the American genus was sometimes called *Eohippus*). This was a small animal, the size of a fox terrier, with three toes of equal size on each hindfoot, and four toes on the forefeet, closely resembling a tapir in this respect. Its teeth bore small cusps (i.e. were bunodont) and the upper premolars were much simpler in crown pattern than the molars, having only three main cusps instead of four. The fossil horses, *Orohippus* and *Epihippus,* from the Middle and Upper Eocene shows the gradual acquisition of the extra cusps on the premolars, so that in *Epihippus* both the third and fourth premolars were four-cusped teeth looking just like the molars behind them. This change in the premolars is called molarization. At the same time, the cusps changed shape somewhat, elongating into ridges called 'lophs'. In the fossil horses, *Mesohippus* and *Miohippus*, of the succeeding Oligocene period, molarization extended to the second premolars as well, and the extra toes of the front feet had been lost, so that all the feet were three-toed. There had also been some increase in size: *Mesohippus* was about the size of a collie. In *Parahippus* which lived in the early part of the succeeding Miocene the side toes were

more slender and shorter than the main central toes on each foot. The more or less contemporary *Anchitherium* was a similar animal which also had slender side toes, but these were not shorter than the central toe. It is of interest because, although not in the direct line of descent of the modern horse, it is one of the few members of the family which migrated from North America into Asia and Europe. *Parahippus* was the earliest of the fossil horses to show the presence of an extra substance, cement, as a component of the crown of the teeth, in addition to the enamel and dentine; in *Parahippus* the cement is sometimes absent, sometimes present, but the genus grades imperceptibly into *Merychippus* of the Middle and Upper Miocene in which, as in all later horses, cement is always present. The cement filled the depressions between the cusps, supporting them and allowing them to be taller, so also allowing heavier tooth wear. In *Merychippus* the surface pattern of the teeth was very similar to that of modern horses but the teeth themselves were very short-crowned (brachydont). *Merychippus* graded into *Pliohippus* of the succeeding Pliocene period, in which the cheek teeth were higher crowned (hypsodont) allowing it to eat grasses, which are very abrasive. The side toes of *Pliohippus* were very slender, and it often lacked the hooves; this dominance of the central toes was an adaptation to running on hard dry grasslands. The contemporary *Hipparion* had molar teeth somewhat more advanced than those of *Pliohippus*, but its feet were less advanced, retaining functional side toes as an adaptation to marshy ground. *Hipparion* is also of interest as another genus which penetrated into Asia and Europe, and at the same time fossil horses also migrated into Africa (*Stylohipparion*) and South America (*Hippidion, Onohippidium* and *Parahipparion*). Finally, at the end of the Pliocene, *Pliohippus* evolved into the modern horses *Equus* which have extremely hypsodont teeth, and only tiny splint bones representing the side toes. *Equus* was found throughout Asia, Europe, Africa, North and South America, but became extinct in the Americas at the end of the Pleistocene. FAMILY: Equidae, ORDER: Perissodactyla, CLASS: Mammalia. For diagram see equidae.   D.W.Y.

HORSE FLIES, so-called because they bite horses, as well as other warm-blooded animals, including man. The name is particularly applied to members of the genus *Tabanus,* which generally have clear wings, while species of *Chrysops,* with banded wings, are called Deer flies, and *Haematopota,* with speckled wings are called clegs or stouts. The eyes of Horse flies are brightly coloured in life: green, often with one to three purple bands in *Tabanus*; spotted in *Chrysops;* with zig-zag bands in *Haema-*

A Horse fly of the genus *Tabanus.*

topota. Only female Horse flies bite, piercing the skin and sucking blood by means of a proboscis formed from mandibles and maxillae. These are drawn out into blade-like stylets, ensheathed in a spongy labium, and it is the withdrawal of the stylets which causes the pain of the bite. The only disease known to be carried exclusively by Horse flies is *Loa loa,* a parasitic worm which affects monkeys and man in the African rain-forest and is transmitted by certain species of *Chrysops.* Diseases that are carried by Horse flies, among other agents, include tularaemia, a bacterial disease transmitted in North America by *Chrysops discalis,* and surra, a blood parasite (trypanosome) of camels and horses in the Middle and Far East, carried by several species of *Tabanus.* The importance of Horse flies as a pest of grazing animals lies mainly in the disturbance and pain of their bites.

Male Horse flies have no mandibles and do not bite. In this respect Horse flies resemble mosquitoes, Black flies and biting midges, and differ from the Tsetse flies and Stable flies, in which both sexes pierce and suck blood.

Tabanus, Chrysops and *Haematopota* seem to be genera of recent origin, and may perhaps have evolved along with the great herds of grazing mammals which arose in the Pliocene Period and of which the African game are the last survivors. Other Horse flies include *Pangonius* and related genera which have evolved a very long proboscis, by which both sexes can probe very deep blossoms, while the female often still has piercing mandibles and can suck blood. There are also many primitive Horse flies, especially in the southern hemisphere, which never take blood. Biting Horse flies occur all over the world, from the equator to the subarctic tundra, and may be a serious pest to travellers during the short arctic summer.

Horse flies lay eggs, usually on vegetation in or near water, and their larvae live in mud underwater, or in wet earth, including the wet debris that collects in rot-holes in trees, where a branch has broken off. The larvae of some genera, including most *Tabanus* and *Haematopota,* are carnivorous. They eat anything living: worms, other insect larvae, even larvae of their own species. A pupa is formed in drier mud near the water's edge. If males and females emerge together they may mate at once, but if males come out earlier than females they gather in mating swarms over the tops of hills and high trees. FAMILY: Tabanidae, ORDER: Diptera, CLASS: Insecta, PHYLUM: Arthropoda.

HORSEHAIR WORMS, or Thread worms, unusual animals closely related to the Round worms (Nematoda). Adult Horsehair worms, 4–40 in (10–100 cm) long but less than $\frac{1}{8}$ in (0·3 cm) across, live in the soil around ponds and streams. They lay their eggs in the water, attaching them to water plants. The larvae are parasitic and usually attack insects. One of the puzzles about their life cycle is that many of the insects acting as hosts for the Horsehair worm larvae are terrestrial not aquatic, for example, crickets, grasshoppers and cockroaches. It could be that these animals become infected by drinking water containing the larvae.

The development inside the host can take several months and the larvae usually leave the host insect when it is near water to lead a free existence in the moist soil. The adults probably do not feed. One of the commonest European Horsehair worms belongs to the genus *Gordius,* so named because the adults can often be found in tangled masses like the 'Gordian knot' cut by Alexander the Great. CLASS: Nematomorpha, PHYLUM: Aschelminthes.

HORSE MACKERELS, also known as scads, jacks, cavallas and pompanos, are not true mackerels (Scombridae) and are distinguished from them by two small spines before the anal fin and the absence of small finlets behind the dorsal and anal fins. The Horse mackerels are usually fast-swimming fishes, well streamlined, but in some species deep-bodied and compressed. The body has a line of little keeled scutes along part or the entire length of the flanks. They are found in temperate and tropical waters throughout the world.

The common Horse mackerel *Trachurus trachurus* of the Mediterranean and eastern North Atlantic grows to about 14 in (36 cm) and is found as far north as Trondheim in Norway. Similar forms are found off the coasts of South Africa, China, Australia and western America. It has a short first dorsal fin, with the first spine directed forwards, and a long second dorsal fin with soft rays. The back is grey-blue or green, the flanks silvery and there is a dark spot behind the gill opening. It feeds on fishes and invertebrates. The young take shelter in the bell of the Sombrero jellyfish *Cotylrhiza,* probably

Young of the Common horse mackerel in the Plymouth Aquarium.

for protection. The derbio or glaucus *Trachinotus ovatus* is a more southerly fish, rarely entering British waters. It is deeper-bodied than the Horse mackerel, the scutes are absent and the first dorsal fin is reduced to a number of isolated spines. Similar isolated spines are found in the leerfish *Lichia amia,* another species from the southerly parts of the Atlantic. Another member of this family is the Rainbow runner, described elsewhere. Amberjacks of the genus *Seriola* are large sporting fishes that can reach 5 ft (1·5 m) in length and are highly prized by sport fishermen. The Horse mackerels are of great importance to fisheries in many parts of the world.

Among the less typical members of this family are the thread-fin *Alectis ciliaris* with streaming filaments from the rays of the anterior dorsal and anal fins, the lookdownfish *Selene vomer* with a curious pointed head and the pilotfish which accompanies sharks. FAMILY: Carangidae, ORDER: Perciformes, CLASS: Pisces.

HORSESHOE CRABS, also called King crabs in North America, are relatively large marine arthropods, up to 2 ft (60 cm) in length, closely related to the extinct *Water scorpions (Eurypterida). Despite their common name they are not crustaceans and, of the various groups alive today, their closest affinities lie with the arachnids. They are placed with the latter in the subphylum Chelicerata, the members of which are characterized by the possession of dis-

tinctive pincer-like mouthparts, or chelicerae, and by the division of the body into two major regions, a cephalothorax, or prosoma, in front and a posterior abdomen, or opisthosoma.

These animals are easily recognized by their horseshoe shape due to the upper surface of the body being covered by a semicircular scoop-shaped plate, or carapace, fringed on the abdominal region with a series of short, stout movable spines, and terminating in a long tail spine which articulates with the posterior end of the abdomen. The mouth is situated on the underside of the

The underside of the Horseshoe crab showing the jointed legs usually hidden beneath the carapace.

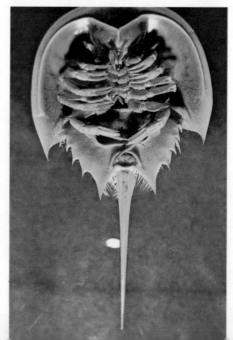

cephalothorax, almost in the centre, and is surrounded by the insertions of six pairs of appendages, namely a pair of chelicerae and five pairs of walking legs. The abdomen also carries on its underside six pairs of appendages in the form of flattened plates, the first pair being fused together as a genital operculum carrying the reproductive pores, and the remaining five pairs bearing leaf-like gills on their posterior faces.

In many of these respects, the Horseshoe crabs differ quite clearly from the arachnids and, furthermore, they possess a pair of compound eyes sited laterally on the prosomal carapace, in addition to a median pair of simple eyes; compound eyes are lacking in the arachnids.

Horseshoe crabs are carnivorous, preying on worms and molluscs. During their search for food they frequently burrow into soft sand and mud by pushing the scoop-shaped carapace into the substratum. The cephalothorax and the abdomen are hinged together so that the body can 'jack-knife', aided by the tail spine. By flexing and straightening in this way, additional thrust for burrowing can be obtained, and the animal often buries itself completely in the sand or mud. The usual method of locomotion is by walking, although small Horseshoe crabs can swim on their backs using the plate-like abdominal appendages as swimmerets.

These curious creatures are truly 'living fossils', for they have remained virtually unchanged for over 300 million years. The four species living today belong to three different genera, namely *Limulus polyphemus* of the Atlantic seaboard of North America and Mexico, *Tachypleus gigas* and *T. tridentatus,* and *Carcinoscorpius rotundicauda* of Southeast Asia. All of these forms live in shallow coastal waters and, within the limits of their distribution, are encountered frequently during the springtime when they come into the intertidal zone to mate and lay their eggs which are buried in a depression in the sand. The larvae hatching from these bear a close resemblance to the extinct *trilobites. In the Far East these animals are often collected for food, and boiled Horseshoe crab is considered something of a delicacy, although it is an acquired taste and often produces unpleasant reactions in those not used to eating them. In the United States the crabs are gathered during their breeding migrations and crushed for chicken food. ORDER: Xiphosura, CLASS: Merostomata PHYLUM: Arthropoda.   J.A.W.

HOUNDS, also known as Smooth hounds or Smooth dogfishes, a family of small sharks externally resembling the Cat sharks but being distinguished by the arrangement of the teeth, which are in the form of a pavement as in the rays. Most sharks have triangular or pointed teeth used for cutting or grasping their prey, but the flat pavement of teeth in the hounds is used for grinding and crushing food found on the bottom (mostly molluscs and crustaceans). They have a world-wide distribution but the best known species of European coasts is the Smooth hound *Mustelus mustelus.* It has a supple, streamlined body with two dorsal fins and one anal fin and grows to 6 ft (1·8 m) in length. It is extremely abundant, as is its counterpart in the western Atlantic the Smooth dogfish *M. canis.* Both are inshore species that frequent shallow waters and mostly browse on the bottom for food. A more colourful member of this family is the Leopard shark *Triakis semifasciata* of the Pacific coasts of North America with a body marked by dark spots along the back and sides. The hounds are viviparous fishes in which the young are not only hatched within the uterus but are nourished through a placenta-like connection between the embryo and the uterine wall of the mother. There are

The Horseshoe crab *Limulus polyphemus* crawling towards the sea on the sandy shore at low-tide. Note the joint between the head and the rest of the body.

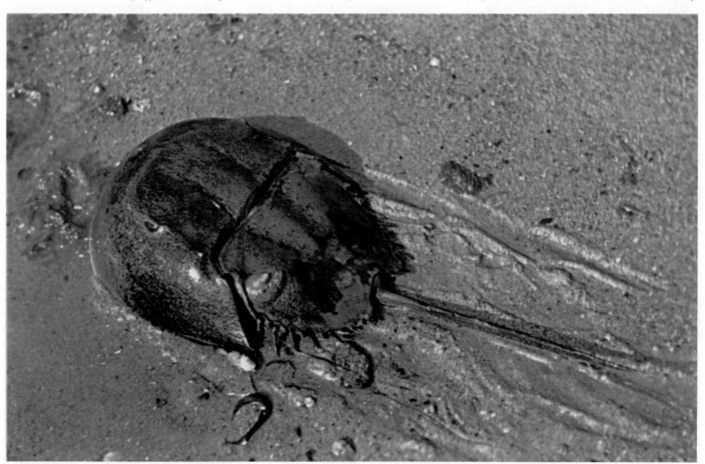

about 30 species known in this family, none of which grow to more than 6 ft (1·8 m) in length. They are a considerable pest to commercial fishermen because of their predation on lobsters, crabs and other fishes. FAMILY: Triakidae, ORDER: Pleurotremata, CLASS: Chondrichthyes.

HOUSE CENTIPEDE, contrasting with all other centipedes in its extraordinarily delicate appearance, being spider-like rather than centipede-like. It can evade capture with a suprising turn of speed; *Scutigera coleoptrata* can cover 20 in (50 cm) in 1 sec. There are 130 species of *Scutigera* and other genera of *Scutigera*-like centipedes.

The head is not flattened as in the three other orders of centipedes. The palps of the second maxillae and the poison claws are more leglike and operate more in the vertical than the horizontal plane. Another unique feature of *Scutigera* is the compound eye remarkably similar to the *compound eye of insects and crabs, each eye consisting of several hundred optical units or ommatidia.

There are 15 pairs of legs and, since propulsive legs diverge, they can be long and, indeed, they are so. Each leg consists of the same elements as the leg of other centipedes but the terminal segment is secondarily divided into numerous tarsi all of which are placed flat on the ground as the animal walks. This contrasts with all other centipedes which walk on the extreme tips of their legs.

As in other centipedes, the propulsive stroke of the leg is shorter than the recovery stroke and there are therefore fewer legs on the ground than off at any given moment. At a point where two legs at opposite ends of one side of the body are propelling and supporting, a leg on the middle of the other side is propelling and completing a tripod of support. This arrangement requires a fairly rigid trunk. The alternation of long and short tergites, the dorsal shields on each segment, which helps to stabilize the trunk of *Lithobius*, is carried a stage further in *Scutigera* where the short tergites are vestigial and the adjacent long tergites (7 and 8) are fused into one. There are thus seven

large shields (the name *Scutigera* means, literally, shield-bearer) covering the 15 leg-bearing segments.

The method of breathing is unique. In the centre of the hind edge of each dorsal shield there is a notch which leads into a cavity and into this cavity two kidney-shaped bundles of fine tracheae open. These tracheae do not take oxygen to the tissues as in all other centipedes but end blindly in the blood space increasing the surface across which oxygen can diffuse into the blood. The oxygen is transported from these tracheal lungs to the tissues by the blood system, which is highly developed. Inspiration of air into the lungs follows the rhythmic contraction of the long tubular heart which runs just beneath the lungs.

The male deposits a spermatophore (containing the sperm) which is picked up by the female. However, the male guides the female and in another genus the male has been seen to pick up the spermatophore with his poison-claws and introduce it directly into the genital pore of the female. The eggs are laid one at a time and abandoned. The young hatch with four pairs of legs; a further pair is added at the next moult and then two pairs at each of the next five moults. A further series of moults take place without further addition of legs.

Small flies are captured and eaten but apparently the compound eyes do not assist much in the capture. The long delicate legs are very vulnerable and can be autotomized (broken-off and shed) but will be regenerated at the next moult. A House centipede which has lost half its complement of legs is still able to accommodate and run rapidly.

Scutigera coleoptrata is probably indigenous to the Mediterranean region but occurs also in the United States, often taking refuge in houses in the cooler months. It has been found as far north as Britain where it has been reported on three occasions in buildings. ORDER: Scutigerimorpha, CLASS: Chilopoda, PHYLUM: Arthropoda.   J.G.B.

HOUSE FLY *Musca domestica,* one of many species of flies a few others of which

are minor pests, in one way or another, although most are harmless, obscure flies that usually pass unnoticed. The House fly is unique, simply because both adult and larva happen to like the sort of surroundings in which man lives, and as a result the House fly has become attached to man wherever he goes. It almost certainly originated in the tropics, but now it occurs throughout the world. The House fly is rather small, ashy brown and grey in colour, with four thin, blackish stripes on the thorax. Indoors it is most likely to be confused with the Lesser house fly *Fannia canicularis,* the males of which fly round and round in the middle of the room. The true House fly can be distinguished from most other members of the family Muscidae by the conspicuous bend in the vein at the tip of the wing.

The Autumn fly *M. autumnalis* is very similar in appearance to the House fly, but has very different habits: it is a pest of cattle in the fields during the summer – it has become known as the 'Face fly' in North America – and only comes indoors in winter to hibernate. The House fly cannot 'bite', and any flies which resemble House flies and also bite are likely to be the Stable fly or Biting house fly *Stomoxys calcitrans.* This has a stiff proboscis projecting forwards from the head, and the vein of the wing is much more rounded than angular. Stable flies are very common on farms, where they breed in straw and manure, and they are responsible for the annoying brown spots of undigested blood which soil the windows and curtains.

The House fly has a spongy proboscis, with large lobes, or labella, richly supplied with branching grooves called pseudo-tracheae, and can feed only by mopping up liquids or semi-liquid food. Solid food must be softened by expelling saliva over it, as well as regurgitating liquid from the crop. These fluids contain digestive enzymes, which predigest the solid food until it can be sucked back into the crop. It is this alternate vomiting and sucking that makes the House fly so dangerous to health, because any disease organisms that the fly has picked up

The House fly *Musca domestica* can be distinguished from most of its relatives by the conspicuous bend in the vein at the tip of the wing. Flies are attracted to excrement, which makes them a factor in the spread of disease.

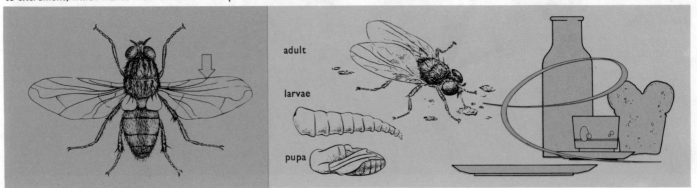

adult

larvae

pupa

A disappearing species in developed countries: the House fly.

with its food are likely to be voided again on to its next meal. A contributory factor is that the House fly is a very general feeder and will settle on anything that is remotely digestible. Thus it will settle on all the foods and drink on a table, and crawl all over the utensils, touching every surface with its wet proboscis, as well as with the hairy pads, or pulvilli on its six feet. It is attracted to faeces, which offer just the right kind of semiliquid nourishment.

The House fly is thus an active agent in spreading bacteria and other disease organisms which infect the mouth and intestine, and which cause many gastric ailments. Wounds, sores, any areas of broken skin, as well as discharges from eyes, ears and other orifices are equally attractive to House flies. It can be seen, therefore, that the protection of food, excreta and the person from the attentions of House flies is very important.

No disease is exclusively transmitted by House flies, as malaria is exclusively transmitted by mosquitoes, but House flies undoubtedly keep many disease organisms circulating more actively than would otherwise be the case. Poliomyelitis is one important disease that has been attributed to House flies, as one of a number of possible agencies. It has been suggested that House flies may be responsible for the mild, immunizing doses that most people receive before they become adult, leaving the acute, paralyzing form of polio as mainly a disease of children; hence its other name of infantile paralysis.

House flies lay eggs in batches of about 150, up to a total of about 600–1000. The larvae are smooth maggots and their natural breeding medium is probably animal dung, particularly horse manure; cow manure is

not so attractive to them. The larvae can also thrive in a wide variety of decaying materials of animal and vegetable origin, far wider than is tolerated by other flies. This is another reason why the House fly is so serious a pest, because human communities produce great quantities of garbage suitable for the breeding of House flies. The disappearance of the horse from towns in recent decades has reduced the supply of stable manure, though the current popularity of horses and ponies for pleasure riding has tended to reverse this process in some areas. Improved refuse-disposal has also cut down the breeding of House flies, but at the same time the increased tendency to sell food in tins, packets, plastic bags and other containers has provided new breeding-sites among the food residues still left in them. Another modern problem is centrally heated buildings. The House fly is essentially a tropical fly, and can continue to breed all the year round if the temperature is maintained. It has been found that even in a cold country such as Norway, the interior of cow-houses is kept sufficiently warm by the body-heat of the beasts to enable House flies to breed in winter. It is part of the versatility of the House fly that it can survive the winter either as adult, larva or pupa, according to circumstances. It is slow to make its appearance during the spring, but builds up rapidly in July, August and September.

Theoretically, enormous populations could arise if all the descendants of a single pair of flies should survive, but this is not likely to happen. On the contrary, the fatality-rate among eggs and larvae is so great that the House flies that we see are only the very rare survivors. These are

enough, however, for heavy spraying campaigns to be necessary in some countries, and it was the House fly that first demonstrated how insects could produce 'resistant strains' against modern insecticides. Proof of the versatility of this remarkable insect. FAMILY: Muscidae, ORDER: Diptera, CLASS: Insecta, PHYLUM: Arthropoda.   H.O.

HOUSE MOUSE *Mus musculus,* probably the most familiar of all rodents. Not only has it followed man throughout the world as a pest, but it is also the ancestor of the domesticated mouse, kept alike as pets by children and as experimental animals by almost every laboratory engaged in teaching or research in genetics, physiology, biochemistry or pharmacology. The House mouse, like the almost equally ubiquitous rat, is a member of the rodent family Muridae, and has many close relatives throughout the Old World (see mouse). Many of these mice enter houses, more or less sporadically but especially in winter, and one cannot assume therefore that any mouse caught indoors is a House mouse. Nor is it true that members of this species are found only indoors.

Most wild House mice that infest buildings can be distinguished from other species of mice by having the fur smoky greyish brown above and below. This does not apply, however, to many of the ancestral races of the species that continue to live predominantly outdoors. These races, e.g. in eastern Europe and in the Mediterranean region, have the underside white or pale grey as in most other wild mice. One characteristic that is useful for distinguishing the species from its relatives is the presence of a notch in the upper incisor teeth when seen from the side, while another dental peculiarity is the extreme reduction in size of the third (last) molar teeth so that the mastication is done almost entirely by the very large first molars.

The House mouse probably began its association with man soon after he first began to cultivate cereals more than 8,000 years ago. It is therefore difficult to know what was the original distribution of the species, but it seems likely that it included the grassland areas of the Near and Middle East, and probably also the Mediterranean region and the steppes of eastern Europe and southern Russia, perhaps as far as western China. In most of this area small, pale-bellied, short-tailed outdoor forms are still found, but often in company with the larger, darker, longer-tailed forms that seem to be more closely adapted to an indoor or farmyard existence. Throughout most of the rest of the world it is the larger and darker forms that have been spread by man. Provided ample food is available house mice are adaptable animals. They occur from the Arctic to the Equator and have even been found living and breeding in frozen meat stores.

House mouse, a rodent pest taken by man all over the world. In some countries, for example Australia, it sometimes reaches plague proportions, in countless thousands.

House mice are no more prolific breeders than many other species of mice, given the same conditions, but when they are living indoors or in corn-ricks with an abundance of food and protection from cold they continue to breed throughout the year. Under these conditions five or six litters per year of five or six young is quite normal and the potential rate of increase is therefore enormous. But if the surplus population is not removed by predators or by mouse-traps, the increase is very soon arrested by the mice themselves. With a low density, the males tend to be territorial, each occupying his own area. But under crowded conditions a social hierarchy develops and the younger or less aggressive males are tolerated by the dominant male, provided they behave with proper deference to him. Crowded conditions also prevent females from breeding and cause high infant mortality quite irrespective of the abundance or scarcity of food.

House mice are capable of surviving on almost anything edible, animal or vegetable, although their preference is undoubtedly for grain and other seeds. They remain a major pest on farms and in warehouses, where control is more difficult than in houses. The major problem is the amount of food that is lost through soiling or through damage to containers rather than the amount eaten by the mice. FAMILY: Muridae, ORDER: Rodentia, CLASS: Mammalia. G.B.C.

HOUSE SPIDERS, three long-legged spiders of the genus *Tegenaria* living or coming into houses in the autumn. Their mysterious appearance in baths is due to their creeping up the overflow pipe and not being able to climb out of the bath. The largest and most hairy species *T. parietina* used to be known as the Cardinal spider because it frightened Cardinal Wolsey at Hampton Court. There was a 16th century Dr. Muffett who prescribed these spiders as pills to be swallowed for many ailments and it is supposed that his only daughter, Patience, grew up with the fear which inspired the Nursery Rhyme:

Little Miss Muffett sat on a tuffet
Eating her curds and whey
When down came a spider
And sat down beside her
Which frightened Miss Muffett away.

FAMILY: Agelenidae, ORDER: Araneae, CLASS: Arachnida, PHYLUM: Arthropoda.

HOUTING *Coregonus oxyrhinchus,* a salmon-like fish of northern Europe that spends the larger part of its life at sea. It was formerly common in the North Sea, ascending rivers to spawn, but pollution has made the houting rather scarce. It is silvery and has an adipose fin but can be distinguished from its relatives by the pointed snout. It grows to about 16 in (40 cm) in length. FAMILY: Salmonidae, ORDER: Salmoniformes, CLASS: Pisces.

HOVERFLIES, characteristically seen hovering, especially around flowers where they are a familiar sight, their wings beating so quickly they are more or less lost to sight. Some are more common in woods where they remain poised at different heights above the ground apparently motionless, but occasionally darting away in any direction to a new position, and back again. From the hovering position they can fly forwards, backwards, sideways, up or down with equal ease. Many of them are coloured with black and yellow bands rather like bees or wasps so that they are not immediately recognized as flies.

Flowers are essential for hoverflies. The constant activity requires a high intake of carbohydrate, and they feed freely on the nectar. At the same time they pollinate the flowers and are next in importance to bees for this.

The larvae of hoverflies have very varied habits. One type, the rat-tailed maggot, lives in water or mud, feeding on decaying organic matter. This has a long telescopically extensible breathing tube so that it can breathe atmospheric air while remaining submerged at some depth. The adult of one of these is the Drone fly, so called because it resembles the drone of the honeybee. Other hoverfly larvae live in ants and wasps' nests where they feed on excreta, while a large group are actively carnivorous, feeding largely on aphids. These aphids are easy prey for a blind hoverfly maggot as they move so little, and do not notice if a neighbour is devoured, Only the soft, easily digested body contents are sucked out and up to 60 may be eaten daily. Thus hoverfly larvae are economically important in controlling these pests. FAMILY: Syrphidae, ORDER: Diptera, CLASS: Insecta, PHYLUM: Arthropoda. R.F.C.

HOWLER MONKEYS, several species of South American monkeys renowned for their loud voices. See New World monkeys.

HUCHEN *Salmo hucho,* the migratory salmon of the Danube basin. This species is only slightly smaller than the Atlantic salmon and in their general biology the two are also similar. Pollution has now made the huchen rather rare and some that were introduced into the Thames in the last century did not become established. FAMILY: Salmonidae, ORDER: Salmoniformes, CLASS: Pisces.

HUEMUL, two species of *deer living in the Andes.

HUIA *Heterolocha acutirostris,* a bird which is almost certainly now extinct, the other two genera in its endemic New Zealand family being now very rare (see wattlebird). The early European settlers found this

A Hoverfly, master of helicopter flight, at rest on a flower. The ability to fly forwards, backwards, sideways, upwards and downwards is essential to its life.

bird confined to mountain forests at the southern end of the North Island. A striking bird, with its glossy black plumage and orange wattles, it used to bound through the forest, rarely flying, searching bark, decaying logs and the ground for food. The huia was remarkable for the sexual dimorphism of the bill. The male's bill was much shorter than that of the female and it would chisel away rotten wood, while its mate probed holes in the sounder parts of a log.

The Maoris found them easy to snare, attracting them with an imitation of their flute-like call. The black and white tail feathers were highly prized for Maori leaders to wear in their hair.

Huias became extinct at about 1910. This has been attributed to hunting, and to extensive collection for museums, but introduced predators probably contributed to the extinction. FAMILY: Callaeidae, ORDER: Passeriformes, CLASS: Aves.   D.G.D.

HUMMINGBIRDS, a family of 319 species of tiny, nectar-drinking birds of the New World, which take their name from the noise made by their incredibly rapid wing-beats. They are mainly aerial, feeding on the wing, and are related to the swifts. Like the swifts they have very small legs and feet and the bony structure of the wings is also very much reduced, the greater part of the visible wing consisting of a large area of elongated

primary flight feathers. The hummingbirds move about by flying, the short legs and little feet merely being used for perching. The head is large in relation to the rest of the body but this is not obvious in most species because of the relatively large size of the wings and tail.

Hummingbirds are, in general, small, fast and extremely active. The largest species, the Giant hummingbird *Patagona gigas* of the Andes, is a little over 8 in (20 cm) long of

which half is tail. The smallest, the Bee hummingbird *Mellisuga helenae* of Cuba, is virtually the size of an insect. The body is about 1 in (2·5 cm) long, the bill and tail adding another inch to this. In a majority of species the body size is about 2 in (5 cm) or less.

As a general rule, the smaller the animal the faster the wings need to move to keep it airborne. In addition the hummingbird has a

How to keep the sexes together. The Huia bird feeds on grubs living in the wood of trees. Only the male has a beak strong enough to chisel a hole through the bark, and the female a beak slender enough to reach the grubs.

The wings of this hummingbird are almost invisible in the picture because of the speed at which they beat, about 100 times per second, to enable the bird to hover with perfect precision.

problem associated with its mode of feeding. When taking nectar from blossoms there is no convenient perch nearby so it must hover while feeding then move backwards to withdraw its bill from the flower. As a result the flight is specialized. The wing-beat is highly efficient and, proportionally, the hummingbird uses fewer beats than other birds. Some of the larger hummingbirds have a rate of 20–25 beats per sec, comparable with that of the considerably larger and slower tits. In small hummingbirds the rate rises to about 70 beats per sec but in the Giant hummingbirds it is the surprisingly slow 8–10 beats per sec. The wings are kept more rigid and extended throughout the beat than those of other birds and they rotate through a narrow ellipse during each beat.

In normal forward flight the body is horizontal and the wing-beat almost vertical, but in hovering the body is more vertical and the wing-beat horizontal, the wing-tip moving through a figure-of-eight. To reverse, the wings are raised and rotated and the hummingbird may momentarily fly on its back before rolling over. The speed of direct flight is from 30–40 mph (50–65 kph).

The bill is long and fine, an exceptionally short one being only about half as long again as the head, while the longest, that of the Sword-billed hummingbird *Ensifera ensifera,*

is straight and as long as head, body and tail combined. Such a bill is designed for probing long tubular flowers. A number of species have the bill slightly decurved, while in the sicklebill *Eutoxeres aquila* the bill is long and strongly arched downwards and a few hummingbirds have a slight upward curve to the bill. The tongue is slender and elongated. It can be extended well beyond the tip of the bill and the edges are rolled in to form a double tube up which the nectar is sucked.

The variety of bills in the hummingbirds indicates their adaptation to different types of flowers as sources of food. In taking nectar from the flowers the birds may transfer pollen from one flower to another and be important agents of fertilization. It would seem that some plants may have become adapted to attract hummingbirds to aid cross-fertilization as in areas where hummingbirds are migrants the flowers needing such pollination tend to have a similar red colour so they can be quickly recognized by a bird new to the area. Where hummingbirds are resident the flowers are more variable and there may be a more direct relationship between one type of flower and a particular hummingbird species. Although nectar forms the staple part of the diet, a large number of tiny insects are also taken, usually snatched in mid-air.

Many hummingbirds are forest-dwellers,

but they may also occur in a wide range of habitats, extending into open country where flowering plants are present and also to high altitudes in mountain regions. In some areas they are nomadic or subject to seasonal movements in order to take advantage of the flowering seasons of different plants. Several species are migratory and three move into North America to nest in the southern parts of Canada or Alaska. Other species, and particularly those of tropical or subtropical mountain regions, may be very localized in distribution at all times.

With their small size and fierce activity the hummingbirds quickly burn up their reserves of energy. During active periods they appear to feed about once in every 10–15 minutes. Like swifts, hummingbirds are at a disadvantage in prolonged periods of rain and low temperatures, but may compensate for this by their ability to become torpid, appearing lifeless and saving energy until the weather improves. Migrating hummingbirds overcome the need for frequent feeding by laying down sufficient fat reserves to enable them to undertake a long journey.

Hummingbirds usually bathe on the wing, in fine spray or rain, or by brushing against wet foliage. They do not tuck the bill into the feathers of the back when they sleep, but squat on a twig with body feathers fluffed, the head tilted back a little and the bill pointing up at an angle. Although they may occur in numbers where food is plentiful they are aggressive and quarrelsome among themselves. They are territorial when nesting, and outside the breeding season may defend smaller feeding territories. Not only do they attack and chase each other but they will also boldly attack much larger birds, which their speed and agility enable them to dominate.

The displays of the hummingbirds are relatively unspectacular in terms of movement, usually being very rapid swoops terminating in a hover in front of the female, but the brilliance of the display lies in the vivid iridescent colours of the male's plumage and the often elaborate plumage decorations such as crests, ruffs, beards and tail-streamers. Most of the more vividly iridescent plumage is on the throat and crown—brilliant shapes of red, yellow, pink, purple, blue or green. In many cases this is only really conspicuous from one angle, usually from the front, so that it shows to best advantage when the male hovers before the female. The head colour may be enhanced by decoration such as the long tapering green or violet crests of the plovercrests *Stephanoxis,* the green and red paired horns of *Heliactin cornuta* or the black and white paired crest and pointed beard of *Oxypogon guerinii*. In addition to a bright crest, the coquettes *Lophornis* have erectile fan-shaped ruffs on the sides of the neck, boldly coloured and with contrasting bars or spots at the feather-tips. When the male

The Ruby-topaz hummingbird *Chrysolampis mosquitus*, of Brazil.

The Black-throated train bearer, *Lesbia victoriae*.

hovers before the female the other visible parts of the plumage are the undersides of wings and tail. The body plumage of most hummingbirds is glossy green or blue and the underwings may have a contrasting chestnut-red tint. The tails of some show an overall bronze or purple iridescence on the undersides of tail feathers, visible in display but not obvious from above, while on others the feathers may be tipped, streaked or blotched with white.

In addition the tails may have a variety of shapes. Broad fans are frequent, and forked tails vary from blunt forks to the long scissor-shapes of the trainbearers *Lesbia* and the slender tail streamers of the streamer-tail *Trochilus polytmus*. Others show different degrees of tapering and elongation of the central tail feathers, as in the hermits *Phaethornis*. The racket-tails *Ocreatus* have the two outer feathers elongated to long wires terminating in large rounded vanes and show the additional decoration of white down patches like powder puffs around the legs, which are also found in some other species.

The nests of hummingbirds are built of fibres, plant down and similar fine material and moss and lichen, bound together with spiders' webs. Some nests are smooth neat cups on twigs, others are domed, and some are pendent, or built onto hanging plants. Nests are often decorated externally with lichens. The female undertakes the building of the nest and the incubation and care of the young. She lays two white eggs, which are very large in proportion to her body size and very bluntly elliptical. Incubation takes about a fortnight and the young are born naked. The female feeds them by inserting her bill well into the chicks' gullets and regurgitating food. The young take three to four weeks to fledge, the period varying, apparently in response to

the food supply available. FAMILY: Trochilidae, ORDER: Apodiformes, CLASS: Aves.

HUMMINGBIRD MIGRATION. It is incredible that such small and, seemingly, frail birds such as hummingbirds should be capable of migrating long distances. The Rufous hummingbird nests as far north as southeast Alaska and migrates to Mexico for the winter, moving along the Pacific side of the Rocky Mountains at heights of up to 12,000 ft (3,500 m). Before it sets off it lays down a store of fat of 50% its normal body weight. The Ruby-throated hummingbird is another expert traveller; it crosses the Gulf of Mexico, a journey of around 600 miles (960 km) non-stop.

HUMPBACK WHALE *Megaptera novaeangliae,* a whale with many similarities to the rorquals but enough differences for it to be placed in a separate genus. It has long flippers, hence *Megaptera*—large wings, with serrated hind edges, which are about a third the total body length of some 50 ft (16 m). Nodules are present on the head and, in addition, the body is usually covered with large barnacles. As the body is black dorsally and white ventrally the barnacles are very obvious on the back, giving a rough black and white spotted appearance. The humpback is a bulky animal and appears to hunch its back on diving, hence its name.

Humpbacks are widely distributed throughout the oceans and follow the rorqual migratory pattern. This follows coasts in certain parts of the world, for example, in New Zealand, where the schools move close inshore frequenting bays and inlets. In spite of this the humpback rarely becomes

The Broad-tailed hummingbird of southern North America.

stranded. The coastal movements mean that much more detail is known of its migration than of most species and this knowledge is helped by its regular habits.

An indication of its bulk compared with length is given by its oil yield. The amount of oil obtained from one Blue whale is obtained from two Fin whales, two and a half humpbacks and six Sei whales. But the Sei whale exceeds the humpback by 10 ft (3·3 m) in length, and the Fin whale by 30 ft (10 m).

In spite of the great bulk, humpbacks may be seen sporting in the sea, often leaping and rolling to fall back in the water with an enormous splash.

The gestation period of about one year is rather longer than that of the rorquals and in this the humpback compares with the Californian grey whale. However, like them it breeds in alternate years. Also, like all the migrating whales, the milk is extremely rich, which allows the young to build up fat before moving to the cold waters in the summer migrations. See Whalebone whales. FAMILY: Balaenopteridae, ORDER: Cetacea, CLASS: Mammalia.   K.M.B.

HUNTER'S ANTELOPE *Damaliscus hunteri,* of the grassy plains of Somalia and Kenya. They live in groups of 6–40 individuals, stand 4 ft (1·2 m) at the shoulder and measure the same in head and body length. They are reddish with white underparts, their ringed horns somewhat lyrate are worn by both sexes, and they have a white line across the forehead, from one eye to the other. FAMILY: Bovidae, ORDER: Artiodactyla, CLASS: Mammalia.

HUNTING WASPS, usually large and, typically, with relatively long legs which hang down below the body in flight. They are often common in hot desert regions. As their common name implies, they are active predators and show a particular predilection for spiders which they paralyze with a sting, prior to storing them in their underground nests for their larvae to feed on. This feeding preference is reflected in an alternative name, the Spider wasps. Some of the larger species provision their nests with the largest of the so-called Tarantula spiders, agilely paralyzing the spider before it can retaliate with its poison fangs. FAMILY: Pompilidae, ORDER: Hymenoptera, CLASS: Insecta, PHYLUM: Arthropoda.

HUTIA, fairly large terrestrial rodents of the genera *Capromys* and *Geocapromys,* of primitive form, restricted to the West Indies with one species in Venezuela. Other species live in Jamaica, Little Swan Island, Isle of Pines, Cuba and the Bahamas. They look very like the coypu, and their continued survival is threatened by dogs, cats and introduced mongooses as well as by being hunted for food by man. FAMILY: Capromyidae, ORDER: Rodentia, CLASS: Mammalia.

HUXLEY, J. S., born 1887, British biologist, philosopher and author, grandson of the great T. H. Huxley. He has influenced the development of embryology, and the study of behaviour, and evolution, and has contributed significantly to contemporary thinking on man's place in nature. Educated at Eton and Oxford, he has held numerous influential academic positions including the Professorship of Zoology at King's College, London, 1925 – 1927; Fullerian Professor at the Royal Institution, 1926 – 1929; Secretary to the Zoological Society of London, 1935–1942; and was the first Director-General of UNESCO, 1946–1948. He was elected a Fellow of the Royal Society in 1938, and knighted in 1958.

HUXLEY, T. H., 1825–1895, English biologist, educator, administrator and scholar; major architect of modern academic biology; and self-styled 'Darwin's Bulldog'. T. H. Huxley, who founded a dynasty of scholars to accompany that of Darwin, was a man of very rare and very great gifts. He was born into a world in which biology, as a science, did not exist. When he left it, biology was an established discipline in centres of learning in many parts of the world—largely as a result of his influence. He was educated in a haphazard manner until he took the matter into his own hands, teaching himself languages and philosophy as well as science and entering medical school in London on a free scholarship. He was awarded his First MB in 1845, having collected numerous awards on the way, and entered the Royal Naval Medical Service as an Assistant Surgeon. From 1846 to 1850 he served on HMS *Rattlesnake,* exploring to New Guinea, and made good use of his time by working on marine organisms and making discoveries for which he was elected Fellow of the Royal Society in 1851.

On his return from the Antipodes, Huxley began the work which was to make him the most important figure in biological science. To start with he had difficulty in obtaining a post but was appointed Fullerian Professor to the Royal Institution in 1855. From then on he occupied several high-ranking positions in academic and public life. He also refused several, including professorships in Edinburgh, Oxford and Harvard, and a seat in Parliament. He built up the small School of Mines in London into the great Royal College of Science; he played a leading part on the first London School Board; he acted as a governor of Eton and Rector of Aberdeen University—in the latter post he was the first to take his duties seriously. He was president of several academic societies, and fellow or honorary member of numerous others throughout the world. He was appointed secretary of the Royal Society in 1871, and president in 1883. In 1892 he was appointed Privy Councillor.

While being a brilliant teacher and orator, a gifted investigator, and an active and influential administrator in academic and public affairs—all of which take considerable time to do properly—Huxley's published works include 171 papers, 87 essays, 22 books, and nine volumes of collected essays. In the five years following the appearance of Darwin's *The Origin Of Species* his 46 publications included nine significant contributions to the debate on evolution. Huxley in fact, more than anyone else, was instrumental in preventing Darwin's work from being rejected out of hand. His immediate support in the public media, his courteous but decisive victory over religious prejudice in the famous Oxford public discussion on Darwinism, and his own academic work, have all played a major role in bringing the facts of evolution to the forefront of biological thought. But, as with Darwin's own work on evolution, these efforts tend to overshadow the very valuable work he did in other areas of natural science. His work on invertebrate morphology was outstanding; his invertebrate text and the brilliant monograph *The Crayfish* can still be read with profit. His interest in what he called 'biological engineering' resulted not only in some fine invertebrate discoveries but also some pioneering work on the origin of the vertebrate skull, the functional anatomy and taxonomic value of the bones of the bird's palate, and the evolutionary development in the primate skeleton leading to man. In other areas his work ranged from hybridism in gentians to the physical anthropology of the Patagonians, from his text *Physiography* to fisheries economics. His energy and wide interests resulted in his effective participation in many organizations, one of which was the Anthropological Institute which he practically founded. But, perhaps most important of all, the educational influence he had was profound. Whether he was lecturing at the Royal Institution or at a Working Men's College he forced home the importance of the search for truth and the need for an understanding of nature.   P.M.D.

HYAENAS, a much reviled group of animals owing to their habit of eating carrion and to their rather unlovely appearance. There are three species: the Spotted or Laughing hyaena *Crocuta crocuta* of Africa south of the Sahara, the Brown hyaena *Hyaena brunnea* of southern Africa, and the Striped hyaena *H. hyaena,* which ranges from northern and northeast Africa through Asia Minor

A Spotted hyaena of southern Africa feeding, with vultures, on the carcase of an elephant.

A mass of bones, taken from a hyaena's lair in Kenya, included human remains which were probably carried from a nearby cemetery.

to India. A feature of all the hyaenas is the shoulders being noticeably higher than the hindquarters, giving them a somewhat ungainly, hunchbacked appearance. They are also remarkable for their gait, which is usually associated with camels. This is known as pacing and it involves moving both limbs of one side of the body together, instead of the normal quadrupedal action. All three species have massive heads with large ears and powerful jaws equipped with large teeth that are capable of shearing through a zebra's thigh bone. Their tails are short and each foot bears four toes.

The Spotted hyaena is the largest and most aggressive of the three species. The male may be 5 ft (1·5 m) long in head and body with a 13 in (33 cm) long tail and 3 ft (91 cm) at the shoulders. It can weigh up to 180 lb (81 kg). The female is slightly smaller. The fur is scanty varying from grey to tawny or yellowish-buff broken by numerous brown spots. There is only a slight mane. Spotted hyaenas are nocturnal spending most of the day in holes in the ground.

They live in clans of up to 100 in defined territories marked by their urine and droppings. Members of other clans are driven off. They often hunt in packs and can run up to 40 mph (65 kmph). The usual call of the Spotted hyaena is a mournful howl, made with the head held near the ground, beginning low but becoming louder as the pitch rises. When excited it utters what can only be described as

The Brown hyaena of southern Africa.

a demented cackle, and it is this that has earned it the name of the 'Laughing hyaena'. It also appears to have the ability to project its voice, thus making it hard to locate the animal from its call. Spotted hyaenas eat carrion and although their sight is poor their sense of smell is remarkably acute and it is believed they can detect a carcase over a range of several miles. They also kill sheep, goats, calves, young antelopes and even smaller prey. They may even eat locusts. They have been observed at night in a pack of up to 20 following a herd of wildebeest and harassing them until they have managed to slow down one of them, after which all the hyaenas concentrated on it. This refutes the idea that hyaenas are cowards and live only by feeding on the remains of the lion's kill. Immensely strong in the jaws and shoulders they are said to be able to carry away a human body or the carcase of an ass.

Mating occurs in January and after a gestation of 110 days one or two young are born. At the time of birth, the young are blind but covered with a thick brown woolly coat. At this stage there are no stripes or other markings, but after about a month, the fur starts to lighten in colour in some areas, leaving the characteristic brown spots. The Spotted hyaena has no natural enemies apart from man and in the wild the lifespan may be as much as 25 years.

The Striped hyaena is the smallest species being not more than 4 ft (1·2 m) long in head and body with an 18 in (46 cm) long tail. It stands 30 in (76 cm) at the shoulder and a full grown male may weigh up to 85 lb (38·2 kg). The coat is grey to yellowish-brown broken by dark, almost black stripes. Along the line of the spine there is a crest or mane of longer hairs. The variation in the thickness of the coat bears witness to the variation in climate that this species encounters throughout its range. In the southerly parts of its range the coat is thin and sparse, while the more northerly individuals may have an almost woolly coat. The diet is similar to that of the Spotted hyaena but the breeding differs in that the gestation period is only 90 days and there are two to four young in a litter,

sometimes as many as six. The babies are born in a hollow in the ground, blind and with their eyes closed. The coat is woolly and unmarked. The Striped hyaena is remarkable for its habit of shamming dead when cornered by dogs. It will lie perfectly still until the vigilance of the dogs wavers. As soon as an opportunity presents itself the hyaena will leap to its feet and make off with all speed.

The Brown hyaena is halfway in size between the Spotted and Striped hyaenas. Its coat is dark brown with indistinct stripes but with dark rings round the lower part of the legs. Like the Striped hyaena it has a long-haired erectile mane. Its feeding and breeding habits are like those of the Striped hyaena but it lives near the shore and feeds on carrion and marine refuse left by the receding tide, eating anything from dead crabs to the carcases of stranded whales. For this reason it is also known as the strandwolf. FAMILY: Hyaenidae, ORDER: Carnivora, CLASS: Mammalia.   N.J.C.

Striped hyaena of Africa and Asia.

HYAENA ODDITIES. Scavenging animals, such as vultures, generally earn our revulsion but the hyaena is perhaps particularly disliked because it sometimes feeds on human corpses. Since mediaeval times hyaenas have also had a bad reputation for being unclean animals because they were said to alternate between male and female, an idea that arose from the superficial similarity of the external reproductive organs of the two sexes. According to Sir Walter Raleigh, hyaenas appeared after the Flood as offspring of the union of a cat and a dog and it was thought that they mated with lionesses to produce an animal called a crocote.

HYBRIDIZATION, the crossing of individuals belonging to two distinct species. The horse and the ass, for example, are crossed to produce the *mule. The term is also used for individuals belonging to two unlike natural populations that have secondarily come into contact, as in long isolated populations of the same species, which are often *phenotypically different and certainly have different gene pools.

Under this definition a number of different kinds of hybridization may be recognized. Most frequently crosses between two different species produce sterile individuals which do not backcross with the parental species. Occasionally the hybrids of such matings are fertile and do backcross to one or both of the parental species, a phenomenon termed introgressive hybridization. Although fairly frequent in the plant kingdom introgressive hybridization is rather rare among animals. When it does occur hybrid populations representing 1–5% of the total are formed and these provide a useful means of transferring genes from one species to another. See genetics.

Rather different consequences result when there is a complete local breakdown of reproductive isolation between two species. Large hybrid populations are formed which exhibit the total range of variability of the parental species. No examples of such large hybrid populations have been found in mammals but they are well known among birds, fishes and a wide range of invertebrates. The phenomenon is also rather more common among plants than among animals. The peculiarities of this sort of hybridization are illustrated by the case of the House sparrow and the Willow sparrow of southern Europe

and western Asia. In most areas the two species coexist side by side without any interbreeding. In a few areas, however, more or less unrestricted hybridization between them is taking place. The resulting hybrid population includes individuals phenotypically the same as both parents and with all combinations of the parental characters, with indications of complete random mating.

The production of a completely new species can occur as the result of hybridization but it is virtually restricted to plants and is made possible by the doubling of the chromosome number which invariably accompanies hybridization thus isolating the hybrid population. It is this latter facility which animals on the whole lack.

The question of how important hybridization has been in evolution is best considered separately in animals and plants. Hybridization is probably an important evolutionary process in plants, and among animals too it has been claimed that many species owe much of their genetic variability to introgressive hybridization. But most of the direct evidence available on the frequency of first generation hybrids in animals suggests they are rather rare. Among hundreds of thousands of Fruit flies *Drosophila* examined, where hybrids can be unequivocally recognized, only three species pairs are known to have produced wild hybrids, with no more than a few score individuals involved overall. Among well known and intensively studied groups of birds in which species differ from each other in colouration, in song, or both, hybrids readily attract the attention of ornithologists and yet they are few and far between. There have, however, been instances of large populations of two

species of ducks living on a lake and hybridizing where the two populations overlap. Other animal groups similarly provide evidence of low levels of hybridization.

In fact in most animal populations where zones of intra-specific hybridization do exist they rarely become broader, indicating that there are marked genetic differences between differentiated populations even within a species. This results in imbalance in the hybrids such that they are at a selective disadvantage and so die out. Introgression in the case of interspecific hybridization is probably much more difficult and therefore, overall, hybridization is of minor evolutionary importance in animals.   K.F.D.

HYBRIDIZATION IN FISHES, the natural or artificial crossing of members of different species, genera or even subfamilies. As a general rule, it has been found that where the parents differ noticeably in any particular character, then the hybrid offspring will be intermediate. This has been recorded for colours, numbers of body parts (fin rays, gillrakers, vertebrae, etc.), and the shape and proportions of the body or individual bones. In many cases, hybridization results in progeny that fail to develop properly. Those that do reach adulthood often show skewed sex ratios, males or females predominating, sometimes to the complete exclusion of the other. This is a most useful attribute in fast-breeding pond fishes since it prevents overpopulation and thus stunted growth. Few reports are available of hybrid fertility, but total infertility has been recorded in trout × char hybrids, in many toothcarp hybrids and in generic crosses between darters (Percidae). Reduced fertility has occurred in crosses between certain salmon-like fishes. Hybrid vigour may be shown by a faster growth rate or greater tolerance to environmental conditions. Hybridization is rare in natural populations but may result when exotic species are introduced. In Lake Erie, carp and goldfish have hybridized; both are introduced fishes that do not cross where their natural ranges overlap in Asia.

Hybridization has been studied in a number of groups of fishes. Amongst the darters, natural and artificial hybrids between species and between genera have been investigated. In the cichlid fishes a number of hybrids have been recorded between species of *Tilapia,* usually in ponds or lakes where an exotic species has been introduced. In the carp-like fishes hybridization is also fairly common and has been achieved artificially between members of different subfamilies.

In nature, barriers to hybridization are numerous and usually effective. Apart from the geographical separation of different species, there is often a separation of spawning grounds or spawning times. If these coin-

Trout hybrid, result of crossing Brown trout *Salmo trutta* and Brook trout *Salvelinus fontinalis.*

cide, then species may be kept apart by various aspects of breeding behaviour, breeding colouration or, in the case of live-bearers, by differences in the structure of the gonopodium, or copulatory organ. Even if mating takes place, the sperm head may not match the size of the micropyle of the egg. Occasionally, however, apparent hybridization has been the result of the sperm triggering off development of the egg without actually joining the female gamete. Finally, the crossing of two species may be prevented by an incompatability of the developmental pattern of the embryo. Since the evolution of new species has involved isolating mechanisms capable of perfecting themselves, it is perhaps not surprising that hybridization is both rare and rarely productive.

HYDRA, a solitary *polyp, not typical of although belonging to the Cnidaria, of which it is one of the few freshwater members.

In a letter written to the Royal Society in 1702, Antony van Leeuwenhoek gave the first description of *Hydra* and described the first instance of asexual reproduction seen in animals. Later, in 1744, Abraham Trembley produced a monograph of experiments on regeneration and grafting in *Hydra*. Since then hydras have been found by many searchers of freshwater habitats and seen by many generations of schoolchildren, but it has been only recently that *Hydra* has been used as a research animal. The result is that it is now one of the best known members of the phylum *Cnidaria.

Hydra is able to cope with the osmotic problems of life in freshwater, although the mechanisms by which it controls water and salt content are unknown. Placed in the class Hydrozoa, *Hydra* lacks any medusoid phase but it is a typical hydrozoan polyp, with a long cylindrical body, closed at one end and with a mouth borne on a projection or hypostome at the other. However, it does not secrete a chitinous coat or perisarc and the polyp is naked. Surrounding the mouth are tentacles, generally five or six in number, of differing lengths. As in all members of the Cnidaria the body wall of the polyp is composed of two cell layers, an outer ectoderm and an inner endoderm separated by a thin, non-cellular layer, the mesogloea. This body wall encloses a single enteron or body cavity and the body is a simple tube, there being no projections or septa dividing the enteron, as in Sea anemones.

The tentacles bear 'batteries' of nematocysts, or stinging cells, which are used to capture small Crustacea. The nematocysts are of four kinds with different functions. The penetrants or stenoteles are probably the best known variety of nematocyst with a long, barbed thread arising from a thick basal region, also bearing barbs; they are used in the paralysis of prey. The volvents or

desmonemes have a long, coiled thread and are used for holding the prey, while the holotrichous izorhizas with long barbed threads are used for defensive purposes. The fourth type or atrichous izorhiza, which was believed before the advent of electron microscopy to have a bare thread, is used to anchor the polyp to the substrate, together with mucus secreted by the basal region of the polyp. An interesting response to the capture of food has been observed in *Hydra*. On the capture of prey, the tentacles curve towards the mouth, which opens wide, and this opening of the mouth has been called the 'feeding reflex'. This is brought about by the presence in the water of molecules of reduced glutathione, a tri-peptide. Once in the enteron, the food is broken down extra-cellularly into small particles by proteolytic enzymes secreted by endodermal cells. These small particles are taken up by other endodermal cells and digested intracellularly.

The nervous system in Cnidaria is a nerve-net of multi-polar nerve cells. In *Hydra* it has been difficult to obtain any histological evidence of this nerve-net, although recently electron microscopists have claimed to have identified nerve cells. However, at least three physiological systems exist, each of which can be recorded electrically. If *Hydra* is observed over a period of time the muscles of the ectodermal system show a series of co-ordinated contractions, the polyp alternating between a small ball and a long cylinder. These contractions may occur every ten minutes and can be recorded as sequences of electrical activity. They have been termed the 'contraction burst' and the activity cannot at present be assigned to any morphological structure. Other systems called 'rhythmic potential system' and the 'pre-locomotor burst' have been noted, and they also cannot be assigned to any morphological structure; the behaviour of *Hydra* is much more complex than was originally thought.

Hydras are noted for their power of

regeneration. Almost any piece cut from the polyp will reorganize and form a complete, although small, individual. Each piece will retain its 'polarity'; a head will always be formed at the head end with respect to the original piece of tissue. It is thought this polarity is maintained by gradients, quantitative differences in certain constituents along the longitudinal axis of the animal. Similarly tentacles, if removed, will be replaced by the polyp. As noted by van Leeuwenhoek, hydras when well fed will reproduce asexually by budding. A small protuberance arises somewhere along the long axis of the polyp, the site depending on the species. This bud grows and develops mouth and tentacles at the end furthest from the parent polyp. When fully developed the new animal is constricted off the parent.

Hydras also reproduce sexually, although their life-history is atypical of the Cnidaria and is a secondary adaptation to life in a freshwater pond which is liable to dry up. Sexual reproduction is seasonal, although cultures maintained in the laboratory will become sexual if they become overcrowded. It is thought that in this instance the amount of carbon dioxide in the environment is an important factor. Species of *Hydra* may be dioecious or hermaphrodite. The gonads on the long body of the polyp are derived from accumulations of interstitial cells, that is undifferentiated cells. Testes produce large numbers of spermatozoa, which are liberated into the water, but ovaries contain, when mature, only one large ovum. After fertilization, radical cleavage occurs and a ball of cells is produced which remains attached to the parent polyp. Then a thick, chitinous shell is secreted around the cells to form a theca, which may be spiny or smooth, and the structure of the theca is used as a taxonomic character. When the theca is complete, the shelled embryo drops off the parent and remains dormant. In this way the embryo can survive the drying up of the pond. Before hatching the theca is softened

Section through a hydra polyp showing two-layered body wall and (right) portion of body wall enlarged.

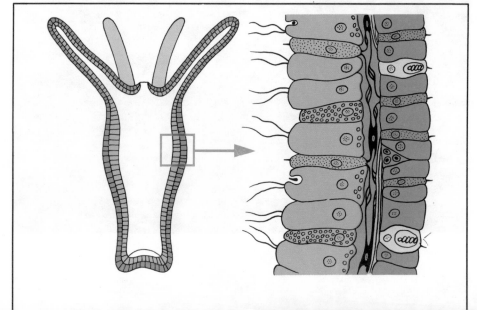

A Green hydra *Chlorohydra viridissima* with young budding from its base.

and the embryo emerges. This embryo is hollow and possesses small protuberances where the tentacles will arise.

There are many species of *Hydra,* found in lakes and ponds throughout the world. Their classification is not easy and involves microscopy to examine the nematocysts. One species is green, *Chlorohydra viridissima,* and contains symbiotic algae, zoochlorellae, in the endodermal cells. *Pelmatohydra oligactis* appears brown due to the presence of symbiotic algae, zooxanthellae, while others are pinkish in colour, for example *Hydra littoralis.* Under natural conditions, each cell of the endoderm in *Hydra viridis* invariably contains 15–25 cells of zoochlorellae. These unicellular algae are green, about 6–12 μm in diameter, with a cup-shaped chloroplast, pyrenoid and thin cell wall. The algae probably belong to the genus *Chlorella,* a common genus of freshwater algae. The algae live inside vacuoles in the endodermal cells and reproduce there by simple cell-division. Since the number of algae per gastrodermal cell normally never rises above about 25, it is believed that the animal can exert some form of control over the size of its algal population, but it is not known how this control is achieved. When small portions of endoderm are removed from the animal, they can regenerate into whole new hydras. When this happens, those gastrodermal cells which de-differentiate and then become ectodermal cells invariably cast out their algal cells, showing that the algae are specifically confined to the endoderm. The algae are passed from one generation of *Hydra* to the next either asexually through the buds, or sexually through the eggs. Infection of *Hydra* by free-living algae has never been observed and, so far, attempts to grow the symbiotic algae in pure culture have failed.

Some, but not all, strains of *Hydra* can be freed from their algae by incubating them in a dilute glycerol solution for a week to produce so-called 'albino' *Hydra.*

When 'albino' *Hydra* are compared with the normal green forms, there is no difference in their growth rates if grown under conditions of ample food supply (e.g. feeding with Brine shrimp larvae every day). Under conditions of starvation or limited food supply, the growth of green *Hydra* is much greater than that of the albino forms, provided the green *Hydra* are illuminated. This suggests that the animal can make use of the products of photosynthesis of the alga. Direct proof of this can be obtained by incubating green *Hydra* in the light in radioactive carbon dioxide, $^{14}CO_2$. The radioactive carbon fixed in photosynthesis moves rapidly out of the endoderm into the ectoderm which is free of algae.

The algae can be isolated from *Hydra* as a pure suspension by gently homogenizing the animal, so that its cells are broken up without damaging the algae, and then precipitating down the algal cells by spinning the homogenate in a centrifuge. Using radioactive carbon-dioxide, it has been shown that the pure suspensions of algae are capable of active photosynthesis, and that under certain conditions, the algae excrete substantial amounts of photosynthetically fixed carbon to the medium.

The principal compound excreted is maltose, a sugar never found in such abundance in free-living algae. The animal tissue contains maltase, an enzyme which hydrolizes maltose to glucose, and experiments with intact animals have shown that the animal tissue converts the maltose to glycogen and protein. FAMILY: Hydridae, ORDER: Athecata, CLASS: Hydrozoa, PHYLUM: Cnidaria.　　　S.E.H. and D.C.S.

HYDROBIA, a group of small Spire snails and Bithynia snails belonging to the family Hydrobiidae. In common with other prosobranch molluscs, *Hydrobia* has a whorled shell into which the animal can withdraw. The shell aperture is closed by an operculum which is horny and spirally-grooved in the Spire snails but limy and concentrically-grooved in Bithynia snails. There is a single gill which has leaflets along one side of the axis only; this is known as a 'pectinibranch' type and occurs in all mesogastropods. There are many different species of *Hydrobia,* few exceed $\frac{1}{2}$ in (1·2 cm) in length and all occur in estuarine, brackish or freshwater conditions. The commonest estuarine species are the Laver spire snail *Hydrobia ulvae,* the Spire snail *H. ventrosa* and another Spire snail *H. neglecta,* each of which tends to occur in different ranges of salinity. The Laver spire snail occurs in vast numbers, commonly 15,000–46,000 per sq m, in bare muds with a salinity range from 10–33%

and forms an important food for shelduck and wading birds. *H. neglecta* occurs on vegetation in areas where the salinity range is 10–24% whilst the Spire snail also occurs mainly in the vicinity of vegetation but tolerates salinities in the range of 6–20%. These species are replaced in very low salinities, of 0–15%, by the Jenkins' spire snail *Potamopyrgus jenkinsi.* Each of these species is widely distributed throughout northwest Europe. Other, rather rarer, Spire shells include the Swollen spire snail *Pseudamnicola confusa* which has a very thin pale brown shell rather less than $\frac{1}{5}$ in (4 mm) long. It lives in nearly fresh water in east and southeast England, certain estuaries in Ireland, in southwest Europe and in north Africa. Another widely distributed but not abundant Hydrobia is the Looping snail *Truncatella subcylindrica* – so called because it loops along rather like a leech alternately attaching the foot and the snout. This animal lives on salt marshes near the high water mark amongst seablite, *Suaeda,* and Sea purslane *Halimione.* It can breathe either in air or in water. The small shell is characterized by its truncated tip which occurs because the terminal three whorls break off in the adult leaving the shell terminated by a limy plate. Finally, there is Taylor's spire snail *Bythinella scholzi* which is the smallest of the Spire snails, the shell length being only $\frac{1}{10}$ in (2·5 mm). Taylor's spire snail lives in canals in Britain, having been introduced from North America in about 1900. It also occurs in north and central Europe and southwest Russia and feeds on decaying meadow grass *Glyceria.* A characteristic feature is that the tentacles can be withdrawn to two small spheres. In common with all other operculate snails, the eyes of this animal are at the bases of the tentacles.

The mode of reproduction of the Laver spire snail and the Jenkins' spire snail are markedly different. In the former the sexes are separate and the eggs are stuck onto the shell of the female to form a gelatinous mass from which planktonic larvae emerge. The Jenkins' spire snail, however, is parthenogenetic and broods the young which are then liberated as miniature adults. Only one male has ever been found and the species was first recorded in the mid-19th century as a brackish water form. In the late 19th century it appeared to be moving into freshwater where it is now a dominant freshwater snail.

The behaviour of the Laver spire snail is known in some detail. When uncovered by the tide the snails crawl and browse on the surface of the deposits, orientating by means of the sun. At a later stage they burrow and feed on material just below the surface of the substratum then finally emerge just as the flowing tide reaches them. Then they launch themselves afloat by means of a mucus raft which is continuously formed and periodically eaten along with entrapped food particles. When the tide ebbs, the snails are stranded where the gradient of the shore is shallow and the cycle of behaviour is repeated. Such floating may also serve to distribute the snail towards freshwater, but contact with low salinities evokes sinking so that the Laver spire snail rarely occurs in brackish conditions.

Closely related to the Spire snails are the freshwater Bithynia snails. They also belong to the family Hydrobiidae and include the Common bithynia *Bithynia tentaculata* and Leach's bithynia *B. leachi*. Both are distinguished from the Spire snails by the possession of a limy operculum. The shell of the Common bithynia is yellowish in colour and large, reaching a length of ⅗ in (1·5 cm). It occurs in hard waters and lakes in Britain and central Europe, western Siberia, northwest Africa and has been introduced into

North America. The shell of Leach's bithynia is approximately half of the length of the previous species. It lives characteristically in hard, densely-weeded waters and occurs throughout England (except in the southwest), in central Ireland, in Europe and northern Asia. FAMILY: Hydrobiidae, ORDER: Mesogastropoda, CLASS: Gastropoda, PHYLUM: Mollusca. R.C.N.

HYDROCORALLINES, an order of hydrozoans which lay down a calcareous skeleton, in contrast to the chitinous perisarc or sheath of the other orders. (See Hydrozoa.) They look like a kind of small coral. There are two suborders: Milleporina and Stylasterina. In the former there is only one genus, *Millepora*, which forms extensive reefs in tropical shallow seas and may contribute to coral reefs. The white or whitish-yellow branching skeleton is pitted with pores of two sizes. There are large pores surrounded

Above: a group of polyps of *Tubularia larynx*.

Left: one of the Trachymedusae, *Gonionemus murbachi*, barely 2.5 cm across. Its polyp stage is very much reduced.

by a circle of small pores. The *polyps which occupy these pores are very small, and include a central feeding polyp, with four to six reduced tentacles bearing only clusters of *nematocysts, and protective polyps or dactylozooids. The latter are slender and mouthless with alternating knobbed tentacles, and they arise from the ring of smaller pores. They have two or three types of nematocyst, one of which is found only in *Millepora*. Tiny reduced *medusae are produced which live only for a few hours and release gametes.

The Stylasterina resemble *Millepora* superficially, forming pink, red or purple branching, calcareous growths and living in tropical and subtropical seas, from shallow to deep waters. The distribution of pores is different. There is a larger, central pore with slit-like pores radiating from it, making a star-shaped pattern. Also, free medusae are not produced, instead young planulae escape from the colony. CLASS: Hydrozoa, PHYLUM: Cnidaria.

HYDROZOA, one of the three classes of Cnidaria, comprising over 2,700 species. Many members are polymorphic, both *polyp and *medusa being present in the life-history (see alternation of generations), although often the medusa is reduced and never leaves the parent colony. Some hydrozoans are oceanic, drifting with the currents and seen only occasionally – for example, siphonophores – while others are inhabitants of the lower shore or shallow

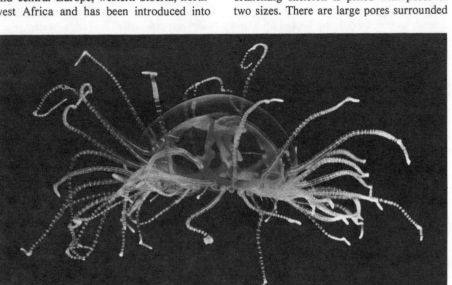

Colonies of Feather polyps *Kirchenpaueria* (= *Plumularia*) *pinnata*, one of the thecate Hydrozoa.

waters – for example, Sea firs (hydroids). Most hydrozoans are marine, an exception being the freshwater *Hydra, and they may be solitary or colonial. In general Hydrozoa are small, polyps and medusae measuring only a few millimetres across, but some members do attain greater size. The ectodermal cells secrete a skeleton, either of chitin round the colony, termed the perisarc, or of calcareous material.

The class is divided into seven orders as follows:

Order Athecata	*Tubularia* (Oaten-pipes hydroid), *Hydra*, *Velella* (By-the-wind-sailor)
Order Thecata	*Obelia*
Order Limnomedusae	*Craspedacusta*
Order Narcomedusae	*Cunina*
Order Trachymedusae	*Geryonia*
Order Siphonophora	*Physalia* (Portuguese man-o'-war)
Order Hydrocorallinae	*Millepora*

In the orders Athecata and Thecata the polyp is the simplest found in the Cnidaria, being made up of two cell layers separated by a thin layer of mesogloea. It is cylindrical with a mouth and tentacles at one end, and is either closed at the other, aboral, end or is extended to form a stolon connecting adjacent polyps in the colony. There are no projections or mesenteries from the body wall in the central enteron or body cavity.

In the thecata hydroids each polyp has a ring of elongated, solid tentacles surrounding the mouth and it is situated in a chitinous cup or theca which is an extension of the perisarc. In the athecate hydroids the polyps are naked – the old name for the order was Gymnoblastea – and they show a greater variety of tentacle type and arrangement. The tentacles may bear a terminal knob packed with nematocysts (capitate) or be elongate, bearing nematocysts along the whole length (filiform). Capitate tentacles are usually distributed over the polyp, while filiform tentacles may form a basal circle with capitate tentacles strewn over the top of the polyp, or there may be two sets of filiform tentacles present.

Hydrozoa are carnivorous and small invertebrates, such as crustaceans, are caught by the nematocysts on their tentacles and conveyed by the tentacles to the mouth. Inside the enteron digestion is extra-cellular at first and then intra-cellular, particles being taken up by the endodermal cells.

There are no well developed muscles, movements being brought about by musculo-epithelial cells which bear muscle fibres in the part of the cell lying on the mesogloea. The nervous system consists of a diffuse nerve-net, whose properties are only just being investigated.

The medusae are generally minute saucer or thimble-shaped jellyfishes with only a moderate increase in mesogloea. The mouth is borne on a central manubrium, like a handle on the underside of the jellyfish, from which radiate canals, few in number when compared with those in a large jellyfish. These are lined with cilia and join into a circular canal round the margin of the medusa. This canal system allows the circulation of food materials and oxygen round the medusa. Round the margin also are a varying number of tentacles and generally present is a circular shelf projecting inwards from the margin, known as the velum. Food organisms are paralyzed by the nematocysts scattered over the upper surface of the medusa. These are passed by cilia to the edge of the medusa and collected from there by the manubrium.

The medusae produced by athecate hydroids are known as anthomedusae and are thimble-shaped, with their gonads developing on the manubrium. Thecate hydroids produce saucer-shaped leptomedusae and the gonads develop on the radial canals.

The free-swimming medusae possess sense organs round their margins. Ocelli, red, brown or black spots at the bases of the tentacles, are connected to the nerve-net and are sensitive to light, the medusae being unresponsive to light if they are removed. In addition, leptomedusae possess statocysts, pits sited at the base of the velum. These pits contain concretions of calcium carbonate in special cells. The simplest types are open to the sea, but the others are enclosed. All are thought to be organs of equilibrium and responsible for orientating the medusa if it becomes moved out of a horizontal position.

In medusae there is evidence of two separately-conducting nerve-nets. One is a 'through-conducting' system overlying a ring of striated muscle fibres in the bell margin. These nerve cells are bipolar and one of them being stimulated leads to the contraction of the whole bell. A nerve-net composed of multi-polar nerve cells spreads over the upper and under surfaces of the medusa and is responsible for local contractions of the bell.

The method of production of the medusae depends on the order. In the thecate hydroids the medusa is budded off asexually from a modified feeding polyp known as the blastostyle, which is enclosed in a protective case, an extension of the perisarc, called the gonotheca. This blastostyle may be produced from the stolons of the colony or from stems of the polyps. Many medusae are produced in one gonotheca, the oldest bud being nearest the top of the blastostyle. All develop in a complex way from protuberances which include both ectoderm and endoderm. In the athecate hydroids, the medusae are produced singly as asexual buds or gonophores. Gonophores are oval, stalked bodies which lack any protective perisarc and which arise in a variety of places, from stolons, from the head of the polyp, or less commonly from specially modified feeding polyps. However, only 30% of the Athecata and 20% of the Thecata produce free-living medusae. The others produce medusae in varying stages of reduction which remain attached to the parent colony and the ova they carry are fertilized in situ by incoming spermatozoa. In many species the planula larva which develops from the fertilized ovum grows to an actinula larva before release into the sea.

The planula or actinula swims about for a while then settles down and in athecate and many thecate hydroids gives rise to a polyp which then buds off other polyps and forms a colony. In some thecate families the planula never becomes a polyp but becomes a continuously-growing stolon from which arise branches bearing polyps. Growth in colonial forms may give rise to hydrorhizal colonies, polyps springing from a basal mat of stolons, or various branching colonies looking like plants and giving rise to the popular name 'Sea fir'. Some athecate polyps are solitary; for example *Hydra,* which is atypical and lives in freshwater. There are also some floating forms which used to be classified as members of the order Siphonophora, namely *By-the-wind sailor, Velella,* which resembles an inverted polyp with a large float.

Three small orders of medusae are also placed in the Hydrozoa: the Limnomedusae, Trachymedusae and Narcomedusae. In these there is usually no polyp the planula larva developing via an actinula larva direct to a medusa, broad and flat, and in the Trachymedusae the medusa has a long pseudomanubrium, an extension of the sub-

A group of polyps of *Clava squamata*, one of the athecate Hydrozoa, growing on seaweed.

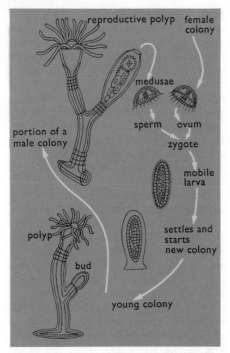

Ostrich-plume polyps *Aglaophenia myriophyllum*, 7.5 cm high.

Life-cycle of marine colonial hydroid *Obelia*, showing medusa and polyp stages which constitute the alternation of generations.

The Rock hyrax *Heterohyrax brucei*, or Yellow-spotted dassie, of eastern and southern Africa.

umbrella or under surface. The planula of an interesting narcomedusan *Cunina* is parasitic on the trachymedusan *Geryonia*. It attaches to the *Geryonia* medusa and develops a stolon from which bud off medusae. In the Limnomedusae is a rare freshwater medusa, *Craspedacusta*, which grows up to 1 in (20 mm) in diameter. It was first found in London in 1880 in a pond containing an Amazonian water lily brought from Brazil. It has since been found in ponds in America as a minute polyp, *Microhydra*, which buds off small medusae.

The *Siphonophora are colonial forms showing the highest degree of polymorphism found in the Cnidaria. These swimming or floating colonies are composed of both polyps and medusae. These include feeding polyps, palpons or 'feelers', bracts and swimming bells. Often a chitinous float is present and is the only part of the colony visible above the waves. The Portuguese man-o'-war, *Physalia*,

is the best known siphonophore with very powerful nematocysts borne on trailing tentacles several metres in length.

Some members of the Hydrozoa produce a calcareous skeleton. These are the *hydrocorallines, for example *Millepora*, and are generally found in tropical seas. *Millepora* is an important contributor to coral reefs. PHYLUM: Cnidaria. S.E.H.

HYLIDAE, a large family of frogs. Most are arboreal and are dealt with under treefrogs.

HYNOBIIDS, among the most primitive of living salamanders, they are confined to Asia, most species having a restricted distribution, often in high mountains. See White dragon. FAMILY: Hynobiidae, ORDER: Caudata, CLASS: Amphibia.

HYRAX, rabbit-sized relatives of elephants living in Africa and southwest Asia. There are two species of Tree hyrax and a half-dozen species of Rock hyrax. See dassies.

IBEX, the name given to seven species of wild goat living in high mountains. They mostly differ from the true wild goat in the smaller amount of black in their colouration, in their flattened foreheads, and in their broad-fronted horns, although this last difference does not apply to the Pyreneean or Spanish ibex.

The Alpine ibex *Capra ibex* is 32–34 in high (80–85 cm), with backcurved horns averaging 26 in (67·5 cm) long. The horns have a broad front surface with even-spaced knots on it; the outer angle is somewhat bevelled off, so that the knots fade towards the outer side. Alpine ibex are dark brown, darker on the underparts and face. Like many ungulates they tend to develop a hard stomach concretion of indigestible matter, called the 'bezoar stone' and in former days this was considered to be an antidote to poison, among other things, and because of it ibex were nearly exterminated. At the beginning of the century the Gran Paradiso National Park in northern Italy was founded for their preservation; from there ibex have been reintroduced all over the Alps.

The Siberian ibex *Capra sibirica* is larger, 40 in (101 cm) high, with horns averaging 53 in (133 cm) in the large southern race. Big males may weigh 200 lb (90 kg). The horns curve more than those of the Alpine ibex, forming at least a semicircle, and the outer angle is not bevelled off, so that the front surface is square with the knots very prominent. The northern race *C. s. sibirica*, from the Altai system, is light yellow-white in winter, usually darker on the shoulders, lumbar region, throat, breast and front of the legs. It is smaller, with horns not above 3 ft (91 cm) long. The southern race *C. s. sakeen*, from the Tienshan, Pamir and Kashmir ranges, is dark brown in winter with a whitish 'saddle' in the male, and long horns. Both races are darker in summer. In the Pamir, ibex ascend to 16,000 ft (5,000 m); elsewhere, they go less high.

The Caucasian ibex, known locally as tur, are about the same size, but more heavily built. There are two species there, whose interrelationships have recently become clear thanks to the work of Vereschagin, Zalkin

and Heptner. The Kuban tur *C. caucasica* is found in the western Caucasus; its horns resemble the Alpine ibex (as does its colour pattern), but the knots are lower, less accentuated, and the horns are shorter and thicker. The Daghestan tur *C. cylindricornis* is found in the eastern Caucasus. Its horns are thick and rounded, with no trace of knots. They turn out and up, then back and down, finally the tips turn in and up—quite unlike any other ibex, but more like the Blue sheep or bharal. In the central Caucasus, the two species interbreed, and as much as 10% of the central ibex population consists of

Siberian ibex.

hybrids. However, the hybrids do not themselves appear to breed—they are very uniform in appearance, with an intermediate type of horn—so that there is no actual gene exchange between the two species. The two species of tur are fairly similar in other respects, but the Daghestan tur differs slightly more from other ibex, and it seems likely that it has diverged fairly recently.

The Nubian ibex *C. nubiana* is small, only 33 in (84 cm) high, with horns 43–47 in (109–119 cm) long; it is light fawn, with the dark markings well pronounced, especially on the front of the legs. It is found in the mountains on both sides of the Red Sea: northern Eritrea, north to Cairo, Sinai and Arabia.

The walia or Abyssinian ibex *C. walie* is 38 in (96 cm) high with horns 40–45 in (101–114 cm) long. Like the Nubian and Siberian ibex, the front surface of the horns is broad and square with prominent knots. It has a marked bony boss on the forehead and is reddish-brown in colour with well-pronounced leg-markings. It occurs only in the Simien mountains of Ethiopia, at 13°N, 38°E. In 1965 only 150–200 were thought to have survived.

The last and most distinctive species is the Spanish ibex *C. pyrenaica*. This is a small species, 28–30 in (70–75 cm) high, weighing about 100 lb (45 kg). The male has horns 48 in (120 cm) long, not dissimilar to the Daghestan tur but closer together and more upright, compressed, with a sharp anterior keel. The colour pattern is sharp, like a true wild goat, with clearly marked black flank-band and black legs and face and a white belly. Spanish ibex are extremely rare and the only places where they are at all common are on some of the high ranges of Southern Spain, such as the Sierra de Gredos and Sierra Nevada. The Pyreneean race has been reduced to a herd of about 20 in the Mt Perdido area. Ibex from other localities have recently been released there and although they are of different races, at least the species will survive in the Pyrenees.

In spring, ibex live below the snow-line in separate-sexed herds; the old males live near the female/kid herds, however. In late summer, the males retreat to high altitudes, where they live alone or in groups of three or four. In October to January (which is the rutting season; the exact time depending on the locality) the males rejoin the females, collecting harems of 5–15 females around them. At this time the males feed little, but fight fiercely, rearing on the hindlegs and bringing their horns clashing together. The young males, whose horns are not yet fully developed, usually fail to win harems; accordingly it is mainly the five to six year old males who rut. The rut lasts seven to ten days, during which time most of the females are covered; but some strong males with huge harems cannot cover them all, so each year 15–20% of the females stay barren.

The Alpine ibex in Switzerland, a wild goat living in high mountains.

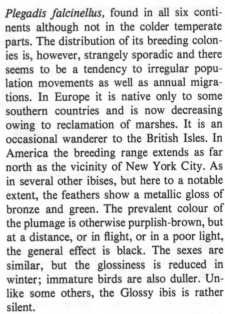

In the mating ceremony, the male holds his tail up against his back, so that the white underside is visible; he stands with neck outstretched in front of or behind the female, making stroking motions towards her with his foreleg (laufschlag); he sticks his tongue out, flipping it from time to time. The female makes symbolic butts with the horns, then the male mounts, clasping the female with his forelegs, his head held up. This is clearly a simplified version of the gazelle ceremony.

Newborn ibex weigh 8–9 lb (3½–4 kg); one or two are dropped per female, from May to June. They continue suckling until autumn, but begin to graze at one month. Females begin to breed at two years old in captivity, but in the wild not usually until they are between three and six years old. FAMILY: Bovidae, ORDER: Artiodactyla, CLASS: Mammalia.   C.P.G.

IBISES, stork-like birds of moderate size characterized by long, thin and markedly decurved bills, resembling that of the curlew and similarly used. The smaller species are also comparable with the curlew in general dimensions; others are considerably larger. The neck is long, as are the legs; the feet are slightly webbed, between the three forward-directed toes. There is a considerable range of plumage colouration among the species. The ibises are placed in the same family as the spoonbills, but in a separate subfamily. The Wood ibises (to which the generic name *Ibis* belongs) are, however, classed with the true storks.

This group of 24 species has a world-wide distribution in tropical, subtropical and some temperate countries (absent from New Zealand). There is one cosmopolitan species; the others are restricted either to the Old World or the New. Their usual habitat is in the neighbourhood of fresh water and their food consists largely of small animals, aquatic and otherwise.

Ibises tend to be gregarious at all times and breed in colonies. The nesting site may vary even for a single species, but is commonly in trees, bushes, or reedbeds and sometimes on cliffs, or on stony islands. There are usually three or four eggs. In the different species the eggs range in colour from off-white to blue, and they may be marked or plain. The sexes share parental duties.

The world-wide species is the Glossy ibis

The Sacred Ibis of southern Africa in flight.

Plegadis falcinellus, found in all six continents although not in the colder temperate parts. The distribution of its breeding colonies is, however, strangely sporadic and there seems to be a tendency to irregular population movements as well as annual migrations. In Europe it is native only to some southern countries and is now decreasing owing to reclamation of marshes. It is an occasional wanderer to the British Isles. In America the breeding range extends as far north as the vicinity of New York City. As in several other ibises, but here to a notable extent, the feathers show a metallic gloss of bronze and green. The prevalent colour of the plumage is otherwise purplish-brown, but at a distance, or in flight, or in a poor light, the general effect is black. The sexes are similar, but the glossiness is reduced in winter; immature birds are also duller. Unlike some others, the Glossy ibis is rather silent.

The Hermit ibis *Geronticus eremita,* also called Waldrapp, is now found only in the Middle East and North Africa, but until the 17th century it bred in Switzerland and other parts of Central Europe. It is peculiar in living in dry country and nesting on cliffs. It has a very disagreeable and persistent smell, which has been likened to that of putrid carrion, and its flesh tastes equally bad. The food consists mainly of insects, especially beetles. The plumage is mostly bronze-green and purple, with a metallic sheen, but the face and crown are bare of feathers, the skin being dull crimson like the bill. There is a related species in the mountains of southern Africa.

The best known species is undoubtedly the Sacred ibis *Threskiornis aethiopica*. It is now extinct in Egypt, but it was revered there in ancient days and many mummified bodies and mural pictures have been found, some showing eggs and young. Farther south in Africa, it is still a common bird, feeding in flocks on the river banks or on open ground. Its contrasting pattern of black and white makes it conspicuous and easily recognizable. The plumage is all white, except for dark wing-tips and dark plumes on the lower back. The head and neck are bare of feathers, with black skin, and the dark red legs may appear black from a distance. The birds fly, often in V-formation, with necks outstretched as do other ibises. Nesting is in trees or on the ground.

Three similar species of white ibises are found in southern Asia and Australia. Of these, the Straw-necked ibis *T. spinicollis* has stiff buff-coloured plumes on the lower neck.

The hadada *Hagedashia hagedash* is an African species with a loud yelping cry, uttered in flight or at rest and sometimes at night. The plumage is dark olive-brown, with a green metallic sheen on the wing-coverts and a blue-black sheen on flight feathers and tail. It is found especially on the banks of rivers and it frequently perches in trees.

The Warty-headed ibis *Pseudibis papillosa* of India, which has bare areas of strongly pigmented skin on the head and neck, also has a patch of red papillae on the bare black skin of the crown. A related

The White ibis of tropical America.

The rarest of all ibises, the Bald ibis *Geronticus calvus*.

species inhabits Southeast Asia. Some ibises have crests, for example the Olive ibis *Lampribis olivacea* and the Spotted-breasted ibis *L. rara* of Africa and the Crested ibis *Lophotibis cristata* of Madagascar. The Wattled ibis *Bostrychia carunculata* of Ethiopia has a wattle hanging from the throat.

Of the now very rare Japanese ibis *Nipponia nippon,* a white bird with a red face, only one small colony is known to exist. The Giant ibis *Thaumatibis gigantea* of Southeast Asia is notable for its size.

The most beautiful species is the Scarlet ibis *Eudocimus ruber* of the Caribbean area, the adults of which are bright scarlet. The related White ibis *E. albus* has a range extending northwards to the southern United States; the young are dark, but the adults are white except for dark wing-tips, dull red bare skin on the face, and pink legs.

Seven other ibises are found in South America, chiefly in the tropical parts. FAMILY: Threskiornithidae, ORDER: Ciconiiformes, CLASS: Aves.   A.L.T.

IBIS PUZZLE. In Konrad *Gesner's *Historia animalium* there is a chapter entitled *De Corvo Sylvatico*—about the Wood crow. Gesner explains that this bird is known commonly as *Waldrapp*—Forest raven, *Steinrapp*—Stone raven or *Meerrapp*—Sea raven. The Waldrapp was about the size of a hen, black tinged with green, long legs, long red bill, short tail and almost bare head. It ate insects and was migratory. Later authors copied Gesner's description, calling it Gesner's wood-crow. But by the 18th century there had been no new firsthand description of the Waldrapp and its existence was denied. Then in the latter part of the 19th century the similarity of Gesner's Waldrapp to the recently discovered Hermit ibis of Africa was noticed and a search of old manuscripts, including Pliny's *Natural History,* showed that the Hermit ibis had once lived over most of southeastern Europe as far as Switzerland and Bavaria. Gesner was vindicated.

ICEFISHES, or bloodlessfishes, antarctic fishes that appear to lack blood. Reports of these bloodless fishes by men back from whaling expeditions were not believed until about 1930 when scientists examined specimens on the spot. They found that the fishes were not, in fact, without blood but that the blood contained no red cells. This was most noticeable in the gills, which were a pale cream instead of the usual red. The common name icefish is preferred to the older name of bloodlessfishes. A number of genera are included in this group (*Chaenocephalus, Chaenodraco, Cryodraco,* etc.) which is placed in the family of antarctic cods. All

The Scarlet ibis has been slain mercilessly because of the beauty of its feathers.

are slim-bodied fishes, less than 12 in (30 cm) long, and have large heads and mouths. The shape of the head has given rise to another common name, the crocodilefishes.

The red colour of blood is caused by the presence of haemoglobin, a chemical agent capable of uniting with oxygen, transporting it around the body and releasing it where it is required for muscle action, etc. It is difficult at first to see how the icefishes can survive without any oxygen carrier. Their blood is almost colourless and contains only a few white corpuscles. Experiments have shown that the only oxygen in the blood is the very small amount that is dissolved in the blood plasma, the watery fluid that normally carries the red blood cells. In active fishes in warmer waters this would certainly not be sufficient for the normal body requirements. In the icefishes, however, the environment is very stable, with the water only a little above freezing point, and the fishes themselves are rather sluggish in their habits. In addition, there is an unusually large amount of blood in the body. These seem to be the principal factors that enable the icefishes to survive without red blood cells. FAMILY: Nototheniidae, ORDER: Perciformes, CLASS: Pisces.

ICHNEUMON *Herpestes ichneumon,* name commonly used for a species of *mongoose, also called the Egyptian mongoose and Pharaoh's cat. It was equated by the Ancient Greeks with an animal revered by the Egyptians because it destroyed crocodile's eggs, but that animal was probably a monitor lizard. Nevertheless, the name is still used for the mongoose.

ICHNEUMON FLIES, parasitic wasps of the superfamily Ichneumonoidea. In common with the bees and wasps, female ichneumons have a spine-like ovipositor which is used as an organ of penetration. Whilst this is modified as a sting in bees and wasps it is used by ichneumons primarily to lay their eggs inside or close to the bodies of their hosts, usually other insects.

There are 11 families of which two, the Ichneumonidae and the Braconidae are abundant and relatively well-known. Ichneumons are largely parasites of caterpillars of moths but they also attack aphids and beetles. Like all the higher Hymenoptera, ichneumons have a wasp-waisted appearance owing to the very slender first and second segments of the abdomen. They are generally red, black or yellow in colour and are active fliers. They have long, many segmented antennae which are not elbowed. The wings are divided by veins into a number of small distinct cells, often having a hardened patch called a stigma near the apex on the leading edge of the forewing. The ovipositor protrudes from the ventral part of the abdomen some way before the tip.

Adult ichneumons are free living and as liquid feeders they are often to be found in the summer visiting flower heads, especially those of the Umbelliferae. They are active, quickly flying insects whose behaviour seems to be highly purposive. Indeed this is a necessary part of their lives, for the adult females are very specific in the host caterpillars they attack and consequently have to be able to find suitable hosts for the development of their offspring. When egg laying, the female unsheaths the ovipositor and thrusts it into the body of the host, thus depositing the egg hypodermically. The young ichneumon larva grows rapidly inside the host, feeding first on its blood and later on other body tissues. Eventually the host is entirely consumed from inside and the Ichneumon fly larva breaks through the now shrunken skin of the caterpillar to make its own cocoon and to pupate. Thereafter it leads a free living existence. Almost every species of caterpillar is liable to attack by some species of Ichneumon fly. A few examples may be given. The Mediterranean flour moth *Anagasta*

kuhniella is commonly attacked by *Nemeritis (Devorgilla) canescens*. The Wheat stem sawfly *Cephus cinctus* an important crop pest is attacked by *Hemiteles hemipterus*

Many ichneumons attack wood- and stem-boring larvae of moths, beetles and other Hymenoptera. One such Ichneumon fly is *Rhyssa persuasoria,* a parasite of Wood wasp larvae, which can attain a total length of 4 in (10 cm). Adults may be seen in conifer forests in spring and early summer, feeding on nectar at flower-heads. The males emerge from the timber first, flying up and down infested trees searching for signs of emerging females. After mating, the female seeks trees containing larvae or pupae of the Wood wasp which lie in small chambers within the wood at the end of long, frass-filled tunnels. The wasp probably finds the infested tree by responding to odours emanating from the wood, which is permeated by a symbiotic fungus introduced by the Wood wasp when she lays her eggs. Having located a tree, *Rhyssa* uses her antennae to find indications of the larvae beneath the surface, and having found a suitable place, she drills her fine, hypodermic-like ovipositor through the bark and into the wood. Detailed study of this behaviour has shown that it is the frass from the gallery, not the host larva, that stimulates drilling, but the frass nearest the host is the most attractive. Because the parasite will drill into cultures of fungus only, it is likely that she responds to chemicals produced by the

fungus and its interractions with the wood, and host larva. When the ichneumon larva hatches it feeds on the immobilized host until it is consumed, and then spins a cocoon within which it passes the winter months before becoming adult in the spring and chewing its way out of the wood.

Many ichneumons are hyperparasitic, that is they attack only caterpillars that have already been parasitized by another parasitic species; and their larvae feed on the contained parasite larva. A very common braconid parasite *Apanteles glomeratus* attacks larvae of the Cabbage white butterfly *Pieris brassicae*. These parasites are very small and

Larvae of an endoparasitic ichneumon emerging from a Small white butterfly caterpillar.

An adult ichneumon *Rhyssa persuasoria* with her long ovipositor with which she is able to bore into wood in search of suitable hosts for her young.

as many as 20–30 of their larvae can develop inside one caterpillar. When mature they emerge through the skin of the dying host and construct bright yellow cocoons in irregular masses on walls, stones or tree trunks.

One remarkable Ichneumon fly, *Agriotypus armatus,* a parasite of Caddis fly larvae which live in streams, dives into the water and swims until a host is found and parasitized. The ichneumon develops in the host, spins a cocoon within the caddis case, and completes its development underwater.

The larger Ichneumon flies are solitary parasites, probably because the host provides only enough food material for the complete development of one parasite larva.

Because of their selective attack on many crop eating caterpillars Ichneumon flies have been used extensively in the biological control of insect pests. ORDER: Hymenoptera, CLASS: Insecta, PHYLUM: Arthropoda.

J.P.S. and R.C.F.

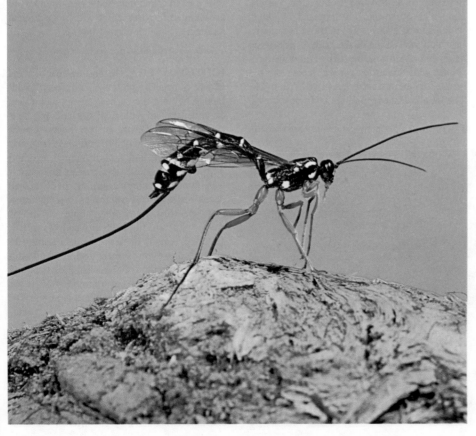

ICHTHYOLOGY, the study of fishes (Gk *Ichthys*—fish, *logos*—discourse or knowledge). It is of interest that the word was first used in 1646 whereas ornithology, the study of birds, was not used until 1706, entomology, the study of insects, was first used in 1766, and herpetology, the study of reptiles, in 1824. If nothing else, these dates show the order in which these studies achieved scientific popularity.

ICHTHYOPTERYGIA, subclass of extinct marine reptiles sometimes known as fish-lizards but better known as *ichthyosaurs. They were shaped like fishes and like them were fully aquatic but they breathed by lungs, so were surface swimmers, and their skin was without scales. All four limbs were modified to form flattened turtle-like flippers, by a big increase in the numbers of finger and toe bones. CLASS: Reptilia.

ICHTHYORNIS, the earliest known fossil species of non-toothed birds. In the history of birds there is a long gap between the toothed *Archaeopteryx,* which lived in the Jurassic period, ending 135 million years ago, and *Ichthyornis* of the Cretaceous period which succeeded the Jurassic and lasted until 70 million years ago. The fossils which have been given the name *Ichthyornis* come from the Niobrara chalk beds of Kansas which were laid down during the upper Cretaceous. The silts laid down in the seas over which *Ichthyornis* flew were excellent for the reception of materials for fossilization; whereas animals dying on land would be dismembered, dispersed and consumed by scavengers and decay. At that time these beds were at the bottom of the sea over which flew large reptiles, such as *Pteranodon,* and at least six species of *Ichthyornis.*

The best-known of these, indeed one of of the best-known of all fossil birds in spite of its great age, is *I. victor* which was a bird of very modern appearance, something like a tern, but about 8 ft (2½ m) high. The structure of its 'arm' and pectoral girdle show quite clearly that it flew well and its skull structure indicates that it was a fish-eater, or perhaps a scavenger.

Ichthyornis was originally stated to have possessed primitive teeth in its jaws, as did *Hesperornis*—another bird living in the same area at the same time. Subsequent more detailed investigation of the fossil material has shown that the toothed jaws found with the fossil *Ichthyornis* material almost certainly belonged to a contemporary aquatic reptile and there is no real evidence that *Ichthyornis* had teeth. However, whether it possessed teeth or not, it gives us a clear indication that the avian stock had produced specialized forms at that very early period. The *Ichthyornis* finds suggest that other avian specialists were then extant, particularly when taken with *Hesperornis,* which was much larger, flightless and an underwater swimmer. FAMILY: Ichthyornithidae, ORDER: Ichthyornithiformes, CLASS: Aves.   P.M.D.

ICHTHYOSAURS, extinct marine reptiles that lived in the Jurassic and Cretaceous periods, 180–70 million years ago. They were fish-shaped or, better still, porpoise-shaped, the head having a beak-like snout, the body tapering to a fish-like tailfin and with a triangular dorsal fin, unsupported by bone, which can be clearly seen in those specimens in which the outline of the body is preserved as an impression in the rock. The jaws were armed with numerous conical teeth, striated on the surface and set in a groove in each jaw. The skin was brownish and without scales.

The limbs were flippers, those in front larger than the rear flippers. The limb-bones were short and broad, the bones of the digits pentagonal or hexagonal and set in a mosaic. Ichthyosaurs were 1–30 ft (0·5–9·9 m) long or more. They swam near the surface, using the tail for propulsion and the flippers as balancers or for changing direction. They were worldwide, and small skeletons inside the larger skeletons in some specimens leave little doubt they bore living young (ovoviviparous). ORDER: Ichthyosauria, CLASS: Reptilia.

ICHTHYOSAUR DISCOVERY. In 1811, Mary Anning then a girl of twelve years of age, living at Lyme Regis in Dorset, found the first ichthyosaur. Her father, a cabinet-maker, used to take her along the cliffs collecting fossils which he sold to visitors coming to his shop in Lyme Regis. He died while she was still young, and shortly after his death she sold an ammonite for two shillings and sixpence and was quick to realize that this might help to relieve the family's financial difficulties. She sold the skeleton of the ichthyosaur for £25 to the lord of the manor, and it was finally bought by the Duke of Buckingham for £200. Not only did Mary Anning find the first ichthyosaur, she also found the first plesiosaur and the first pterodactyl, two more large fossil reptiles which were also unknown until then, and this at a time when women were not expected to take part in scientific discoveries, even less to go clambering over cliffs with a geological hammer.

ICHTHYOSTEGA, the best known of three genera of fossil amphibians from East Greenland. They are the earliest tetrapods known, coming from a geological horizon which is either Upper Devonian or basal Lower Carboniferous (about 350 million years ago).

Ichthyostega had well-developed legs and limb girdles. In most details of its anatomy it was typically amphibian: it had a well developed vertebral column and strong tetrapod-type ribs. However, some structures show that it was not far removed from its fish ancestry. Among these are a tail bearing a fin supported by fin spines and a skull still carrying vestigial bones behind the jaw articulation which are remnants of those which in fish support the gill covers. ORDER: Ichthyostegalia, SUPERORDER: Labyrinthodontia, CLASS: Amphibia.

ICTIDOSAURS, an extinct group of highly advanced mammal-like reptiles found in rocks of uppermost Triassic age in southern Africa. They are only known from fragmentary skull and jaw material but their characteristics are of great interest for their

Ichthyosaur remains from the Lower Jurassic rocks of Germany, so perfectly preserved that the skin and other soft parts can be studied.

close approach to the mammalian structure. *Diarthrognathus* is the best known genus. Ictidosaurs are best considered as a lateral and sterile offshoot of the mammalian line.

IDE, a carp-like fish otherwise known as the orfe.

IGUANAS, the largest and most elaborately marked group of lizards in the New World. The family is almost totally restricted to that area, except for two genera in Madagascar and one genus in Polynesia. Iguanids range from species 3 in (7·5 cm) long to those 6 ft (2 m) in length. Their diets may be insectivorous, carnivorous, herbivorous or omnivorous. Many forms are territorial. All are oviparous except for the Swift lizards *Sceloporus* and Horned lizards *Phrynosoma* some of which are ovoviparous. The eggs are soft-shelled and buried underground.

The Common iguana *Iguana iguana* ranges from the lowlands of central Mexico south into southern South America. It lives in the vicinity of ponds or rivers at altitudes from sea-level to the mountains. Iguanas bask on branches of trees during the day, usually over water so that if danger appears the reptile can drop (sometimes for a considerable distance) into the river or pool, dive, and remain submerged on the bottom for many minutes. These reptiles are fast runners, good climbers, swimmers and divers. Although well equipped for survival, this species has a reputation as a dietary delicacy. To hunt the iguana, young boys will follow a river, then while one of them climbs a tree to frighten the reptile into the water, two or three others dive in to catch the iguana where it is concealed in the rocks or debris on the bottom. This method is very effective, and in many regions this lizard is now very scarce or extinct.

This species has been sold in marketplaces in the tropics by stringing the animals together alive by the tendons of their hind limbs on poles for sale to the public. Because of this inhumane practice and their increased scarcity, the department of conservation of Mexico strictly protects this species, and it is now hoped that in many areas the iguana will begin to re-appear in numbers.

A number of species of large Ground iguanas *Ctenosaura* occur throughout Mexico and range farther north than the Common iguana. They are also found south into Central America. Although they do ascend trees, they prefer to hunt for food on the ground as they are mainly carnivorous. One form, the Black-and-white ground iguana *Ctenosaura similis* has large muscular jaws enabling it to prey on small rodents, other lizards and an occasional bird. These iguanas are also used as food by the local people.

In the Caribbean area, island forms of the

The Common iguana is one of the Green iguanas.

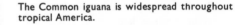

The Common iguana is widespread throughout tropical America.

Ground iguanas of the genus *Cyclura* have remained isolated from one another for long enough to evolve into several distinct forms. All of these primitive forms have a similar body build, are mainly ground-dwellers, and feed both on vegetation and small animal life. However, on the Lesser Antilles and the Virgin Islands near northern South America, the Ground iguanas are extinct and are known only from fossils found in caves. These islands are occupied by the Common

iguana, and it is possible that some overlap in competition resulted in the eventual extinction of the cyclurids in these areas.

One of the largest of these insular iguanas, is the Rhinoceros iguana of Haiti and neighbouring areas, which attains perhaps the greatest weight (although not the greatest length) of the iguanids. This reptile has heavier jaws than other members of this group. This, plus a grotesque pattern of enlarged scales on the head, including three prominent pointed scales on the snout, accounts for its popular name. Despite its formidable appearance, it is quick to run from man, and is hunted with trained dogs, which may result in the capture of one lizard in a day after hours of hunting. However, when cornered it can strike out with its tail with considerable force, and can bite hard when handled. It is becoming extremely rare because of extensive hunting for use as food and for zoological gardens. *Cyclura macleayi*, the Cuban Ground iguana, is another lizard rapidly becoming depleted in numbers. Current economic difficulties in Cuba and the Isle of Pines have resulted in increased pressure on populations of this lizard which will no doubt continue.

Island forms of these iguanas or, indeed, any other reptile can be depleted far more rapidly and with much less effort than mainland forms. Each island species is distinct and if it becomes depleted, there is no other source from which its numbers can be rebuilt. On the mainland, however, while local predation on a species may dent an overall population, if protection is introduced members of the species will often return to fill the gap. For this reason, it is doubtful if many insular forms of iguanas will long survive within the limited confines of islands that are being increasingly heavily populated.

One island form of iguana in the Pacific, the Marine iguana *Amblyrhynchus cristatus* has evolved on a number of the Galapagos Islands. A lack of natural enemies has resulted in a reptile that is apparently unafraid of man, but an inhospitable environment has produced some alterations in the basic iguana pattern resulting in a unique reptile. The Marine iguana, although possessing a very workable and strong (but little understood) territorial attitude, occurs in large herds, sometimes piled many deep on coastal lava rocks. It is vegetarian, but feeds mainly on various seaweeds growing at the bases of cliffs and in vast underwater 'fields'. These lizards submerge to graze on these beds of seaweed and are the only ones that have become adapted to a marine environment. Until Brookfield Zoo, Chicago, succeeded in maintaining a colony of these reptiles for more than three years, these intriguing reptiles had never before been successfully maintained in any number as an exhibit in a zoological park.

All iguanas have conventional legs and feet, and there appears to be no evidence that these are being lost, as is the case with many other lizard groups.

The tail of the Common iguana is edged with a row of sharp, serrated dorsal scales resembling a 'saw tooth'. When the long, slender, whip-like tail is swung toward an enemy, the blow can cause pain, and the sharp edge can cut through a cloth shirt. The iguana can shed its tail as a defence measure as can many lizards but the regenerated tail may not develop the 'saw tooth' characteristic.

Iguanas are voiceless, as are most reptiles, but a cornered iguana (particularly the cyclurids) can emit very audible gurgling hisses.

The ornamental scalation, enlarged and erectile throat fan, and dorsal fringe of the Common iguana produces a most fearsome appearance and is used by the males to indicate that territories are occupied without the need to resort to fighting. In the more primitive cyclurids which lack such conspicuous ornamentation, battles are rather commonplace. In fact, the startling ornamentation of the Common iguana has resulted in its being employed in film-making to play the role of 'dinosaur' in many science-fiction movies by magnifying the size of the beast on the screen to many times that of the humans it encounters.

Although the dark-coloured Ground iguanas are not capable of changing colour to any detectable degree, the Green iguanas can alter their shades of green or red considerably. In captivity, and even under artificial light, these lizards remain a dull green or shade of grey or brown. However,

in the tropics and in their natural environment, these lizards are often a brilliant, almost fluorescent green or bright orange. Unfortunately, these colours begin to fade over a period of days after they have been captured. FAMILY: Iguanidae, ORDER: Squamata, CLASS: Reptilia. R.P.

IGUANODON, ornithischian *dinosaur of the Upper Jurassic to Lower Cretaceous. It was a large bipedal herbivore with a maximum length of about 35 ft (10·5 m). The hindlimbs were powerful and the thumb bore a bony spike used in defence. The fossil skeletons and footprints have been found widely in Europe, and in North Africa and Asia. *Iguanodon* is of great historical interest as it was one of the first dinosaurs found, the original description by Mantell being based on teeth and bones from southern England. A remarkable collection of close on 30 skeletons was recovered in the 1870's from a subterranean deposit discovered in a coalmine at Bernissart in Belgium. ORDER: Ornithischia, CLASS: Reptilia.

IMITATION, is said to have occurred if an animal carries out an act or makes a sound which it has observed another individual making and when that act or sound is not one which the first animal would normally make in the situation.

It has been shown that some animals can solve a problem more quickly if they have previously observed another individual solving the same problem. This is particularly true of higher animals such as cats and monkeys but even fishes may show this facility. It can be taken as evidence of an ability to imitate the actions of the other individual.

Occasionally traditions arise through imitation; an example of this is the sweet-potato washing habit of a group of Japanese monkeys, *Macaca fuscata*. The monkeys were fed by Japanese scientists with sweet potatoes on the sandy shore of an island. The sweet potatoes were consequently gritty. One young individual learned to carry each sweet potato into the sea and wash it. The habit spread by imitation to other young monkeys and then to the adults so that, finally, 70% of the members of the colony had acquired the habit.

A species of Pacific dolphin, the Spinning dolphin *Stenella roseiventris* has the habit of spinning when it leaps out of the water. A Bottle-nosed dolphin *Tursiops truncatus* which does not normally do this was introduced into a show tank containing a Spinning dolphin. After watching the Spinning dolphin performing tricks for a food reward the Bottle-nosed dolphin leaped out of the

Young Japanese monkey learning to wash a sweet potato before eating it.

A Common iguana, climbing a manchioneal tree, strikes an aggressive attitude.

water and spun in a similar but much less expert fashion. Previously this dolphin had never been known to spin.

The best examples of imitation are those which have been observed in birds, many of which learn to reproduce sounds by imitation.

The ability of the Grey parrot *Psittacus erithacus* and the Indian hill mynah *Gracula religiosa* to imitate human speech is well known. Some 30 species of British birds are said to mimic the sounds made by other birds. Starlings *Sturnus vulgaris* are accomplished mimics and one has even been known to imitate the ringing of a telephone so accurately that a human observer was deceived by it.

A number of biologists have studied the way in which birds develop the ability to sing the song of their own species. Some birds learn their song by imitating birds of their own species, an example being the chaffinch *Fringilla coelebs* which is unable to sing its characteristic song if it has never heard another chaffinch sing. A young bird unable to sing its own song will, after a few months, be able to reproduce a perfect version of a chaffinch song after being allowed to hear another chaffinch singing. This is, therefore, a special case of imitation in which, although the animal is unable to imitate the song at the time, it is able to do so later as a result of its earlier experience.

T.B.P.

IMMORTALITY, in the usual sense of the word, that is, the indefinite continuation of the life of an individual, is unknown in science. Unicellular organisms that do not reproduce sexually and in which the entire body divides into two new organisms with nothing left over are sometimes said to be potentially immortal.

The continuity of the life of all types of organisms from generation to generation implies that a part of the living substance of one individual (in sexual reproduction, two individuals) forms the original piece of living matter of an individual of the next generation. Some biologists hold that the protoplasm of the germ cells is separated early from the rest which forms the remainder of the body, and thus that the germ plasm has a sort of potential immortality.

IMMUNITY, the ability of an organism to resist the invasion of its body by another organism. Traditionally the word has been associated with resistance to communicable disease. Thus it was long known that an attack of smallpox, if it did not kill, protected the individual from further attacks for the rest of his life. The patient was said to be immune to smallpox, a disease now known to be caused by a virus. More fundamentally we currently regard immunity as the ability of

the organism to distinguish between 'self' and 'non-self'. Thus immune mechanisms not only protect against disease but as a rule make it impossible to transplant skin, heart, kidney and other organs from one individual to another. In recent years research into methods of overcoming this natural immunity to transplants has been one of the most active aspects of biomedical studies. These experiments have added considerably to our knowledge of many fundamental processes in the living body.

An English physician, Edward Jenner, demonstrated in 1796 that by infecting patients with cowpox they were protected against smallpox. This was the first experiment in artificial immunization using a living organism *(Vaccinia)* and from it we get the term vaccination. With the discovery in the 19th century that bacteria caused many diseases, research into immune mechanisms began in earnest. Bacteriologists in the period 1880–1900 were divided into those who, following Metchnikoff, regarded immunity as being due to the ability of certain white blood cells (phagocytes) to destroy the invading bacteria by engulfing and digesting them, and those who led by Koch regarded chemical changes in the blood as the prime factor in immunity. The truth lay in a combination of the two theories. Phagocytosis occurs in all animals and indeed was first described in the Water flea *Daphnia*. On the other hand chemical protective substances (antibodies) can be produced by vertebrates but probably not by any invertebrates.

The toxins elaborated by some bacteria, notably diphtheria and tetanus, caused the production of antibodies by the patient. These antibodies reacted with the toxin and neutralized it both in the body and in the test tube. Whereas an injection of toxin would kill an experimental animal a mixture of toxin and antibody did not do so. It was then shown that the injection of many macromolecules (especially proteins) into experimental animals would result in the production of antibodies. Substances which caused the elaboration of antibodies were termed antigens. The study of blood groups showed that, in some cases, blood contained not only antigens on the red blood cells but that the plasma contained antibodies to the alternative antigen. Thus in the simple ABO blood grouping, group A individuals have anti-B in the plasma, group B have anti-A and group O have both anti-A and anti-B. The blood groups are inherited in a simple Mendelian fashion. See genetics.

Antibodies were later found to consist of special proteins termed gamma globulins which nowadays are often referred to as immunoglobulins (Ig). These Igs may react in a variety of ways with the corresponding antigen (e.g. by causing precipitation of a toxin or the agglutination or haemolysis of

red blood cells or bacteria). Such reactions occur in both the test tube and in the organism. Thus the different types of antibodies may be termed precipitins, agglutinins etc. according to their mode of action. In all cases antibodies combine physically with the corresponding antigen. The surfaces of the two molecules are believed to have complementary shapes and are often regarded as fitting each other as do a lock and key.

In the 1930's Landsteiner made up a series of artificial antigens by linking small chemical groups to a pure protein. Experimental animals would produce antibodies which distinguished between these often closely related, chemical groups as well as forming antibodies to the protein carrier. Indeed these antigen-antibody (Anab) reactions were (and for some substances still are) the most sensitive method of detecting and determining the concentration of organic compounds present in very low concentrations. In 1937 Landsteiner suggested that when an antigen entered the body it was taken up by phagocytes and served as a template against which the gamma globulin antibodies were formed.

It was known for some time that injection of an antigen into a newborn animal failed to stimulate the production of antibodies. It was thought that no response to the antigen occurred in the animal in such cases. However in 1956, Burnet and Medawar made the discovery that the animal so treated was unable to produce antibodies to the injected antigen for the rest of its life. This is the phenomenon of immunological tolerance for the discovery of which Burnet and Medawar were later to get the Nobel Prize. Earlier, in 1945, Owen had observed that most twin cattle have a mixture of each other's red blood cells and thus must have exchanged the embryonic precursors of these cells when their foetal circulations became mixed in the overlapping of their placentae. This phenomenon was an example of naturally occurring immunological tolerance, called blood chimerism. Although common in cattle the condition has only been recorded in eight sets of human twins throughout the world. Medawar and Billingham subsequently showed that most twin cattle would accept skin grafts from each other. Later Medawar demonstrated that if newborn or foetal mice of one strain were injected with the cells of another then the recipient mice would accept skin grafts from the donor. Immunological resistance was not therefore genetically determined but is acquired during development, as Burnet had predicted a decade earlier. The newborn mammal gets its antibodies from the colostrum and milk of the mother just as it gets its antibodies in utero from the maternal blood.

A human genetic abnormality, which occurs only in males, is known in which the individual is unable to produce any anti-

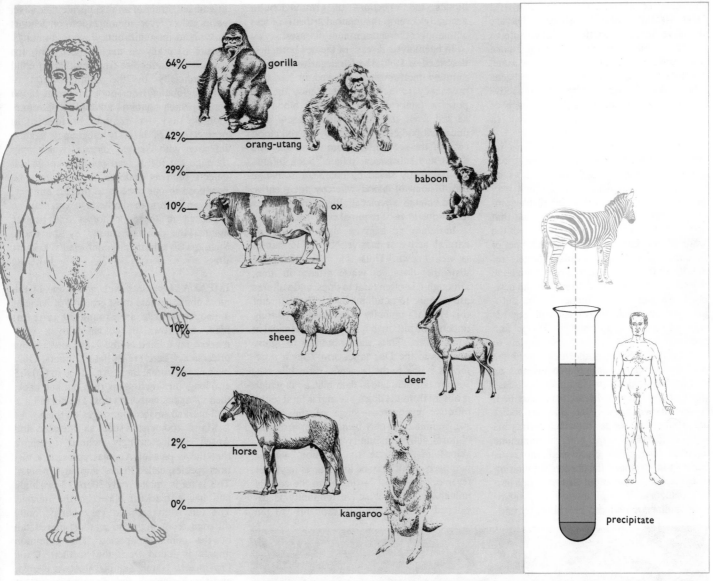

64% — gorilla
42% — orang-utang
29% — baboon
10% — ox
10% — sheep
7% — deer
2% — horse
0% — kangaroo

zebra

precipitate

Immunity tests as a tool in the study of evolution. The addition of blood from one animal to that of another causes a precipitate to be formed, the degree of precipitation reflecting the affinities of the two species tested.

bodies. This condition was always fatal in the days before the discovery of antibiotics since the individual was unable to resist invasion by the common pathogenic bacteria and viruses. The condition is termed agammaglobulinemia and is due to the inability to produce plasma cells. It is of interest, however, that these children may become sensitized to substances that cause hypersensitivity such as 2,4 dinitro-fluorobenzene (DNFB), which sensitizes the skin. Such hyper-sensitivity can be transmitted to normal children by the transfer of cells and is an example of tissue immunity which does not depend on circulating antibodies in the blood.

Antibodies are produced by the plasma cells which migrate in the post-natal period in large numbers from the thymus gland into the spleen, lymph nodes, lining of the intestine and many other areas. Antibodies are not produced by the most primitive of the living vertebrates, the hagfishes *Myxine* which lack

lymphoid cells although the related lampreys, which have lymphoid cells, can produce antibodies.

The lymphocytes and the monocytes of the blood and macrophages of tissues as well as the plasma cell are all derived from a common stem cell and it is known that they can change from one type to another. The digestion of antigens occurs in antigen-sensitive cells in areas such as the lymph nodes and the spleen and lymphocytes from these areas carry the blueprint (probably as RNA) for the manufacture of specific antibody by the plasma cells. These cells which have been shown to manufacture antibody (indeed their cytoplasm contains little else than Ig molecules) occur in large numbers throughout the body. Antibodies are produced in response to the micro-organisms encountered by the animal during its life. Germ free animals kept in a sterile environment only have about $\frac{1}{10}$ of the amount of Ig found in normal animals.

Lymphocytes play a major role in the body's defences against infections and tumours and in the rejection of transplants of foreign organs, and are of fundamental importance in the body's antibody and tissue types of immunity. It has recently become clear that lymphocytes, despite their structural similarity, are of diverse origin and function. They include cells that are short-lived, arise in the bone marrow and are the precursors of the antibody-forming cells, as well as cells responsible for tissue immunity. Other lymphocytes are long-lived spending months or even years circulating from one lymphoid organ to another via the blood and lymphatic systems. These long-lived cells are called antigen-sensitive cells and respond to the presence of antigen by multiplying.

In recent years a great deal has been learned about the nature of Igs. Thus most Igs have two identical antibody-combining sites which cover less than 0·1% of the surface of the molecule where total surface area is at least 100,000 square angstroms. Igs are therefore bivalent, reacting with two antigen molecules, but they are monospecific since both antigen molecules fixed are the same. Igs, therefore, differ markedly from antigens which have many different antibody-determining sites on their surface each of which may provoke the manufacture of a different antibody.

Sometimes the immune mechanisms instead of protecting the organism damage it as is the case in hyper-sensitivity to drugs such as DNFB or to plant pollens which may produce hay fever and other allergic phenomena. Coombs has recently pointed out that von Pirquet, who in 1906 introduced the word allergy, intended it to cover all types of immunity not merely harmful immune reactions to foreign antigens. The autoimmune diseases and haemolytic disease of the newborn are similar conditions. In the autoimmune diseases the body mistakenly regards some of its own components as 'foreign' and proceeds to use its immune mechanisms to destroy them. Some authorities regard the primary cause of autoimmune diseases as non-immunological. In Hashimoto's disease (the first autoimmune disease to be described) it was shown about 1960 that antibodies are produced by the patient which destroy his thyroid gland. Several other autoimmune diseases have been discovered and it is believed that some of the chronic debilitating diseases, like rheumatoid arthritis, fall into this category. It is of interest that agammaglobulinemic children kept alive by anti-biotics and injections of gammaglobulin generally develop rheumatoid arthritis or less commonly other autoimmune diseases.

In haemolytic disease of the newborn, first described in 1940, the Rh negative mother's immune mechanisms, exposed in her first pregnancy to a foreign substance the Rh positive factor of the embryo's blood inherited from the father, subsequently produces antibodies which destroy the red blood cells of the second (or more commonly the third) and subsequent infants. Such infants are frequently saved by complete exchange transfusions of blood whereby their entire blood volume is replaced. Blood transfusions may sometimes be required even before birth.

Immunity to a given organism may be natural, active or passive. Natural immunity is well known. Thus the virus of canine distemper does not cause disease in man, although it is often fatal to dogs, and vultures are immune to botulinus toxin. The nature of this type of immunity is however very rarely understood although it may be biochemical in some cases. Thus the immunity of many animals to the Dog tapeworm *Taenia pissiformis* is due to the presence of the bile salt, sodium taurocholate in their bile, a salt which is absent from the dog's bile and is fatal to the infective cysticercus stage of the worm. Active immunity may be natural or artificial. Natural active immunity the individual develops in response to infection with a pathogen and it may be life long as in yellow fever or very short lasting as in the case of influenza. Artificial active immunity is developed in response to exposure to an attenuated strain of an organism either alive, as in yellow fever immunization, or dead as in typhoid immunization. Passive immunity occurs naturally in the newborn with the transfer of antibodies from mother to child or artificially by the administration of gammaglobulin from pooled human blood serum which contains antibodies. Gammaglobulin may, for example, be injected to protect women in early pregnancy against infection with German measles which may damage the foetus, and produce congenital defects such as deafness. Antisera may be produced in one species to protect another. Thus antiserum to diptheria toxin may be produced in sheep or horses and protect against the damage caused by the toxin. Such passive immunity only lasts a short time.

E.J.O'R.

IMPALA *Aepyceros melampus,* one of the most abundant and most graceful of African antelopes. Impala are around 39 in (1 m) high, red-brown in colour with a well-marked fawn band on the flanks and a white underside. There are no lateral hoofs. Only males have horns; these are 20–30 in (50–75 cm) long, turning first up, then out and back, then up again, with long tips. The horns have well-marked, spaced-out ridges on them.

Many zoologists, such as Meester and Ansell, are increasingly inclined to believe that the impala of Angola represent a distinct species, called Peters' impala *A. petersi.* This latter is smaller, only 30 in (75 cm) high, and has a blackish blaze on the muzzle. The tail is longer and very bushy, quite different from the slender, short-haired tail of the common species. The Common impala is found from the northern Cape Province to Natal, Zambia, western Kenya, and the Karamoja and Ankole districts of Uganda. Peters' impala is found only in southwestern Angola and the adjoining districts of Southwest Africa. It is nowadays a rare animal, and it is thought that there are only some 700 remaining.

In the dry season, impala live in big herds of hundreds of individuals; in the wetter months these big herds break up into small one-male units, with 15–25 females to every male. The surplus males live in bachelor bands, up to 50 or 60 strong. The male herds his females by walking around them with a nodding motion of his head, roaring as he does so; he has at all times to be ready to defend his possession, and fierce fights take place. Sometimes the one-male units may join together for a while, then split up again; and in open grassland they may associate with the bachelor bands. However, the females stay close together, herded by the male, while the bachelor males may wander

Left: impala. Opposite top: herd of impala ewes. Below left: young impala rams. Below right: impala rams rubbing faces, a trial of strength.

as much as 200 yds (180 m) from the main herd. Young males are chased out of the one-male unit at about a year old, often not because of a challenge they have offered the herd male so much as by 'displacement chasing', the result of redirection of aggression when the herd male is threatened by an outside male.

The impala's habitat par excellence is the woodland edge, the area of transition from which they can reach the grasslands to graze and the forest and shrubbery for refuge. In many areas, impala form a kind of symbiosis with baboons: the impala are the wary partners, the baboons provide the protection with their fearsome canine teeth. When disturbed by predators, impala make huge bounds, making a confusing picture for the lion or cheetah whose hunting technique involves singling out one animal to chase; the herd then runs together, leaping distances of up to 30 ft (9 m).

Mating takes place between January and March, in the early dry season just before the one-male herds unite to form the huge conglomerates. In the Nairobi National Park, where impala have been studied, there is a second rutting peak, in August to October. When a female is in oestrus, the male sniffs or licks her urine, adopts the 'flehmen' posture, then urinates or defaecates himself. The two may then lick one another alternately for several minutes. He then walks after her, nose forward, 'empty-licking'; if she is lying on the ground he paws at her with his hindleg causing her to rise and move off, or laterally displays to her with a wagging tail, turning and sniffing. Every time the female stops walking, the male licks her genitalia, smells her and adopts the flehmen pose if she urinates. Then he rises to his hindlegs and follows her in this position and mounting. At first there is no copulation but finally he rushes forward and copulates but without clasping the female. Intromission lasts about a second. Immediately after, the male becomes aggressive and chases the female. Threat behaviour by another male stimulates the herd male to court, after driving off the rival, and he rubs objects with his face—although he has no face-gland!

Many zoologists have disputed whether the impala is more closely related to the gazelles, to the reedbuck, or is more *sui generis*. Gentry has recently shown that the impala should be regarded as a primitive member of the Alcelaphini (the hartebeest-gnu tribe). Not only does it have skeletal and dental characters recalling this group, but its horns are very similar to those of Hunter's hartebeest; and like the gnu it shows symbolic mounting behaviour, a peculiarity unique to alcelaphines. FAMILY: Bovidae, ORDER: Artiodactyla, CLASS: Mammalia.

C.P.G.

IMPRINTING, the process whereby certain animals become psychologically fixated upon the parent, or parent substitute, during the first few hours or days of their lives. This is particularly well-known in young chicks, ducklings, and goslings, but is also seen in other birds and some mammals such as sheep, goats, and cattle. It may even play a part in the formation of the mother-child bond in man, depending on how widely one interprets the term.

In many animals the survival of the young depends, at least in part, upon a close association between parents and offspring. In some species the young are relatively helpless and need a considerable amount of attention from the parents. In these altricial species the behaviour of the young plays little part in the establishment and maintenance of the parent-young bond; as in perching birds and primates, including man. In precocial species, however, the young are active and can walk, run, climb, or swim very soon after birth or hatching. Thus they are able to follow the parents from the nest or birthplace. This following behaviour necessitates the recognition of the appropriate parent-object, and as the animals do not come into the world with these powers of recognition they must develop them rapidly in order to survive. Imprinting may thus be said to be a means of promoting the survival of precocial young by ensuring that they become attached to the biologically appropriate parent-object.

Precocial young animals, particularly the nidifugous species of birds (those which can 'flee the nest' soon after hatching) including chicks and ducklings, do not have an innate recognition of the parent-object. They become fixated upon any relatively appropriate object in their immediate vicinity and the deliberate substitution by man of an alternative may result in the young becoming imprinted to an inappropriate parent-object. Thus nidifugous birds have frequently become imprinted to man, or other animals, and under experimental conditions may become imprinted to all kinds of bizarre objects from ping-pong balls to nesting boxes.

Imprinting has been recognized as a definite behavioural phenomenon by biologists and naturalists from Aristotle on, but it was Konrad Lorenz who first used the term 'imprinting', in 1937, as a translation of the German 'Prägung'. He also brought the phenomenon of imprinting to the attention of a great many people by his descriptions of his imprinting experiments in his book 'King Solomon's Ring' (1952). In this he described how a maximal imprinting effect is achieved by being as much like the natural parent as possible. He found he could imprint young mallard ducklings only if he reduced his size by squatting and by quacking almost continuously. All animals in fact come into the world equipped with certain sensory attune-

ments and animals which imprint respond most readily to natural stimuli. An understanding of this enabled the present writer to imprint eider ducklings to himself in the Canadian arctic so successfully that the ducklings preferred him to their natural parents.

The nidifugous birds are the animals in which the imprinting phenomenon is most clear-cut and in which it is best understood. A number of factors are involved in the development of the imprinting response; these include the sight of the parent, the sound of the parent, the expenditure of energy in following the parent, and, first of all, the feel of the parent under which the chicks hatch.

It is known that nidifugous egg-young respond to sounds produced by their neighbours and/or their parents, but the first discrete stimulus affecting the newly-hatched or hatching chick is the contact stimulus of the parent's feathers around its head. Given this contact the chick remains quiet and still. This ensures that the chick does not wander away from the parent during the critical hatching period. It also begins the general process of imprinting, for the auditory and visual stimuli to which the chick responds emanate from an animal to which it already has a positive tactile reaction. Thus full imprinting is the result of a complex of factors involving the natural parent, or something very like it.

Imprinting may be regarded as a special kind of learning with certain very definite peculiarities. First of all, the process of imprinting is usually, if not always, confined to a very short period of the individual's early life known as the 'sensitive period'. After this the imprintability of the animal drops very quickly and is soon lost. Secondly, full imprinting is irreversible; the fixation is permanent. Thirdly, it is a learning of species characteristics rather than individual ones, for it would be a distinct disadvantage if the offspring, on reaching maturity, tried to mate with their parents. And fourthly, it involves the learning of the characteristics of species which will be responded to in later life in sexual contexts but which cannot elicit a sexual response in the bird undergoing the imprinting process. In this respect imprinting is of future as well as present importance to the animal being imprinted.

The full imprinting seen in nidifugous birds would seem to have much in common with the process whereby young ruminant animals become attached to their parents, or some substitute. The attachment of lambs to human nurses is well-known, and an attachment to inappropriate parent-objects has also been noted in the young of moose, buffalo, zebra, and mouflon. Such animals may become fixated upon horses or motor vehicles, as well as upon humans. This also bears out the supposition that the primary function of imprinting is to ensure that the young animal develops a following response to its parent: in the vast majority of cases the parent-object is the appropriate one, and any attachment to it will promote survival. P.M.D.

INCUBATION IN BIRDS, the process of promoting the development of the embryo inside the shell of birds' eggs through the provision by the parent bird of suitable conditions of temperature, humidity and mechanical protection. Normally these conditions are provided by the body of the parent bird, but in some cases foster parents are used or the parent deposits the egg in such a way that other agencies, such as the heat of fermentation of plant material, the sun or volcanic heat serve the purpose.

Incubation in birds is functionally equivalent to gestation in mammals. The fertilized egg cell has to have certain carefully-controlled conditions of temperature, fuel supply, waste removal and mechanical protection in order to develop properly and these conditions must continue to be met throughout the period of incubation or gestation. In mammals these requirements are satisfied inside the female parent which carries the developing embryo around with her. In birds they are met inside a calcareous shell which is expelled from the parent and deposited in a nest where there is a less intimate connection between embryo and parent. The mammal has the advantage of being able to keep the embryonic environment strictly under control, but the bird has the advantage of a certain degree of independence from its embryos.

The incubation period is usually regarded as that time which elapses, under normal conditions of regular incubation, from the laying of the eggs to the emergence of the young from the shell. Several groups of birds, however, begin incubation with the laying of the first egg. These include divers, grebes, pelicans, parrots, hummingbirds and many birds of prey. The result of this is that the young hatch out successively and are of different sizes. Later young are thus at a disadvantage in the competition for food and nest space and under conditions of food shortage may die. On the other hand this does mean that the older young normally do survive under these conditions, which they might not do if the food was shared equally between all.

Most birds do not begin to incubate until the clutch is complete, and in these cases all young hatch at more or less the same time, with obvious advantages from the point of view of parental care. Incubation in these cases, therefore, begins with the laying of the last egg, and the incubation period for an individual egg is not equivalent to the length of time for which the egg is in the nest.

In all cases the incubation period for the species is constant and represents the time necessary for the embryo to develop to the point of hatching with the parent 'sitting' regularly. The length of the incubation period in birds has been a subject of considerable confusion until quite recently. Aristotle assumed that the size of the egg determined the length of the incubation period and gave a number of incorrect incubation periods for birds which were copied for 2,000 years. We now know that the period required for the proper development of the bird embryo depends upon a number of factors operating in a complex manner, and is not necessarily reflected in the size of the egg. Small eggs of some birds take as long to hatch as others 30 or 40 times their size.

The extremes of incubation period are from about 80 days in the Royal albatross *Diomedea epomophora* to around 10 days in the smallest of the perching birds. Other well established incubation periods are 77 days in the kiwi *Apteryx australis*; 53 days in the Emperor penguin *Aptenodytes forsteri*; 35 days in the Eagle owl *Bubo bubo*; 21 days in the Domestic fowl *Gallus gallus*; 15 days in the Wood pigeon *Columba palumbus*; and 11 days in the Brown-headed cowbird *Molothrus ater*. When eggs are placed in artificial incubators the natural incubation period cannot be reduced by more than a day, suggesting that the natural incubation regime works at nearly optimal efficiency.

The incubation temperature—the temperature which the egg requires in order to develop properly—is maintained by the sitting bird within very narrow limits. In many birds this is about 93°F (34°C) with a variation of ± 0·6°F that is ± 1°C. In cold weather the sitting bird sits tighter, and in excessively hot weather the bird will rise off the eggs but shade them with the wings. The Emperor penguin, which breeds in the antarctic winter in temperatures as low as −108°F (−60°C) and in biting winds, maintains the single egg around 93°F (34°C) for 53 days. The 'sitting' bird (the Emperor penguin incubates standing up) supports the egg on the feet and covers it with a feathered abdominal fold. A nighthawk *Chordeiles minor*, nesting on a flat roof (as is common in this species), has been known to keep the temperature of its eggs down to 115°F (46°C); the roof temperature was as much as 142°F (61°C).

Feathers are poor conductors of heat and most incubating birds develop special brood patches by a local moult of the feathers, giving an unfeathered area of skin with a rich supply of blood vessels. There may be one, two or three brood patches in the belly region, according to species, although a number of aquatic birds, such as ducks and gannets, have none, doubtless because they would lose too much heat via brood patches when in the water. The highly vascularized area is brought into contact with the eggs so that they are warmed by heat from the blood. The heat generated in and around the clutch is kept from dispersing by the mantle of feathers which the incubating bird arranges around the eggs—this being one of the purposes of the shuffling movements made by a bird settling onto eggs. Ducks produce a type of brood patch by plucking some of the breast feathers, and these are also used to form a warm lining to the nest. Gannets and boobies incubate their eggs by covering them with their large, highly vascularized, webbed feet.

The difference in temperature between the upper part of the eggs in contact with the incubating bird and the underside of the eggs may be considerable, particularly in ground-nesting birds, and this is one of the reasons why eggs need to be frequently turned during incubation. Turning of the eggs also prevents the embryos from becoming attached to the inside of the shells, which would prevent proper development. In the natural state eggs are turned very frequently: in the pheasant *Phasianus colchicus* once an hour; in the sparrowhawk *Accipiter nisus* once every 20 min; and in the American redstart *Setophaga ruticilla* once every 8 min. Eggs of the Domestic fowl, in artificial incubators, may be turned as often as every 15 min with increased hatching success and they should be turned—in alternate directions—at least five times in 24 hr. If they are not turned only 15% hatch. In the natural state the brooding bird turns the eggs deliberately or incidentally every time it adjusts its position, which is very frequently. The eggs are rearranged by the bird moving them with the bill and feet and the result is a random turning and shifting of the eggs in the nest. Towards the end of the incubation period the incubating bird sits much tighter, with less movement, and it has been found in artificial incubators that leaving the eggs unturned in the last few days before hatching does not reduce, and may even increase, the hatching success.

In most birds both sexes play a part in incubation, though the female tends to be involved more than the male. However, many different kinds of arrangement may be seen in the class as a whole. In species with reversed sexual dimorphism, such as the phalaropes, the male incubates. In other species the sexes take turns, sometimes at intervals of a few hours and in other cases, particularly in seabirds, every few days. Sometimes, as in the Red-legged partridge *Alectoris rufa*, the female may lay two clutches and the male and female incubate a clutch each. In other cases, as with the African waxbill *Estrilda astrild*, the two sexes incubate the one clutch simultaneously.

Through all these complexities of parental behaviour during the incubation period it must be remembered that the parent birds must consistently perform the 'correct' activities if the brood and the species are to survive. The various kinds of incubation behaviour therefore involve instinctive acts developed as a result of natural selection and genetically incorporated into the basic make-up of the species. P.M.D.

INCUBATOR BIRDS, or megapodes, 11 species of chicken- or turkey-like ground birds, almost entirely restricted to Malaysia and Australasia. They are grouped together in the family Megapodidae and in all the eggs are incubated, not by the bird but by some form of natural heat. Other terms for the group are 'Mound birds' or 'Mound builders' and various species are known as 'Brush turkey', 'scrubfowl', 'Mallee fowl' (or 'lowan') and even 'junglefowl'—a term best restricted, however, to certain members of the pheasant family, Phasianidae.

Seven genera are currently recognized in the family and these may be arranged in three groups according to their ecology: the junglefowl—*Megacephalon* (1 sp), *Eulipoa* (1 sp) and *Megapodius* (3 spp); the Brush turkeys—*Alectura* (1 sp), *Aepypodius* (2 spp) and *Talegalla* (3 spp); and the Mallee fowl —*Leipoa* (1 sp). The junglefowl are found in a variety of habitats but never far from the shore for they usually deposit their eggs in pits which they dig in sand, leaving them to be incubated by the heat of the sun. This habit is modified in volcanic areas, the egg-pit being dug in soil through which volcanic steam filters. On one island off Queensland eggs are laid in rock crevices exposed to the sun—the rocks retaining the sun's heat by night. In the denser jungle areas *Megapodius freycinet* rakes together piles of earth and vegetation in heaps up to 35 ft (10½ m) in diameter and 15 ft (4½ m) high. The composition of the mound apparently varies with the need for heat production, heavily shaded mounds, for example, having much vegetation. Several pairs of birds may contribute to the mound, in which they lay their eggs in tunnels up to 3 ft (0·9 m) long. The incubation period is eight to nine weeks—a period only exceeded by the largest albatrosses, the Emperor penguin and the kiwi.

The Brush turkeys are confined to New Guinea and the east coast of Australia, living largely in the tropical rain-forests. They build mounds composed largely of plant material, about 12 ft (3½ m) in diameter and 3 ft (0·9 m) high. The vegetation ferments rapidly and the male keeps the female away until the temperature has dropped to a level which will not overheat the eggs. The male is able in some way to test the temperature of the egg-chamber and to control it by digging over the top of the

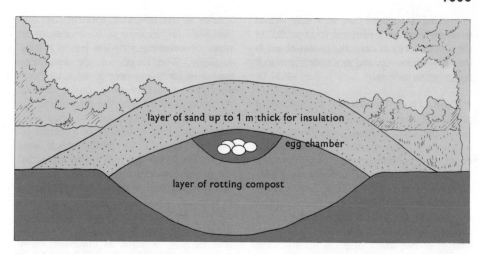

layer of sand up to 1 m thick for insulation

egg chamber

layer of rotting compost

The Australian Mallee fowl *Leipoa ocellata*, one of the megapodes or mound-builders, maintains the egg chamber at a constant temperature of 33°C by opening or closing air vents in the layer of sand above; heat is provided by the layer of rotting compost below.

mound, but the exact mechanism of this is unknown.

The Mallee fowl lives in arid regions of Australia where the temperature fluctuates widely and mound material is not readily available. During the winter birds collect vegetation from a wide radius and deposit it in a pit up to 15 ft (4½ m) in diameter and 4 ft (1·2 m) deep. After it has rained they cover this with sandy soil and the vegetation then ferments. Through the season there are considerable changes in the pit temperature due to changes in fermentation and in environmental temperature and the male controls the egg temperature by manipulation of

the materials in various ways. Details of egg-laying are only known in the Mallee fowl where they are laid over a period of several months and hatch at intervals. See also Mallee fowl. FAMILY: Megapodidae, ORDER: Galliformes, CLASS: Aves. P.M.D.

INDOSTOMID FISHES, a highly specialized family of freshwater fishes containing a single genus and species, *Indostomus paradoxus* known from about 50 specimens discovered in Lake Indawgyi of the Myitkyina District of Upper Burma. This tiny species, which reaches only 1¼ in (30 mm) in length, is covered in bony plates and when it was

The Mallee fowl *Leipoa ocellata* at work building its mound.

first discovered in 1926 it was thought to be intermediate between the pipefishes and the sticklebacks, having the bony plates of the former and the spines along the back of the latter.

Recent studies at the British Museum (Natural History) have shown that the relationships of *Indostomus* are far more complex and cannot be properly understood until the anatomy of many other possible relatives has been examined in much more detail. These studies have also shown that *Indostomus* is highly unusual in being able to move its head both sideways and up and down, actions which are normally impossible in fishes since there is no neck. Not much is known of the biology of these fishes, but a fishery officer in Thailand who kept some in an aquarium, noticed their curious habit of jumping when frightened and sticking to the glass sides of the tank above the water line. FAMILY: Indostomidae, ORDER: Gasterosteiformes, CLASS: Pisces.

INDRI *Indri indri,* a large, grey-and-black lemur which with the *sifaka and the avahi makes up the family Indriidae, characterized by a vertical clinging and leaping habit and a specialized diet of leaves, buds, flowers, fruit and bark. It is the largest of the Madagascar lemurs, with a head and body length of 28 in (70 cm), and is peculiar in having a very short tail, 1 in (3 cm) long. Its long back legs, used for its enormous vertical leaps, give the impression it is much bigger, and in the villages of the east coast rain-forest it is regarded as one of man's distant relatives, which is not far from the truth.

Indris live in small social groups, probably family units, of 2–4 adults. These seem to be territorial, and the indri is most famous for its eerie howls, which carry over great distances and are answered by howls from neighbouring groups. A group of indri can be induced to produce this howl by playing a tape-recording of their own calls. It also utters short, intermittent grunts as a mild alarm call. There is a single offspring at birth, which is carried on the mother's fur. The indri is only found in the northern part of the east coast rain-forest and, after the *aye-aye, it is probably the most threatened species at the present time. If forest destruction continues at its present rate, it could become extinct in a decade.

The avahi *Avahi laniger* is a greyish or brownish, soft-coated, slightly smaller lemur with a head and body length of 12 in (30 cm) and a tail of 16 in (40 cm) long. It differs from the indri and sifaka in being nocturnal.

The avahi also forms small groups, probably family units, of 2–4 individuals, although it is most often encountered singly at night. As with all nocturnal lemurs, its eyes reflect a bright red glow, and it can easily be spotted with a torch in the dark. High-pitched, whistling calls are produced at night, and these may serve as territorial advertisement between social groups. There is one baby produced towards the end of the dry season, and the infant is carried on the mother's fur. The avahi occurs all over Madagascar and, as is usual with Madagascar lemurs, there is a rufous rain-forest form *Avahi laniger laniger* on the east coast and a greyish drier forest form in the north-west, west and south of the island. FAMILY: Indriidae, SUBORDER: Prosimii, ORDER: Primates, CLASS: Mammalia. R.D.M.

INHERENT RHYTHM OF BEHAVIOUR. There is a tendency at times to conceive of the behaviour of lower animals exclusively in terms of response to external stimuli, with an animal more or less in a state of suspended animation until a stimulus from outside is received. In fact, any animal has an inherent rhythm of activity which is independent of the environment. This can be best illustrated by the researches on the Plumose sea anemone *Metridium senile*. If we observe one of these anemones at intervals in an aquarium it can be seen to vary its position. It may be stretched out or contracted, its tentacles lengthened or shortened, its body dilated or shrunken. A group of Plumose anemones will, at any moment, show all these positions, and research showed that each individual anemone goes through a sequence of movements.

When the Plumose anemone, so placed that the human observers could watch its movements against a blackened background, was subjected to close and continuous scrutiny, and its shapes drawn at intervals, it was suspected that the anemone was carrying out a continuous rhythm of movement. By keeping the anemones under conditions of constant temperature, in water free of food materials, undisturbed by vibrations, it was shown that their activities were independent of external circumstances, that they constituted an inherent, continuous and rhythmic activity. The continuous nature was confirmed by attaching fine levers to various parts of individual anemones, the outer ends of which were in contact with slowly revolving drums covered with smoked paper. Throughout the day and night, by this means, the anemone gave a graphical record of its own activities. Further confirmation was obtained by the speeded-up cinematograph film.

The inherent rhythm of the Plumose anemone, and the endogenous rhythm of other animals, such as the *circadian rhythms of insects and others, and longer cycles, as in migrant or hibernating animals, are controlled by what is known as the biological clock. The 'clock' is a mechanism which acts as a pacemaker or pendulum and keeps up the inherent rhythm of behaviour even when external stimuli are absent. Thus, many animals with a 24-hour rhythm continue to show rhythmic physiological and behavioural change when kept in constant light or darkness. External stimuli are, however, needed to 'reset' the clock each day. Recent research has shown that the mechanism of the clock lies in the metabolism of individual cells and the essential rhythmicity is produced by an oscillating feedback system in a chain of biochemical reactions. See rhythmic behaviour and circadian rhythm.   M.B.

INHIBITION, a term used by biologists in three ways. Firstly, it is used to describe the suppression of one kind of behaviour by another; animals do not carry out such incompatible acts as feeding and mating simultaneously and these are therefore said to show mutual inhibition. Secondly, inhibition is said to occur in experimental conditions in which an animal shows a decreased response to a learned association. Finally, the term is applied at the cellular level to describe the suppressive action which some nerve cells may exert upon the activity of other cells.

The phenomenon of inhibition was first discovered in 1893 by Sir Charles Sherrington whose experiments showed that, when the hamstring muscles which are responsible for the bending movement of the knee are stimulated electrically, it is not possible to elicit the 'knee-jerk reflex' by tapping the knee-cap. Thus stimulation which results in a flexor response simultaneously inhibits the occurrence of extensor actions. This situation was found to exist in all pairs of skeletal muscles which operate antagonistically, Sherrington termed this 'central inhibition' for he discovered that destruction of the cerebral cortex removed the inhibition so that antagonistic muscles could simultaneously contract.

Inhibition also occurs at a more complex level than that of a single muscle contraction. For example, a bird feeding on bread crumbs in a suburban garden flies away if it sees an approaching cat. The stimulus to feed is still present but feeding is said to be inhibited by the flight response which is a form of behaviour of higher priority in this particular situation. Sometimes two behaviour patterns may be equally appropriate in a situation and if they are mutually inhibiting, the animal may be incapable of carrying out either.

Sherrington also discovered that when inhibition of, for example, the scratching reflex of a mammal, has been removed, the previously inhibited behaviour recurs with increased vigour. This phenomenon of 'reflex rebound' has also been found to occur in more complex types of behaviour in a wide variety of animals.

It has been discovered that the destruction of certain areas of the brain may result in an animal carrying out a particular type of behaviour. For example, ablation of certain regions of the hypothalamus of the cat can induce a state of rage. It is therefore believed that these regions of the brain have an inhibitory effect on the nervous centres responsible for aggression. Similar inhibiting regions may exist in the brain of insects. The female Praying mantis *Mantis religiosa* is a highly rapacious predatory animal. During courtship she may bite off the head of the smaller male; this, however, merely facilitates the process of mating for the headless male copulates vigorously. Normally the brain has an inhibitory effect upon copulation but decapitation removes this.

In his experiments on the conditioned reflex Pavlov discovered a form of inhibition associated with learning. This he termed 'conditioned inhibition'. If an animal has been conditioned, to salivate at the sound of a bell followed by a food reward, repeated ringing of the bell without the reinforcement of food leads to a decrease in salivation so that the animal finally ceases to salivate at the sound of the bell. The conditioned reflex has been inhibited by this process but it has not been completely extinguished for after a period of rest, the ringing of the bell once again elicits salivation.

Pavlov noticed that when an animal was conditioned to respond to a stimulus such as the sound of a bell, other bells also elicited the conditioned response. If, however, the animal was not rewarded with food when the other bells were sounded, the conditioned response to them became inhibited so that it only salivated when the original bell was sounded.

The establishment of a state of inhibition of conditioning does not imply that the learned association has been forgotten. This is shown by the fact that an animal will once again show, after a period of rest, a reponse which had been inhibited. Inhibition, therefore, is a state in which the learned response is suppressed but not forgotten.

The phenomenon of inhibition has now been identified at the level of the nerve cell or neurone. Certain neurones, when stimulated, inhibit the activity of other neurones, making it more difficult for them to be stimulated. As some neurones possess both stimulating and inhibiting fibres it has been realized that the capacity to stimulate or inhibit lies at the nerve ending or synapse which is the point at which the neurone makes contact with another neurone. T.B.P.

INQUILINES, animals which live in close association with others, and thereby derive some benefit, either gaining protection, or ready access to a constant supply of food. Unlike parasites, they do not harm their hosts. They fall within the general category of commensals, but are recognized as a distinct ecological group because of their particular association with social insects, such as ants

and termites. These societies often harbour several different kinds of animals which are tolerated as guests in the nest or colony. Examples of such nest-sharers include certain spiders which live in the nests of tree ants, and resemble the latter in appearance to such a degree that it is often difficult, on casual observation, to tell the host and guest apart. Other inquilines found in ants' and termites' nests include various species of woodlice, millipedes, springtails and crickets. These guests, which are also referred to as 'synoeketes' (Gk *syn*—with; *oiketes*—dweller), enjoy the shelter of the nest and also help themselves to a portion of the hosts' food, although the amount they consume is relatively insignificant. From this type of association it is but a short step to a phoretic one in which the guest actually attaches itself to the body of the host. Certain fly larvae, for example, which occur commonly in ant nests, coil themselves around the body of the ant larvae and literally snatch the food from the latter's mouths. Ultimately, such an association could evolve into an ectoparasitic relationship. J.A.W.

INSECTIVORA, an order of mammals the members of which although basically related are less closely so than the members of most other orders of mammals. All are primitive and there is a tendency among zoologists studying them to transfer some of the Insectivora to separate orders on their own. See mammals: classification. For ordinary purposes, however, it is more convenient to treat the Insectivora as it has been understood for a century or more until our knowledge is more complete and a revised classification is available.

They are mainly small mammals, the largest being only rabbit-sized. All have the muzzle projecting beyond the teeth to form a mobile snout, often liberally provided with prominent whiskers. Ears and eyes are small and frequently hidden in the skin or fur. In many species the urino-genital system has a common opening to the exterior, making sex determination of live animals very difficult. The skull is generally narrow, low and flat with a small braincase that is not much expanded above the level of the 'forehead'.

The Insectivora are regarded as the most primitive order of placental mammals and in many respects they have diverged little from the ancestral mammalian form. They all retain certain primitive features. For instance, they have the full set of five toes (none of them opposable to the rest) on each foot, and in walking the feet are usually plantigrade, with their soles laid flat on the ground. All insectivores have a small simple brain, with smooth non-convoluted cerebral hemispheres that do not extend backwards to overlay the cerebellum. The olfactory lobes are usually large. The jaws hold a

primitively large complement of unspecialized teeth (up to 48), all of which are rooted (not continuously growing as in some rodents). The cusps of the molars are high and sharp and there are at least two incisors in each half of each jaw. The teeth lack specializations, though in many species the incisors may be enlarged and act as canines; the true canine being an insignificant tooth resembling a premolar. Other primitive features include large vacuities in the bony palate and also an open tympanic cavity.

Most groups of the Insectivora have a fossil record extending back at least to the Eocene, the early fossil forms showing some affinities with the extinct creodont carnivores. However, relationships with the Primates are much closer, some of the fossil insectivores being very similar to primitive lemuroids. There are eight groups of living insectivores, many being quite different and having little to connect them. They are sometimes classified as superfamilies grouped in two suborders, but are here listed simply as separate families.

Among the characteristics of the Insectivora, many are not universally applicable and serve to show just how diverse the group is. For instance, most have weakly developed zygomatic arches in the skull, or none at all; yet in hedgehogs and Elephant shrews the zygomatic arches are very prominent. Clavicles are present, but not in *Potamogale*; the forearm bones are separate, but not in Elephant shrews. The Macroscelididae have a caecum and large eyes, the other families do not. The Golden moles, tenrecs and solenodons are similar in having zalambdodont teeth, with the cusps in a 'V' pattern but the other insectivores have dilambdodont teeth, the cusps of which form a 'W'. Some groups, like the shrews and solenodon, are very unspecialized, others are very highly modified. Some families are extremely abundant and widely distributed (moles and shrews) others are very rare and localized (notably solenodon).

As a group the insectivores are found throughout the world except in Australia, Antarctica, Greenland and the greater part of South America. They are almost all nocturnal. They feed extensively on insects, but also take many other invertebrates (especially worms and molluscs). Some will eat almost anything including carrion and even occasional vegetable matter.

Lacking large teeth or claws the insectivores have little with which to effect an active defence against predators; so most are shy and evasive, hiding away and only coming out at night. Some (hedgehogs and tenrecs) have an effective protection of spines, some burrow, and many have very characteristic and potent skin glands which produce objectionable scents making them distasteful at least to mammalian predators.

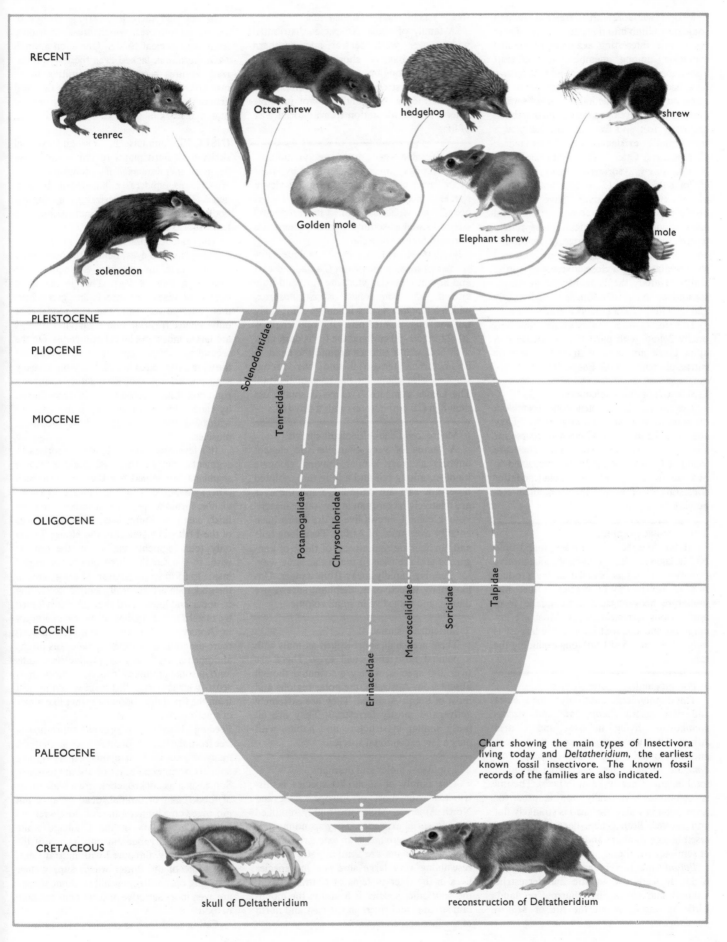

RECENT

tenrec

Otter shrew

hedgehog

shrew

solenodon

Golden mole

Elephant shrew

mole

PLEISTOCENE

PLIOCENE

MIOCENE

OLIGOCENE

EOCENE

PALEOCENE

CRETACEOUS

Solenodontidae

Tenrecidae

Potamogalidae

Chrysochloridae

Erinaceidae

Macroscelididae

Soricidae

Talpidae

Chart showing the main types of Insectivora
living today and *Deltatheridium*, the earliest
known fossil insectivore. The known fossil
records of the families are also indicated.

skull of Deltatheridium

reconstruction of Deltatheridium

Most insectivores are terrestrial, though some may climb into trees and bushes. There are several interesting examples of parallel evolution among members of different insectivore families where individual species have become independently modified for the same way of life. Thus individuals of several families have developed very similar webbed or bristly feet and flat tails and adopted a semi-aquatic existence e.g. Water tenrec (Tenrecidae), Otter shrew (Potamogalidae) Water shrew (Soricidae) and desmans (Talpidae). Moles (Talpidae) and Golden moles (Chrysochloridae) have become highly specialized for a completely fossorial life involving great modifications especially to the forelimbs. Hedgehogs (Erinaceidae) and Spiny tenrecs (Tenrecidae) are protected from predators by a close covering of spines. Only one family, the Elephant shrews (Macroscelididae) have developed a light body and long limbs for a cursorial mode of life.

The insectivore families are reviewed briefly below, with particular emphasis laid upon those not dealt with under separate entries elsewhere in the Encyclopedia.

1 Solenodontidae—solenodon

The two species of solenodons resemble a cross between a rat and a large shrew. They are about 12 in (30 cm) long with coarse fur and an 8 in (20 cm) scaly tail. They are found only in the West Indies, restricted to two islands, Cuba and Hispaniola (the latter consisting of Haiti and the Dominican Republic).

2 Tenrecidae—tenrecs

About 20 species of tenrecs, found only on Madagascar, have undergone an adaptive radiation. This has resulted in the production of several spiny species, rather like miniature hedgehogs, a semi-aquatic form and various terrestrial types. Most are uncommon and not well known; the largest is only 14–16 in (35–40 cm) long excluding the tail.

3 Potamogalidae—Otter shrews

This family consists of only three species and two genera *Potamogale* and *Micropotamogale*, living in west and central Africa. They are very similar to the tenrecs and are sometimes classified as such. *Potamogale* is the largest insectivore having a total length of nearly 23 in (60 cm). The tail is compressed vertically and is used for propulsion in water; the head is strangely flat and narrow. Both genera bear a superficial resemblance to otters and lead a similar sort of semi-aquatic life.

Potamogale is very active, especially at night. It feeds on aquatic and terrestrial animals and sleeps in a burrow on land. Little is known about the life of *Micropotamogale*.

4 Chrysochloridae—Golden moles

A family of about 20 species distributed widely over west, central and southern Africa. All have a short compact body covered with long brown, iridescent fur. The forelimbs are strongly modified for digging and their eyes, ears and tail are invisible externally, an adaptation to a fossorial way of life.

5 Erinaceidae—hedgehogs and gymnures

Hedgehogs are characterized by their dense covering of spines. There are eleven species, including five species of Desert hedgehogs, widely distributed in Europe and Africa as well as southwestern, southern and northern regions of Asia.

Gymnures (Moon rats) include five species of insectivores from China, and east and Southeast Asia. Most are rare and little known. The commonest is *Echinosorex*, which looks like a rat with shaggy fur, scaly tail and long, pointed nose. Its total length is 20–24 in (50–60 cm) and the fur is dark grey with bold white patches around the head. It is nocturnal, terrestrial and has strong-smelling skin glands at the base of the tail. The Lesser gymnure *Hylomys* is small (less than 8 in (20 cm) in total) with a tiny tail.

6 Macroscelididae—Elephant shrews

A family of very characteristic elegant animals all very similar, having elongate hindfeet, a long tail and a long thin, pointed nose. The ears are quite large and the eyes are relatively larger than in any other insectivore. Elephant shrews live in dry thorn-bush country over much of Africa. Their long tails and hindfeet are reminiscent of those of kangaroos and are used in much the same way, for jumping rapidly away from danger. Unlike many insectivores, Elephant shrews are diurnal and some live in small colonies.

7 Soricidae—shrews

These are small, short-legged animals with a pointed nose and small eyes. There are over 200 species, widely distributed though absent from Australia, the polar regions and most of South America. They are extremely active and mostly terrestrial. They are all fairly similar in structure and habits, with only a few exceptional species.

8 Talpidae—moles and desmans

This family of about 20 species is distributed over most of Europe, Asia and North America. Moles are highly modified for a fossorial existence. They spend most of their life underground in an extensive burrow system. Desmans are semi-aquatic animals resembling very large shrews. One species lives in the river systems of central Russia, the only other species is found in the mountain streams and rivers in the east and north of the Iberian Peninsula.

In addition there are various groups of extinct insectivores, which are known only from very ancient fossils. One such animal, *Deltatheridium,* lacked even the few specialized features seen in the primitive living insectivores and seems very close to the ideal generalized ancestor for the entire placental mammal stock.   P.A.M.

INSECTS, animals having an external skeleton of hard plates of chitin joined by flexible membranes, in common with crustaceans, spiders, millipedes and centipedes. They are characterized by having the body divided into three distinct regions: the head, thorax and abdomen.

The head bears the mouth, the mouthparts, the antennae and eyes, Behind the head is the thorax made up of three segments each bearing a pair of legs. This is the most diagnostic feature of insects and gives them their alternative name, the Hexapoda. The only other terrestrial animals having six legs are larval mites and larval millipedes. On the second and third segments of the thorax are the wings. In winged insects, the wing-bearing segments are often fused together to form a rigid box. Like the head, this is strengthened by rigid folds in the cuticle, in this case, to withstand the forces exerted by the flight muscles.

In a few insects the abdomen comprises 11 segments, but in the vast majority some segments are joined together or have been otherwise modified so that they are no longer visible. Grasshoppers, for instance, have ten fairly easily recognized segments with traces of the 11th still visible, but the House fly has only four segments visible on the outside with, in the female, three others telescoped inside to form an ovipositor. The segments of the abdomen are generally simple, consisting of upper and lower hard skeletal plates joined by membranous regions at the sides. Except in Apterygota (primitive wingless insects) there are no legs or other appendages on the abdomen apart from the reproductive organs and, in some groups of insects, a pair of short sensory structures called cerci which project from the tip of the abdomen rather like a pair of small antennae.

Feeding. Hardly any organic substance is free from the attacks of one insect or another: many insects feed on plants, others on live animals or on dead plant or animal remains. Some, such as cockroaches, use a wide range of food, plant or animal, dead or alive but most feed on a limited range of closely related foods. Caterpillars of the Cabbage white butterfly *Pieris rapae* eat only plants of the cabbage family, flavoured with mustard oils, and some of the Potter wasps supply their offspring only with caterpillars. Some insects are even more selective and eat only one kind of food.

Eating solid food is considered to be more

basic in the evolutionary sense and insects, such as cockroaches, grasshoppers and beetles, doing so have two pairs of jaws, the mandibles, large and strong for biting off fragments of food, and the maxillae, much smaller and concerned with breaking up the fragments and passing them back to the mouth. These jaws, unlike our own, are outside the mouth. They are bounded front and back by lips, called the labrum and labium, bearing numbers of sense organs connected with taste. In addition, also tasting and manipulating the food, are two pairs of

Insects are characterized by a metamorphosis in the life-history. Here (left) a moth and (right) a butterfly are emerging from their pupal cases.

leg-like structures called palps which are parts of the maxillae and labium. This, then, is the arrangement of mouthparts typical of cockroaches, grasshoppers and beetles.

Insects feeding on fluids have the same basic mouthparts but these are modified to form a tube through which food is sucked as through a straw. In bugs the two maxillae are long and slender and they lock together to form two tubes, one for injecting saliva into the food, the other for sucking it up. The food tube is also formed from the maxillae in butterflies and moths, although in a completely different way from the bugs, while mosquitoes make a wound with long, sharp mandibles and maxillae, inject saliva through a structure called the hypopharynx and then suck blood up through the space between the labrum and hypopharynx.

These fluid feeding insects are faced with the problem, of taking in too much water and having to prevent excessive dilution of the fluids in the body. Some, like Tsetse flies overcome the problem by passing the water through the body very quickly. They feed on vertebrate blood and take a full meal in a few minutes, but even while feeding drops of clear fluid are passed from the anus. In plant-sucking bugs which feed more or less continuously there are special structures for

getting rid of the water as quickly as possible. Butterflies feeding on nectar store it in a watertight sac on one side of the gut and only pass it back for absorption in small amounts.

The gut is a tube running continuously from the mouth to the anus on the last abdominal segment. It is in three main parts, foregut, midgut and hindgut, the first and last being lined with cuticle continuous with the body covering. The foregut is often complex because it has the function of passing the food back to the midgut, of storage, and, in those which eat solid food, of helping to break the food up before it is passed back to the digestive region. Hence it may comprise a muscular pump, a simple tube, a thin-walled and distensible crop for storage, and a muscular gizzard lined with strong cuticular teeth which grind up the food.

From the gizzard the food passes back to the midgut and it is here that enzymes are produced and the products of digestion are absorbed into the blood. There is no cuticle lining the midgut, but usually there is a thin membrane, called the peritrophic membrane. This may protect the delicate cells from damage by the food.

Finally, the remains of the food pass to the hindgut which is divided into a tubular ileum and the rectum from which more water and

salts may by absorbed since the contents of the rectum include not only undigested food, but also the urine.

Insects need the same overall range of foods as other animals – carbohydrates and fats for energy, proteins for growth and reproduction, vitamins and trace elements with small but essential roles in enzyme activity and elsewhere. Some insects can survive on a very restricted diet because they can make other groups of compounds from those they ingest, while quite a large number which cannot do this themselves house bacterium-like organisms which do it for them.

The blood system. Fats, sugars, amino acids, water and salts, from the food, are absorbed into the blood, but the blood system of insects, and of arthropods generally, differs from our own because the blood does not flow round a system of arteries and veins; it simply fills the whole space within the body, called a haemocoel. As a result the muscles, nerves and other structures are bathed directly in blood instead of being supplied by a network of capillaries.

The heart in insects is a long slender tube lying in the upper part of the haemocoel, just above the gut. Blood enters it from the haemocoel through a number of small holes and then is pumped forwards into the haemocoel again near the brain. Sometimes there are smaller pumps to help maintain the flow of blood through the legs and antennae, but the overall flow is very sluggish and irregular when compared with our own.

Insect blood consists of a fluid plasma with different types of cells floating in it. Each cell contains a nucleus, unlike our own red blood cells. The plasma carries the products of digestion from the gut to other organs for storage and use, while some sugars and proteins remain in solution in the plasma which is itself a store. It also carries waste products to the *Malpighian tubules for excretion and hormones to the organs they are to stimulate. Another important role of the plasma in insects with a soft, flexible cuticle, like caterpillars, is that of helping to maintain the body form and being essential in locomotion. This role is especially important in all insects while the cuticle is soft, just after a moult.

The blood cells also engulf micro-organisms and harmful debris which may get into the blood. If the intruder is too big, as parasites often are, for one cell to deal with, large numbers of cells combine to form a capsule round it, The blood cells are also capable of coagulating the plasma to plug wounds.

Respiration. The breakdown of carbo-hydrates and fats to release energy ultimately requires oxygen. Hence animals need to breathe in air containing oxygen and carry this to the tissues, especially the muscles, where energy is being released. In land animals, the surface through which oxygen passes into the body is a potential source of water loss, because if oxygen can pass in, water can pass out. Water loss is reduced if the respiratory surface, where the exchange of gases takes place, is tucked inside the body so that the air soon becomes saturated and cannot easily diffuse away. Instead of lungs, insects have a series of tubes, the tracheae, which open to the outside on the sides of each segment of the body by spiracles. In most insects the tracheae join up to form main trunks running along the body and from these fine branches run to all parts of the body carrying oxygen directly to the tissues. When more oxygen is needed certain sac-like regions of the tracheal system can be ex-panded and contracted by movements of the body to pump air in and out. This is a very efficient system since it can maintain an adequate supply of oxygen to flight muscle which, weight for weight, uses oxygen at a higher rate than any other tissue known in the animal kingdom. Since, however, dif-fusion plays an important role in respiration the size to which insects can grow is limited because diffusion is only adequate over a short distance. Thus, few insects are much over $\frac{1}{2}$ in (12 mm) diameter.

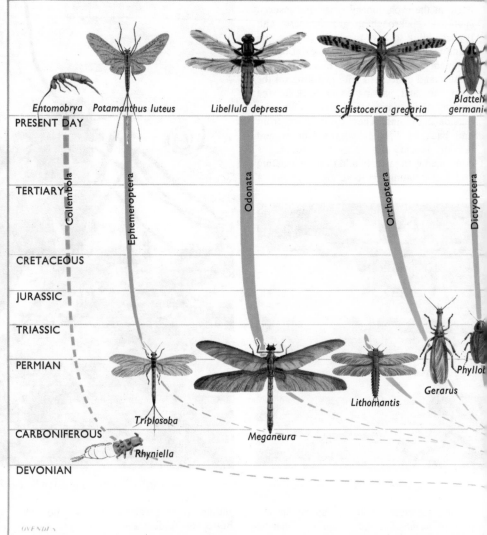

Many insects are aquatic. Some, such as mosquito larvae, still use atmospheric air as their source of oxygen. They have spiracles which open to the air when they are at the surface and close when they dive. Water beetles in addition carry a store of air underneath the wing covers so that they can remain submerged for some time, but ultim-ately insects breathing in this way must come to the surface to renew their air supply.

Other aquatic insects obtain oxygen directly from the water, often having gills which are flaps of the body with a very thin cuticle and a rich supply of tracheae. The oxygen dissolved in the water passes into the tracheae which are gas filled; there is a much more rapid diffusion of oxygen round the body as a gas than in solution in the blood. *Damselfly larvae have gills of this sort and so do dragonfly larvae, but their gills are inside the rectum and the insect keeps a flow of water over them by pumping water in and out of the anus.

Some aquatic insects have a special kind of respiration, through a plastron which consists of a thin layer of air over parts of the outside, held by some device, such as short hairs or a layer of perforated cuticle which is not easily wetted. Oxygen diffuses into it from the water and then into the spiracles. One aquatic bug *Aphelocheirus* has about two million hairs per square millimetre. A plastron also occurs in the pupae of some Crane flies and the eggs of many insects which are laid on land in positions liable to flooding.

In both terrestrial and aquatic insects carbon dioxide formed in respiration leaves the body by the same route as the oxygen entered.

Excretion. An essential role in excretion is played by the Malpighian tubules. These are long slender tubes, lying in the haemocoel, closed off at the free end, but opening into the gut, usually at the junction of mid- and hindgut. Muscles on the outside of the tubules cause them to undulate so that there is a movement of blood all round them. Water and dissolved substances diffuse into the tubules, perhaps with some active pumping of selected substances like uric acid, and these then flow down the tubule into the gut. But the fluid which passes in from the blood will contain many useful substances as well as the unwanted ones and these, together with much

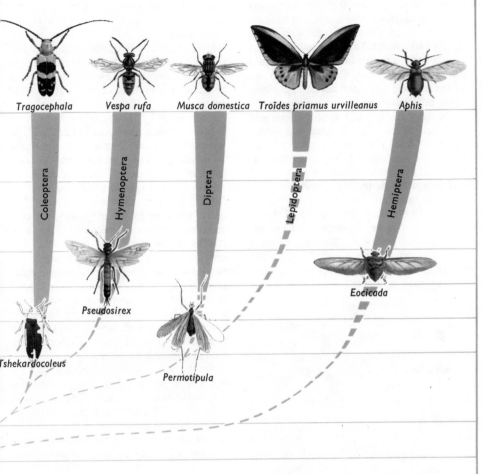

Tragocephala   Vespa rufa   Musca domestica   Troïdes priamus urvilleanus   Aphis

Coleoptera   Hymenoptera   Diptera   Lepidoptera   Hemiptera

Pseudosirex

Eocicada

Tshekardocoleus

Permotipula

Table illustrating the probable evolution of present-day insects from groups long extinct. It also indicates the relationship to each of these groups.

insect's own body. Thus at many leg joints there are groups of hairs which are bent when the leg bends and so they give the insect information about the position of its joints. Other similar groups occur at the neck, on the mouthparts and elsewhere. Sense organs which give the animal information about itself are called proprioceptors.

Often associated with these hairs are oval discs of thin cuticle called campaniform sensilla. These respond to stresses in the cuticle such as are induced by bending or pressing on a surface so these too function as proprioceptors. In addition there are proprioceptors inside the insect which respond to movement of joints or stretching or sometimes just to vibration, and in this case they may be associated with thin membranes to form the organs of hearing.

The nervous system thus gives the insect information about the outside world and also tells it something about itself so that it can adjust its behaviour in an appropriate manner. Longer term regulation of physiology and behaviour is brought about by hormones which regulate moulting and metamorphosis, egg development, colour, urine production and other functions. They are produced by neurosecretory cells in the nervous system, as well as by special hormone producing organs, the corpora allata and corpora cardiaca near the brain and the prothoracic gland in the head or front of the thorax.

Co-ordination between insects involves many factors, but of particular interest are chemical substances called pheromones which may stimulate as smells or be eaten and act on the physiology of the insect. We have seen that such substances may be concerned in mating; they are also very important in social insects, regulating the behaviour of individuals, the production of queens and many other activities in the colony. See bee.

Life-history. Most insects lay eggs large in proportion to their size. A female locust $1\frac{1}{2}$ in (4 cm) long lays eggs $\frac{1}{4}$ in (6 mm) long and $\frac{1}{25}$ in (1 mm) in diameter. The Cabbage white butterfly lays eggs $\frac{1}{25}$ in (1 mm) long. The eggs contain a great deal of yolk providing the raw materials and energy required by the embryo during its development. So much yolk affects development and in most insects the embryo forms as a small streak of cells along one side of the egg and only grows sufficiently to enclose the yolk within itself. In the earlier stages of development it is often possible to make out the segmentation of the insect more clearly than in the adult.

When the larva is fully formed, and the egg is ready to hatch, it swallows liquid or air and blows up the front end of its body by compressing the abdomen. In this way it exerts pressure on the inside of the egg shell until this splits. Sometimes the larva has special structures called egg bursters on the

water, are reabsorbed on the lower parts of the Malpighian tubules or in the rectum. The remains pass out of the anus with waste food material.

Uric acid is the most important of the nitrogen-containing waste products.

The control of activity. All the aspects of insects we have been discussing demand some degree of co-ordination, both of processes within the insect and of the insect with its environment. This co-ordination involves the nervous system and sense organs, hormones and pheromones.

The insect's nervous system is built up from nerve cells, essentially similar to those of other animals, grouped together at intervals to form ganglia arranged in a chain along the length of the body beneath the gut, with approximately one paired ganglion per segment. The biggest ganglion, spoken of as the brain, is in the head and, unlike the rest, it is above the gut, and it is the main co-ordinating centre for all information received by the insect.

Vision depends largely on compound eyes on the sides of the head, but many insects also have simple eyes (ocelli) in the front of the

head, the function of which is not fully understood. Some larvae, such as caterpillars, have simple eyes instead of compound eyes, and inefficient by comparison, on the sides of the head.

Smells and tastes are perceived by tiny hair-like structures, containing large numbers of sensitive nerve endings, scattered all over the body, but are particularly abundant on the head, used to find food and avoid unpleasant situations. An insect has no nose, but has feelers or antennae instead. These are covered with sensory hairs, many concerned with smell. The feathery antenna of the male Silk moth, for instance, has 20,000 sense organs and contains over 40,000 nerve cells. The taste organs are mainly grouped round the mouth.

Most of the minute hairs which clothe the bodies of insects respond to touch, the bending of a hair stimulating the nerve cell beneath it. Some hairs are concerned only with touch and these are usually much larger than those which also perceive smells or tastes. These hairs not only respond to touch by outside things, they may also be stimulated by contact between different parts of the cuticle of its head which help it to tear through the shell.

As the larva grows the intersegmental membranes of the abdomen stretch to some extent, but ultimately growth is limited by the inextensibility of the cuticular plates. For this reason insects and other arthropods moult from time to time, that is they shed the existing cuticle after laying down another, larger one. The new cuticle is produced under the old one before the latter is shed, so at first it is no larger but, having shed the old cuticle, the insect blows itself up by swallowing air to expand the new cuticle before it hardens. This is repeated a number of times during the life-history, each moult resulting in the production of a bigger external skeleton. Apart from the Apterygota, which continue moulting throughout their lives, insects do not moult once they have reached the adult stage.

Broadly speaking, insect larvae fall into two categories: those which, from the time of hatching, have a general resemblance to the adult insect although they are smaller and lack wings; and those which look nothing like the adult. Larvae of the first type generally occur in the same habitat as the adults and eat the same food. In those insects which are thought to have appeared early in the evolution of the group, there may be many moults; mayflies, for instance, commonly undergo 30 or more during their development. More recently evolved forms tend to have fewer moults; four or five in grasshoppers, five in bugs.

Insects in the first category increase in size at each moult and there is also a progressive development of adult features, such as the wings. These are first visible as small projections of the upper plates of the last two thoracic segments and the insects are known as exopterygotes (wings developing outside). The wings also increase in relative size at each moult and the reproductive organs approach the adult condition. The final moult produces more profound changes in appearance and the adult insect emerges, expands its wings and is able to fly.

The exopterygote insects have only a slight change or metamorphosis in the transition from larva to adult, but in other insects, such as butterflies and House flies, the larva looks quite different from the adult and the transition from one to the other involves an extensive metamorphosis.

The difference in appearance between larva and adult in these insects is exaggerated by the fact that the larvae show no sign of developing wings, which develop in folds tucked beneath the cuticle, and this group of insects are called endopterygotes (wings developing inside). This may also be true of the adult legs and some of the mouthparts where these are not present in the larva.

The difference between larval and adult

forms probably arose through the larvae becoming adapted to live in different habitats from the adults. Often this new way of life involved burrowing. This is something which grasshoppers and like insects rarely do and clearly they are not fitted for such an existence; long legs and developing wings would be an encumbrance in a narrow tunnel. By comparison, fly grubs, leatherjackets and even caterpillars with very short legs, or no legs at all, and with their overall worm-like form are much better suited to burrowing. Many, but by no means all of them, do.

The general pattern of growth of exopterygote insects is a series of three, four or five larval stages each terminated by a moult. At the end of larval development, however, there are still profound differences between larva and adult. The transformation, and especially that of the wings, is too great to be accomplished at a single moult and a new

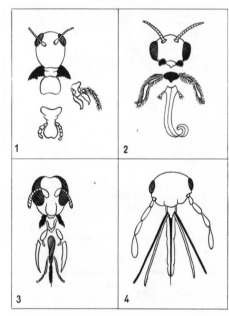

Mouthparts of 1. cockroach (biting), 2. butterfly (sucking), 3. bee (chewing and sucking), 4. bug (piercing and sucking).

stage, the pupa or chrysalis, comes between the last larval stage and the adult. At the moult to the pupa the adult legs and wings, which up till now have been developing beneath the larval cuticle, become apparent. The pupal stage is usually inactive while profound internal changes occur, particularly in the musculature, many larval muscles being destroyed while adult muscles, and especially the flight muscles, are built up.

When the adult is ready to emerge it swallows air to increase its volume and then pumps blood into its various parts to expand them. The most conspicuous expansion involves the wings. When first fully expanded these are soft and the insect cannot fly, but after a time the wings harden and flight is possible.

Adaptations to life on land. Insects are

essentially land animals, although quite a number occur in fresh water. Only a few are found in salt water, but individual species can survive in the most extreme conditions. For instance, the larvae of the fly *Ephydra cinerea* live in the Utah Salt Lake where the salinity is about six times that of sea water, while another member of the same family of flies, the Petroleum fly *Helaeomyia petrolei,* lives in pools of crude petroleum in California. In general, insects have been extremely successful in adapting to life on land, and no other group of invertebrate animals rivals them. To survive on land certain conditions must be fulfilled, the most important being the regulation of the water content in the body and thus the concentration of salts and other substances in the blood and body cells. The restriction of water loss is particularly important in land living animals because water is not always readily available while a good deal is lost by evaporation and a certain amount is lost in the excretory processes. The success of insects on land is due to a very large extent to the efficiency with which they have overcome this problem.

On the outside of the insect's cuticle there is a layer of wax which is largely responsible for preventing water loss. The innermost molecules of this layer are stacked together side by side so closely that water molecules cannot penetrate. Like most other organisms, however, insects need oxygen for their energy releasing processes and a surface through which oxygen can pass in will inevitably allow water to pass out. This loss cannot be altogether avoided, but it is reduced in insects by having the respiratory surfaces, the equivalent of our lungs, tucked inside the body as narrow tubes called tracheae. The air in these tubes soon becomes saturated with water vapour and further evaporation is restricted. The tubes open to the outside by small holes called spiracles and water loss is kept to a minimum by keeping the spiracles closed and only opening them when most of the oxygen is used up or carbon dioxide accumulates in the blood.

Some aquatic insects excrete ammonia which is very toxic and must be diluted, but land dwellers cannot spare sufficient water to excrete ammonia and in most insects the ammonia is converted into uric acid which is only slightly toxic and can be excreted as a solid, so conserving water. The uric acid is passed in solution from the blood into the *Malpighian tubules, but the water is absorbed back into the blood, so that much water is circulated but very little is lost.

Apart from the restriction of water loss there are other problems associated with life on land. Water provides support for the body and this is particularly important in invertebrate animals which lack a discrete skeleton. On land many of these forms tend to lose their body shape because the air, being less dense,

All insects have an exoskeleton of cuticle. Here, a stereoscan photo of the head of a booklouse *Liposcelis bostrychophilus* shows this outer layer in minute detail. The bases of the antennae, and a compound eye, with only seven facets, are clearly seen.

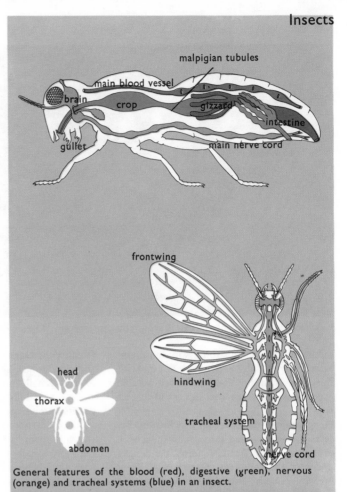

General features of the blood (red), digestive (green), nervous (orange) and tracheal systems (blue) in an insect.

Grotesque adaption of the mouthparts in the beetle *Dynastes centaurus*.   External features of a locust. Right: hindleg, showing the strong muscle system.

does not support them as well as water. In insects, however, the rigid cuticle provides this support.

Not only does the cuticle preserve body form, it can also provide firm legs which raise the body above the surface of the ground. This is important since friction between the body and the ground is greatly reduced and the insect is able to move much faster than any wormlike creature. Indeed this is apparent within the insects themselves where one has only to compare the slowly crawling Blow fly larva with the fast running adult to appreciate the importance of the rigid skeleton.

The ability to run fast is important to insects because it helps them to catch their prey if they are carnivorous or parasitic and also to avoid potential enemies. To some extent it also helps to disperse the insect

within its habitat, which is essential if the food supply is not to be completely used up, but much more important in this dispersal is the ability to fly. This again is dependent on the cuticle since wings, to be effective, must be rigid. Flight also enables the insect to find new and more distant habitats where, perhaps, competition with other organisms for food and space is reduced and the species can flourish. Thus we can see that the ability to fly will have contributed appreciably to the success of insects on land.

Although quite a few insects occur in fresh water, most authorities believe that these are derived from land-dwelling ancestors. The problems of life in fresh water differ from those of life on land in that water loss is of no significance. Many aquatic insects have a cuticle which is freely permeable to water, and there is now ample water to permit the

safe elimination of ammonia and no need to expend energy in producing less toxic substances. One of the main difficulties is, however, that there is too much water. The body fluids of the insect represent a much more concentrated salt solution than does fresh water so that water passes into the insect by *osmosis. This is counteracted by excreting the excess water. There is, however, then the problem of losing salts to fresh water. To counter this, some at least have developed special mechanisms for taking up salt from extremely dilute solutions. The so-called 'gills' on the tails of mosquito larvae perform this function.

In salt water the relative positions of insect and environment are reversed, the water containing a higher concentration of salts than the body fluids. There is thus a tendency for water to be withdrawn from the body of

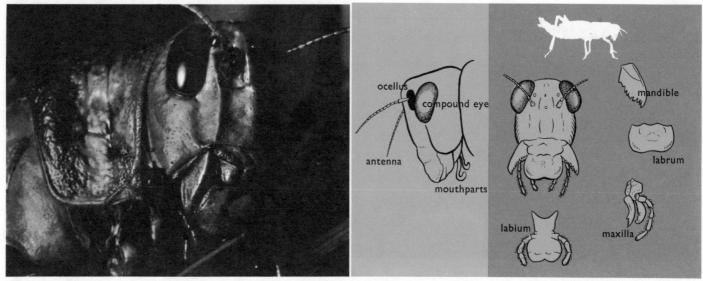

Left: close up of a head of a locust, to show mouthparts. Right: diagram of the same showing main organs which are separated out far right.

the insect and for salts to pass in. In general insects seem to have been unable to cope with this state of affairs and, with a few notable exceptions, they are not successful in salt water.

Geographical and seasonal distribution. Insects are to be found throughout the world, extending to the Arctic tundras, the deserts and even the continent of Antarctica. They are not equally abundant throughout this range or at all times of year. There may be several reasons for this, but the most important is undoubtedly their dependence on suitable temperatures for their body functions to continue. Unlike the mammals, insects are unable to regulate their body temperatures to within fine limits and so, in general, they are only active when outside temperatures are high enough to warm them up and enable their enzymes to work properly. Thus, while in the tropics, where it is always warm, insects are abundant all the year round, away from the tropics the season during which insects are active becomes shorter. This governs the number of generations which can be produced in a year. In the tropics many insects breed continuously, but elsewhere it is usual for a break to occur in development during the unfavourable period. If this is short there may be time for several generations during the warm weather, but towards the poles the period of warmth gets shorter so the number of generations is reduced to one. This does not apply to artificial situations such as occur in greenhouses or rubbish dumps; here the high temperatures may permit breeding all the year round.

Survival over the unfavourable period usually occurs in a particular stage of development, but this varies in different insects. In Britain, moths like the vapourer *Orygia antiqua* overwinter as eggs, others, such as the Yellow underwing *Anarta myrtilli,* as larvae, many others as pupae, for

instance the Dagger moth *Apatele* spp, while some butterflies, like the peacock *Nymphalis io* and Small tortoiseshell *Aglais urticae,* survive as adults. A comparable variation occurs in other groups of insects. Sometimes the stages do not have any particular features which fit them for surviving bad conditions, but more usually there are specializations of structure, behaviour or physiology which enhance their ability to survive.

Although in the tropics low temperature does not limit insect development there are often periods of the year when a shortage of water does so, as in deserts where rainfall is very infrequent. Insects in these regions have their development delayed during the dry season and, as with survival of cold intemperate regions, the unfavourable time is survived by different stages in different species and, again, there may be specializations which make for more effective survival.

Economic importance. Something like $\frac{3}{4}$ of a million species of insect have been described and many thousands more are discovered and described each year. There are probably about 2 million species altogether. There are 250,000 species of beetle, 120,000 species of butterflies and moths, and over 75,000 species of flies and of plant-sucking bugs. No other animal group compares with the insects in terms of numbers of species. The next biggest group of animals, the Mollusca, contains only 45,000 species, while all the vertebrates together only come to about the same number. Indeed, insects make up over three quarters of the total number of animal species.

Insects are not only abundant in species, but also in numbers of individuals. A locust swarm may contain 1,000 million locusts, so as literally to darken the sky, and when they are on the ground there may be 1,000 or more to the sq yd (sq m). Aphids may be even more abundant and over 25,000 have been counted

on a single tomato plant. Even Collembola (springtails) may be so abundant as to carpet the ground with a density of up to 1,000 per sq in, so dense that even these minute creatures are standing on each others' backs several layers deep.

Economically insects are no less important than they are zoologically and their effects are by no means always adverse.

One of the most widely known roles of insects is as pollinators of flowers, of agricultural crops as well as the flowers in our gardens, and many would yield no fruit if they were not pollinated. In this, honeybees and bumblebees are particularly important.

The insects themselves or their products may also be important. Silk is the most notable product, being obtained from the cocoon of the *Silk moth, but others are beeswax, honey, and the red dye cochineal which comes from a Scale insect living on prickly pear. It takes about 70,000 insects to make 1 lb (0·45 kg) of dye.

Insects are also of great economic benefit in the control of pests, both plant and animal. An almost unbelievable instance is the control of the prickly pear cactus in Australia by the caterpillar of a moth, *Cactoblastis cactorum.* Until this insect was introduced the cactus was spreading rapidly, but in two years the caterpillars cleared about 25 million acres of the cactus and have kept it in check ever since.

Many insect pests also are kept in check by bringing in other insect parasites and predators which destroy them, a most notable example here being the control of a Scale insect *Icerya purchasi,* in California, by the introduction of Ladybird beetles to eat them.

It is in this field of biological control that the insects, largely unrecognized, are of greatest benefit to men. While there are numerous examples in which man has deliberately introduced insects to control pests there is an infinity of cases in which insects, by maintaining the balance of nature, prevent potential pests from ever developing into real pests. Another unrecognized, but none-the-less important, beneficial role of insects is as scavengers, hastening the breakdown of dead organic materials and so speeding the return of nutrients to the soil. This is particularly well illustrated by the role of beetles in breaking down cattle dung, usually in a few weeks. When cattle were introduced into Australia, there were no Dung beetles. Consequently the dung dried and persisted for years making large areas of pasture virtually useless until Dung beetles were introduced from other parts of the world.

There are, however, numerous harmful insects: those which carry diseases of man or his animals, those directly harmful and those which destroy crops.

Among the first are many blood-sucking insects, such as fleas which transmit plague from rats to man and from man to man, and mosquitoes responsible for the transmission of malaria and yellow fever. It has been estimated that there are 250 million cases of malaria in the world every year and about 3 million of these are fatal. Tsetse flies transmit the protozoan which causes sleeping sickness, a disease which does not affect man directly but makes it impossible to keep

cattle in some 2 million square miles of Africa south of the Sahara.

Insects directly harmful but not economically significant include blood-sucking flies whose bites cause much irritation and caterpillars with irritating hairs, while the stings of wasps and bees are not only painful but may cause the deaths of people who have become sensitized. Similar annoyance is experienced by domestic animals, often leading to loss of condition and hence reduced yield of meat or milk. The economic loss caused by *Warble flies is more obvious because they render the hides of cattle useless by boring holes through which they breathe and eventually escape to the outside.

Finally, there are the effects of insects on crops, where the economic losses may be enormous. In the United States alone over 125 species of insect attack cotton causing an annual loss of $200,000,000, the best known being the bollworm and the Boll weevil. Indeed, no fruit, vegetable or grain crop is without its population of insect attackers. The larva of the Codling moth *Cydia pomonella* bores into apples and before the use of DDT up to 50% of the crop might be lost through its activities.

Even when a crop has been harvested it is not free from attack and grain is particularly susceptible at this time. Of the world's grain production 5–10% is damaged by insects

during storage and in the tropics the figure may reach 50%, the worst offenders being Grain weevils, Flour beetles and moths.

Classification. Insects probably evolved from a small centipede-like form resembling the *symphylids of today, in which case the first insects would have been without wings. Certainly the first fossil insects, from the Devonian, are wingless. The many wingless insects living today, believed to be descended fairly directly from these early wingless forms, are classified together in the Apterygota (Greek *pteron* – wing, *aperton* – without a wing).

Not all wingless insects are classified in this group. Some being only secondarily wingless, like the wingless grasshoppers and flies, which are obviously closely related to winged grasshoppers or flies. Flies living on oceanic islands are often without wings; if they did have wings they would tend to get swept out to sea by the winds.

In addition, there are whole groups of insects, such as the lice and fleas which, although wingless, are not classified in the Apterygota. These present more of a problem, but they have probably evolved from winged insects and have lost their wings as an adaptation to their special environment. Lice, for example, seem to be descended from ancestors like the winged Psocoptera. In other insects the complex life history suggests an advanced rather than a simple insect, as in fleas with their complex metamorphosis, true Apterygota changing gradually from larva to adult with little or no metamorphosis.

A more positive characteristic of the Apterygota is the presence of leg-like structures on the abdomen of the adults. No other adult insect has these, although the larvae may do so. Like winglessness, these limbs are probably relics of ancestors which, like millipedes, had legs on every segment.

The Apterygota are divided into four orders: Collembola, Diplura, Thysanura and Protura. Collembola or springtails have only six abdominal segments, with a forked tail folded underneath which acts like a spring hurling the insect into the air. Diplura and Thysanura have two and three long 'tails' respectively, while Protura, tiny soil insects, are the only insects never to have antennae.

All other insects are classified together as Pterygota, or 'winged' insects, although as we have seen many have no wings. Wings may have evolved from fixed lobes on the body used for gliding, the insects subsequently gaining the ability to flap these; but they probably could not fold them back over the body as many insects do today because this would involve a more complex hinge than is necessary for just flapping up and down. Hence the Pterygota are divided into two major groups, the Paleoptera ('old, wing') which cannot fold their wings and the Neoptera ('new, wing') which can do so.

Eye spots are a common protective device in butterflies and moths, as in the moth *Automeris io*.

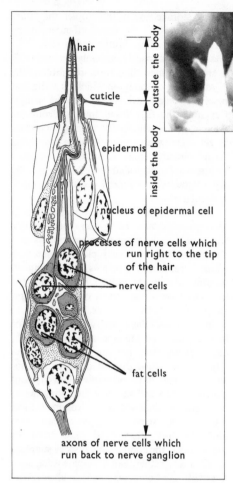

hair

cuticle

outside the body

inside the body

epidermis

nucleus of epidermal cell

processes of nerve cells which run right to the tip of the hair

nerve cells

fat cells

axons of nerve cells which run back to nerve ganglion

1 in (2,5 cm.)

Structure of a bristle from the mouthparts of a locust. Not more than 0.025 mm long, it registers taste.

Order Ephemeroptera	mayfly
„ Odonata	damselfly, dragonfly
Division Polyneoptera	
Order Plecoptera	stonefly
„ Grylloblattodea	Mole cricket
„ Orthoptera	cricket, grasshopper, katydid
„ Phasmida	Leaf insect, Stick insect
„ Dermaptera	earwig
„ Embioptera	(no common name)
„ Dictyoptera	cockroach, mantis
„ Isoptera	termite
„ Zoraptera	(no common name)
Division Paraneoptera	
Order Psocoptera	booklouse
„ Mallophaga	biting lice
„ Siphunculata	sucking lice
„ Heteroptera	true bugs: Assassin bug, Bed bug
„ Homoptera	plant bugs: aphis, cicada
„ Thysanoptera	thrips
Division Oligoneoptera	
Order Neuroptera	Ant lion, lacewing, alder fly
„ Mecoptera	Scorpion fly
„ Lepidoptera	butterflies and moths
„ Trichoptera	Caddis fly
„ Diptera	true flies, mosquito, House fly, gnat
„ Siphonaptera	flea
„ Hyménoptera	ant, bee, wasp, Gall insect
„ Coleoptera	beetle, woodworm, weevil
„ Strepsiptera	(no common name)

R.F.C.

Many orders of Paleoptera are known only as fossils, but modern representatives are mayflies (Ephemeroptera) and dragonflies (Odonata). The Neoptera seem to have developed along three main lines and the remaining insect orders are grouped, according to the line they are on, into Polyneoptera, Paraneoptera and Oligoneoptera, their names derived from features of their wing venation.

Two important features used in classifying insects are the form of the wings and the development of the mouthparts, whether these are modified for feeding on solid or on liquid food. These are often reflected in the name. Isoptera, for instance, have all the wings similar in appearance (Gk *iso*—equal). Lepidoptera have the wings covered in scales (Gk *lepidos*—scale). Siphonaptera have tubular mouthparts for sucking blood (Gk *siphon*—tube, and *a*—without, *pteron*—wing).

The classification of insects is:

Class Insecta

Subclass Apterygota

Order Collembola	springtail
„ Diplura	(no common name)
„ Thysanura	bristletail, firebrat, silverfish
„ Protura	(no common name)

Subclass Pterygota

Division Paleoptera

INSECT PEST BY AIR. Since man started travelling over any distance farther than mere nomadic wandering he must have encouraged the spread of insects, but only since major intercontinental migrations and the wholesale opening of new areas to cultivation has this become serious. One example is the Maize moth *Pyrausta nubilalis* of Europe. When maize was introduced from America in the 16th century it became a favourite host plant of the moth. Then in the 20th century the moth was accidentally introduced into North America and eventually reached the Midwest corn belt. However, the rate of spread was comparatively slow and another introduced pest, the Japanese beetle *Popillia japonica,* was recorded as spreading at 5–10 miles (8–16 km) a year.

Within recent years the dangers of spreading insect pests has been greatly increased by the volume and speed of air traffic and control of their movements is now a considerable public health and agricultural problem. A spectacular example is that of the arrival of cockchafers *Melolontha melolontha* at several airports in the USA from Orly Airport, Paris, where large swarms had been attracted to the lights of the loading bays. Particular care has to be taken in the southern USA to prevent the arrival of mosquitoes from Yellow fever areas and even fruit brought in by tourists as souvenirs is potentially dangerous as theoretically one fertilized female mosquito is sufficient to start a population of pest proportions. With the advent of 'Jumbo' jets and supersonic airliners the problem of guarding against the introduction of pests is bound to become more difficult.

INSIGHT. Wolfgang Köhler was the first scientist to suggest that animals might be capable of arriving at the solution to a problem using insight rather than solving it purely by trial and error. Insight learning and trial and error learning can be contrasted in that the latter involves a series of responses by the animal until it chances to find the solution whereas insight is said to occur when the appropriate behaviour appears in a novel or problematical situation.

Köhler worked on the Canary Islands between 1913 and 1917 at an anthropoid station in Tenerife where he carried out his classical experiments on the intelligence of chimpanzees. In a now famous experiment with the chimpanzee 'Sultan' he hung some bananas from the ceiling of the cage and provided the ape with two large boxes. Sultan moved the boxes around and looked at the bananas; suddenly his behaviour changed completely and he placed one box on top of the other and, standing on the top of this construction, he attempted to reach the bananas with a stick. On a subsequent occasion he placed three boxes one on top of the other and by standing on the top box he succeeded in reaching the bananas by hand.

Other chimpanzees also discovered ways of reaching the fruit, by climbing on one another's backs or by leading their keeper by the hand until he stood underneath the bananas and climbing up on him.

Köhler noticed that the solution to a problem frequently came suddenly to an individual which had been inactive and quietly considering the situation and he regarded this as evidence that the animal had shown insight in its approach to the situation. One chimpanzee playing with two sticks discovered that one fitted into the end of the other. It stopped playing with the sticks at once and, using the extended stick, it managed to reach the fruit.

Köhler's chimpanzees were caught wild and it might be argued that their experience in the wild had assisted them in the solution of some of these problems. There can be no doubt that past experience plays a major role in the process of insight learning. For example, if chimpanzees are provided with a stick and bananas just out of reach outside the cage, individuals which have had experience of playing with sticks solve the problem much more rapidly than individuals to whom sticks are unfamiliar.

This example illustrates the importance of what is termed 'latent learning' which is previous experience during which the animal has learned something of the properties of the situation in which it is now placed.

A second type of experiment carried out to discover if animals can show insight into a problem is that in which an animal is placed in a maze which it learns to investigate in order to reach a food reward. Ingenious experiments have shown that laboratory rats can show insight in this situation. In one experiment a rat was placed in a maze with three pathways to a food reward. The rat soon learned to select the shortest one. A blockage was then placed in such a position that it obstructed both the shortest path and the one of medium length. The rat then returned to the beginning of the maze and without hesitation selected the longest path, thus arriving at the correct solution to the problem.

Harry Harlow of the University of Wisconsin has carried out a series of experiments on what he has termed 'learning sets'. Using Rhesus monkeys he provided the animals with two wooden triangles and a wooden disc and taught them to select the disc. He then gave them two discs and a triangle and rewarded them when they selected the triangle. The correct solution to these problems was to select the unpaired model and, after this training, the monkeys would always select the odd figure, whatever objects were offered to them. In this situation therefore, the animals learned the concept of 'oddness' which gave them insight into novel problems of this type. In doing this they had learned to ignore shape or texture and to make their decision solely on the basis of the relationship between the three objects.

Insight learning seems to differ from trial and error learning in that the relationship leading to the solution to the problem is solved in the brain without the necessity for physical activity. Some psychologists have suggested that insight is a kind of trial and error learning which takes place in the brain without being acted out.   T.B.P.

INSTINCT. A striking feature of some animal behaviour is that it is so characteristic of the species that it serves as a recognition feature. It is easy, for example, to recognize many bird species by their song alone. Thus the conclusion could be drawn that the pattern is fixed by the genetic make-up of the individual which is shared with all the other animals of that species. Often, too, the behaviour appears in its fully developed form on the first occasion of its performance. There seems to be no period of gradual putting together of the pattern by trying to do the action, whatever it may be. If no learning is required, as so often seems, what then brings about the behaviour? The reply can be given 'It is instinct'. But this is in itself non-scientific because when one attempts a definition, the word 'instinct' is indefinable. And it obstructs further research because the statement is itself complete enough an explanation for many people. If instinct is indefinable, it is equally immeasureable. To the novelist an instinctive action has the connotation of being done without reference to the conscious mind; it is 'second nature', in other words. This idea that instinctive behaviour is inborn is strengthened by the apparent fixity of the patterns; once they appear they remain unchanged for the animal's lifetime.

This lack of adaptability shows itself particularly strikingly in quite unnatural situations which a research worker may bring about. A Trapdoor spider makes a flap over the entrance to the hole in which it lives, hence its name; this flap is so made that it blends with the surrounding greenery on the bank. Yet when the area around the hole is cleared down to bare earth, the spider will nevertheless construct a green trapdoor which now contrasts strongly with the surroundings. Clearly, therefore, it is not intelligent action. Similar rigidity of response is shown by a gull which incubates a wooden block in place of its egg. Although animals behaving like this look foolish and seem to be acting in a thoroughly maladaptive way this is only because the conditions are highly artificial; under natural circumstances a gull's impulse to brood objects of a certain size ensures that eggs are properly cared for and they are normally the things which the gull encounters and which fulfil the criteria of objects to be retrieved.

Instinctive behaviour was therefore viewed as being characterized as a pattern common to all members of a species throughout their geographical range, as arising complete at the first performance of the movements and as being innate.

The word instinct is also used to describe the driving force behind behaviour; thus, the maternal instinct is taken to be the reason why a mother cat cares for her kittens. It was in an attempt to reconcile all these aspects of the concept of instinct that Lorenz produced his scheme for typical, so-called, instinctive behaviour. He looked first at the motivation of the behaviour and saw this as being due to 'reaction specific energy', an internal store of nervous energy which became attached to particular behaviour, say, fighting or nesting.

The psychologist's concept of *drive is better invoked for this for at least one can begin to see a possible physiological basis for it; the lack of such a possible explanation for reaction specific energy was one of the causes of strong criticism of Lorenz's theory.

When this internal state has reached a certain level, the animal begins *appetitive behaviour. During this phase it seeks the particular conditions in which the final instinctive act can take place. Many kinds of behaviour can intervene at this point. A dog may learn that food is available at a certain place, so its appetitive behaviour will be influenced by learning. Or, as many invertebrates do, the animal may search randomly, thus, a ladybird larva will wander at random over leaves in its search for the aphids upon which it feeds. Or the animal may be guided by signals from other animals; a female grasshopper is led in this way to a group of singing males of her own species.

Appetitive behaviour comes to an end, according to Lorenz, when certain environmental stimuli are encountered which trigger off the behaviour. These are *releasers which may not necessarily be the whole of the natural stimulus situation which the animal encounters, but may be only a small part of it. It is not the fish shape of another male which releases fighting in a male stickleback but the red underside which all males develop in the breeding season. What follows is the instinctive act, viewed originally by Lorenz as being the innate, rigid, action pattern which formed the hard core of instinctive behaviour. He proposed that, in the performance of this act, the reaction specific energy 'runs away' and thus the motivation is reduced so that the action is not performed repeatedly.

This model of instinctive behaviour was a useful one for it broke free from the restriction on investigation imposed by the invocation 'instinct'. Though nowadays one finds much to criticize in some of its details, the general concept has use as a rule-of-thumb for looking at behaviour.

The crux of the matter is whether one should separate off instinctive behaviour as a category different in kind from the rest of behaviour. To get away from the mysticism of 'instinct', we need to look again at some of its concepts.

Firstly, the extent of individual variation in species-specific behaviour patterns needs to be measured. The songs of birds are a good example. Although chaffinches are recognizable as a species by their song there are individual minor variations and indeed there are dialects. Furthermore, there is evidence that the individual characteristics of the calls of some species are recognized by other birds, and are used, for example, by a mate to recognize his or her partner. Thus species-specific behaviour is not as unchangeable as might have been believed; the behaviour of each individual is not identical to that of all others, but only bears a general resemblance. The suspicion that learning has a part in perfecting such patterns is therefore confirmed by experiments. See heredity and environment.

Secondly, the internal determinants of behaviour need close attention. An animal prevented from performing a piece of behaviour may do it more intensely the longer it has been constrained. Lorenz explained this as a build-up of reaction specific energy but an explanation in terms of levels of activity of centres in the central nervous system, hormone production and the like must be attempted. It is now, for example, clear that much activity on a cyclic basis is stimulated from within the animal.

Thirdly, the development of a behaviour pattern must be studied. Many factors influence the appearance of behaviour; not the least is the maturation process going on in the nervous system of a growing animal. The connections between nerve paths take time to become established. The development of the simple sinuous movements of an axolotl larva can be traced to the joining of nerve cells, first down each side of the body and then by cross connections between the two sides. Equally the role of the environment, in other words, of the experience of an animal, must be taken into account. No animal can develop isolated from environmental experience. Even in the womb a mammalian foetus is being influenced in many ways by its mother. The ability to deal with their newborn young seems to depend in Rhesus monkeys on the amount of time they spend in play with their brothers and sisters. Isolate a female from as near birth as possible and not only will she have difficulty in responding to a male, but when her offspring is born she will be quite unable to nurse it.

Finally, the evolutionary history of reaction must be considered. By comparison with other species it should be possible to offer at least a tentative suggestion for the way in which the behaviour came to show the form that it does and why it should do so.

Geneticists have long accepted that genetic potentialities are expressed only in so far as the environment will permit them to be. The ultimate appearance of an organism is the result of this inter-action of innate characteristics and the environment. To suggest that instinct is behaviour encapsulated against environmental influence is unrealistic. The behaviour which has been called instinctive is the end result of the developmental process in which the genetically determined features of the behaviour have made their contribution but also experience has played its part. Looked at in this way instinctive behaviour is no longer a separate kind of behaviour but one part of the spectrum to be found among animals. J.D.C.

INTEGUMENT, a general term designating the covering of an animal. It is correctly used to describe not only the 'skin' of vertebrates, which comprise a cellular epidermis and a connective tissue dermis, but a range of structures from the pellicle of the unicellular Protozoa to the shell or carapace of crabs.

Even the most primitive of multicellular animals, the sponges, which lack the tissue specialization shared by all other Metazoa, have a surface layer of flattened cells known as pinacocytes. Coelenterates (hydra, jellyfish, etc.) have an ectoderm of cells, some of which may be ciliated, glandular or contain contractile fibrils. Parasitic worms and flukes, while they lack any true epidermis, have a cuticle which may even bear short spines, lying directly on mesodermal tissue. Annelid worms, on the other hand, have both columnar epidermis and overlaying cuticle, as well as an underlying connective tissue bed.

Many molluscs protect themselves by means of a shell, which is formed of non-living, secreted material, and is thus not in the strict sense an integument. The soft parts are covered by a cellular epidermis. The colouration of cephalopods, such as the squid, is due to numerous pigment-holding bodies known as chromatophores. Star fishes and Sea urchins, members of the phylum Echinodermata (spiny skins), are characterized by having calcareous plates, overlaid by a thin epidermis and bearing many spines.

Perhaps the most interesting integuments, apart from those of vertebrates, are found in the Arthropoda, a phylum of animals (including the crustaceans, insects, centipedes, millipedes and spiders) which have jointed limbs and an external skeleton.

The integument of arthropods has an inner single layer of cells, called the hypodermis or epidermis, which is situated on a basement membrane and secretes an outer non-cellular cuticle, varying in thickness from a fraction of a micron to several millimetres. This cuticle is extremely tough and durable. It contains a polysaccharide chitin and a protein 'arthropodin', but the outer part (exocuticle) also becomes infiltrated with additional secreted protein and is hardened and darkened by a tanning process in which the protein chains become cross-linked by quinones which are formed from dihydroxyphenols. To the outside of the exocuticle is the epicuticle, itself formed of three parts, an inner layer of lipoprotein, a middle layer of wax and an outer protective covering of cement, secreted by integumentary glands.

The cuticle of crustaceans, such as crabs and lobsters, contains large amounts of inorganic materials, especially calcium carbonate.

During their development and growth arthropods moult, a process which is under the control of hormones. In insects, moulting is induced by a hormone, called ecdysone, produced by the thoracic glands, which are themselves stimulated by a neurosecretory hormone from the brain. In crustaceans the moulting hormone is produced by the Y-organs; these are normally inhibited by a hormone secreted by the eyestalks; thus removal of the eyestalks results in moulting. See also skin, ecdysis and epidermis. F.J.G.E.

INTELLIGENCE. Not so very long after metal foil caps for milk bottles were introduced, people in Britain found these were sometimes ripped from the bottles standing outside their back doors. This phenomenon spread gradually until many parts of Britain were suffering from this apparent vandalism. The foil was being picked off by Great tits. These birds often use nuts as food and the movements of tearing off the caps were very similar to those they use to open nuts. Now they were applying this ability to a new source of food, the cream which floated just below the cap in the milk bottles.

This is a good example of adaptability of behaviour and would be classified by most people as intelligent behaviour. The word intelligent means many things when used generally but for our purpose we will use the definition usually employed by animal behaviourists. Intelligence is the ability to adapt behaviour to changed conditions. This is also a definition of *learning and indeed learning must be included as intelligent behaviour whether it is shown by a worm, an octopus or a man. Thus a honeybee which learns to visit a paper square of a particular colour is showing intelligent behaviour, just as a rat when it learns to get food by going through a door with a star over it rather than through one with a circle over it.

The psychologist who devises an intelligence test for a group of children is not really trying to find out how much the

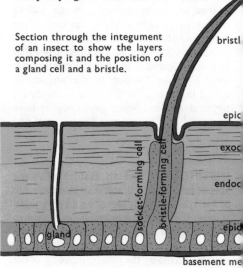

Section through the integument of an insect to show the layers composing it and the position of a gland cell and a bristle.

bristl

epic

exoc

endoc

epid

basement me

children have learned, he is not interested in their capabilities for parrot learning. Rather he is looking for evidence of their ability to see to the heart of a problem and then apply what they have discovered to other similar problems. Now this is *insight, for the problem has to be solved in the first place without practice or trial. Similar kinds of behaviour are to be found in animals but usually only among the vertebrates is there real evidence for insight.

During Wolfgang Köhler's famous experiments on the behaviour of chimpanzees, he hung fruit out of reach over one of the apes at the same time leaving a number of boxes about on the floor of the cage. The ape climbed on one which was near to the fruit but could not reach the appetizing food. Indeed none of the boxes were big enough to be used alone to get the food, The animal retreated to the side of the cage, looked at the boxes, then came forward, placed one beneath the fruit, took another and put it on top of the first one, climbed up and took the banana. Now, the ape had not tried to put one on top of the other and experimented, as it were, but it seemed as if it had done this in its brain and realized how the problem could be solved. Occasionally one of the apes would produce a solution which Köhler had not foreseen, as when one chimpanzee in the same situation as that just described took a keeper by the hand, led him out to stand beneath the fruit and then climbed onto his shoulders. Another kind of problem which Köhler set his chimpanzees was to put fruit on the ground out of reach outside the bars of the cage. Scattered about the cage were various lengths of bamboo, none of them long enough to pull the food into the cage. Again a chimpanzee might try one stick just as it would try one box, then review the situation, coming forward afterwards with a solution, in this case to make a longer stick by inserting one into the end of another.

Great tits are adept at using beak and feet to get their food. They can hang onto a lump of fat suspended from a branch and peck at it. When one was given food hung on a string which was surrounded by a glass tube, the bird had to pull up the string in some way to get the reward. The different ways in which individual birds solved the problem seem intelligent. Thus one would lift the string a little in its beak, hold the string loop under one foot, grasp the string lower down, lift it again, grasp the new loop and so on until the food was raised far enough for it to reach down from the perch and take it. But another bird would lift the string and hold it under one foot, then shuffle along the perch with the string being drawn up under its foot.

Worms can learn to negotiate a simple maze (T-tube offering a choice of soil or an electric shock). Intelligent behaviour, through the capacity to learn, is related to brain size and complexity, reaching a peak in man.

successes

failures

Although Great tits are known to be very able at coordinating their movements, the way in which the birds employed individual solutions using beak and foot suggests intelligent solving of the problem.

Tool using is a kind of behaviour which seems to indicate intelligence. One of the finches to be found in the Galapagos Islands has the habit of using a cactus spine held in its beak to probe for insects in cracks in tree bark. The spines are not taken from the tree but have to be looked for and carried to the tree where they are used. The American naturalists Dr and Mrs Peckham studied the behaviour of solitary wasps in great detail. They frequently saw the wasps closing up their holes after the egg had been put in it with sufficient food. But on one occasion the wasp took up in its mandibles a rather larger grain or 'stone' than usual and appeared to use it to batter down the soil into the mouth of the nest. Stones are obvious tools to use, early man used natural stones before he learned to shape them artificially. Sea otters use them to break open the Sea urchins which are their food; they float on the surface holding an urchin on their chest and pound it with a stone until it breaks. But chimpanzees have been seen to make tools in the wild. They break off a twig, then shred off the leaves and any small side branches. This leaves a thin withy which they poke into the holes of a termite mound. Termites bite it and the ape pulls out the stick with termites attached. The insects are a much appreciated food. Tool using can be said to indicate that an animal has insight into the possibilities of an object.

Perhaps one of the most fascinating sets of experiments which give evidence for higher abilities in animals are the ones carried out by Otto Koehler on the ability of birds and other animals to count. At first he was at pains to make sure that the animals recognized numbers and not patterns; if six spots were to be arranged as they are on playing cards they could easily be distinguished from any other number arranged in the same fashion by the difference in pattern. But if the number was represented by dots of various sizes arranged quite randomly, the animals would not be able to learn a pattern but would have to count the spots. Food was put in one of two basins, each of them having a lid which completely concealed anything inside. On one lid were, say, three blobs, while on the other there were four. Beside the basins was a master card bearing three blobs. A jackdaw could learn rapidly to select the basin which bore the same number as the master card whatever that number was up to seven or eight. But more remarkable results were yet to be found out. Koehler arranged that the animals came down a passage into the open where the basins were. While the animal was moving along the passage, a buzzer sounded

Supply the missing number. Often regarded as 'intelligence tests', these problems are perhaps better seen as measures of aptitude for particular kinds of abstract reasoning (in this case with numbers).

or a light flashed, a number of times. Birds and squirrels could do this equally well. They would match the number of buzzes or flashes to the number of blobs on the lid of a basin and learn to go to that one immediately to find food. Birds would also pick out a certain number of grains according to the signal they had received. Thus, some basins had no food in, others had one or two grains and all of them had indentical plain lids. The bird would come out into the arena, knock the lid off the first basin, take the grain if there was one and go on to the next. This was repeated until the bird had taken the number which corresponded to the one which had been indicated. One jackdaw counted wrongly taking only four grains instead of five. But, though it looked like an error, the bird turned round before leaving the arena and went by the basins again nodding its head for each grain that it had taken previously, then pushed the top off another basin and took a fifth grain. These experiments surely demonstrate that a true concept of number exists in birds and lower mammals.   J.D.C.

INTELLIGENCE QUOTIENT. This is a measurement of a person's general level of intelligence that has many practical uses but some drawbacks. The intelligence quotient, or IQ, is a ratio: $\frac{\text{mental age}}{\text{chronological age}} \times 100$, and by definition the average person has an IQ of 100. The mental age is the ability of a person to carry out successfully tests which the average person of a given age can do. Thus a person who passes tests that 50% of 15 year-olds can pass has a mental age of 15. If his chronological or real age is 15, then his IQ is $\frac{15}{15} \times 100. = 100$. If 10 years old, his IQ is 150. Mental defectives generally have IQ's below 70, while that of a genius is about 180.

INTENTION MOVEMENTS, the preliminary or incomplete actions in a sequence of associated behaviour patterns which are not carried through to completion.

The flight intention movements of birds provide good examples of this phenomenon. When a bird is about to take off and fly it makes a series of movements which were analyzed by Daanje in 1950. Firstly, the bird lowers the forepart of its body and raises its tail, the legs are flexed and the head points slightly upwards. The second action is a springing movement; the bird extends its legs rapidly and raises the front part of the body whilst lowering the tail. This action normally launches the bird into flight. Often however, if the bird is mildly alarmed it may repeat this sequence of actions several times without actually leaving the ground and in this case the actions are referred to as flight intention movements.

In social situations an animal may also make an intention movement without actually completing the activity which is foreshadowed. For example, most social mammals before attacking another individual of their own species firstly look fixedly at it with both eyes and then charge before finally biting or butting. Sometimes however, the animal may not actually attack its opponent but confines its actions to staring and charging. The stare and charge are intention movements of attack.

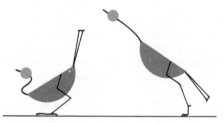

Two stages in the take-off of a bird.

Subordinate individuals learn to associate these patterns with an attack so that they avoid an aggressive individual which makes these movements. Thus the intention movements serve as a threat and influence the behaviour of another individual. Because they may act as social signals, intention movements are common amongst social animals and many of them have become exaggerated and incorporated into courtship or aggressive displays. See ritualization.
                                            T.B.P.

INTESTINE, the part of the alimentary canal extending from the stomach to the anus or cloaca. It is usually long and much coiled and the internal surface is often produced into folds or finger-like structures called villi to increase the surface area. In most animals, the anterior part of the intestine receives the secretions of various glands and is one of the main digestive regions of the gut. The posterior part of the intestine is concerned more with the absorption of the soluble products of digestion, and with water absorption in terrestrial forms.

INVERTEBRATA, a name first used in 1828 for all animals without backbones, the converse being Vertebrata, for animals with backbones, that is, with a spinal column made up of vertebrae. During the present century, as the significance of the *notochord in dividing the animal kingdom became increasingly realized, the term invertebrates became more and more a convenient negative term for all groups (phyla) other than vertebrates. It has now ceased to be used in precise tables of classification and represents a miscellaneous collection of phyla, from the single-celled animals or *Protozoa to the highly specialized insects and spiders. Many of these have little in common except that they can be shown to represent stages in the evolution of animal life. In numbers of species invertebrates far outnumber the vertebrates. Of the one million or more recorded species of animals only 42,000 belong to the vertebrates.

IRRUPTIONS, irregular, explosive migrations, occurring only occasionally but often in spectacular proportions. The term has much the same meaning as *eruption but the latter relates more especially to the centre of origin whereas irruption relates to the destinations of the migrating animals. The stimulus for an irruption appears to be a great increase in population, due to an abundance of food or a mild winter allowing high survival and consequently a large breeding population the following spring. Many irrupting species specialize on certain foods which may be abundant one year, allowing a rapid increase in population, and scarce the next, forcing the animals to move in search of fresh supplies. The best known irrupting species are birds, which are very mobile and often spread far beyond their normal ranges but irruptions of rodents are also common. Examples of irrupting species are crossbills, lemmings, sandgrouse and Snowy owls.

ISOPODA, a distinct but very variable order of Crustacea with over 4,000 species described and probably many others yet to be discovered and described. The order includes the woodlice, gribble and pillbugs or sowbugs, as well as many similar forms lacking common names that live in fresh and brackish water and in the sea.

Isopod means 'equal feet' (Gk *isos*—equal, *pous*—foot) and the name is derived from the thoracic limbs which are very much alike. The isopods are also characteristically flattened from above downwards, but in some, such as *Phreatoicus*, the body is flattened laterally and resembles an

amphipod such as the Freshwater shrimp *Gammarus* and in *Cyathura* the body is cylindrical. The typical flattening is enhanced in many forms by the lateral development of either pleural or coxal plates. The outline is generally oval, as in *woodlice, but elongated forms do occur. Parasitic forms, however, show many varying degrees of departure from the typical condition.

The body is divisible into three regions: head, thorax and abdomen. The head is shield-like and without any obvious division into segments. It carries a well-marked pair of compound eyes which lie level with the surface of the head. The number of ommatidia in each eye is very variable ranging from 20–25 in freshwater and land isopods, for example, the pillbug *Armadillidium*, and up to 3,000 in the deep-sea *Bathynomus*. The thorax consists of eight segments but in all isopods the first thoracic segment is fused to the head and in some forms the first two segments are so fused. The last thoracic segment may be reduced or absent. The abdomen of six segments continues the outline of the thorax so that it may not be clearly demarcated from it. The segments may be free or united to various degrees. Except in *Cyathura*, the last abdominal segment is fused with the telson and although

there is no separate and independent telson, as in amphipods, the last segment is often referred to as the telson, sometimes as the pleotelson. The size varies from $\frac{1}{36}$ in (0·7 mm) to the very large deep-sea isopod *Bathynomus* 15 in (38 cm) long and 5 in (12 cm) broad. A large number of the common species fall within a size range of $\frac{1}{4}-\frac{3}{4}$ in (5–20 mm).

The appendages are in number and position typical of the Malacostraca, the subclass to which the isopods belong. The head carries the usual five pairs of appendages. The antennules are uniramous (single branched) varying in degree of development from being well developed in the primitive freshwater Water slater *Asellus* to mere vestiges in the land-dwelling woodlice. The antennae are often long and generally well developed. In some species they are unusual in being adapted to seizing prey. The mouthparts consist of mandibles, maxillules and maxillae. Isopods are generally scavengers and omnivores with a number of herbivorous species. Intertidal forms feed on seaweeds, for example, the Sea slater *Ligia*, which cuts off pieces of seaweed with its mandibles; others, such as *Idotea*, use rows of specialized setae on the mouthparts as well as the mandibles to scrape and bite off

Common woodlice or slaters, with young ones, and a centipede.

pieces of seaweed or any other organic matter. The carnivorous *Eurydice* tears apart the cuticle and rasps the internal tissues of other living crustaceans. It also feeds on dead organic matter bolting large pieces of tissue with little previous mastication. The gut can store considerable quantities of food.

The seven pairs of thoracic appendages or walking legs are developed as typical walking legs and are all much alike. Each consists of a single ramus or branch which has fundamentally seven joints as in the Water slater but generally the first joint is fused to the body to form a coxal plate and only the last six joints form the movable leg. Each limb has three curves in the same plane, the basal joint is directed inwards, the next joint downwards and the last four joints outwards. The legs are arranged in two groups, generally the first three pairs pointing forwards and the last four pairs backwards. Thus the Water slater can walk with ease over the surface of soft mud in freshwater ditches and brackish pools respectively. It has also been shown that the Sea slater can, when walking on land, execute 16 steps per min which is about the fastest leg movement for any arthropod. Each step takes a shorter time than corresponding steps in water, so greater speeds are attained, equivalent to over 1 mile (1·8 km) per hour. Some isopods can climb over seaweeds and hydroids, others are sand-burrowing with joints on the last four pairs of legs expanded serving to push sand grains aside. In some species of *Munnopsis* two of the joints of the last three

A slater *Philoscia muscorum*.

The Sea slater *Ligia oceanica* among Acorn barnacles.

pairs of legs are leaf-like and fringed with long setae which form efficient paddles and, by a rotary movement, drive the animal backwards through the water. Many isopods use their walking legs for holding large particles of food in contact with their mouthparts and the first pair may be modified to assist the mouthparts in breaking up the food.

The first five pairs of appendages on the abdomen are known as the pleopods (Gk *plein*—swim) and are respiratory structures. They are thin flattened, leaf-like, two-branched limbs in all free-living forms, and

enters the pleopods from a ventral sinus and is, as oxygenated blood, returned direct to the heart to be pumped around the body. The pleopods are also used for swimming, the effective stroke area increased by the fringe of setae on the margins and by the right and left members of a pair being linked together at their bases by coupling hooks so that they act as one paddle.

Most isopods are marine and are found from the intertidal zone of the shore to the abyssal depths of all the oceans. In the Philippine and Tonga trenches isopods are well represented at depths up to 30,000 ft (10,000 m). In the intertidal region they may be found in many habitats, climbing over seaweeds, under stones, in empty barnacle shells, in salt and brackish water pools, in sandy soils of open beaches and estuaries or forming burrows in silt-clay soils of estuaries. The *gribble burrows into wood, and others have adopted a parasitic habit. See article on parasitic isopods.

Some isopods have invaded fresh water and a number are cave dwellers and, like isopods living at the bottom of deep lakes, are without eyes or pigmentation.

All isopods lay large yolky eggs which, when fertilized, are passed into a ventral brood-pouch usually formed by the overlapping of pairs of thin flat plates, or oostegites, borne normally on the first five thoracic segments. Some species have the habit of rolling into a ball and in them the brood-pouches are formed by an infolding of the body wall. The young leave the pouch as miniatures of the adult except for the development of the last pair of thoracic legs. This stage is the post-larval or manca stage, which moults to give the juvenile form in which the last pair of legs are shown.

As the juveniles develop through successive moults males become distinguishable from females by the development of an appendix masculina on the second pair of pleopods, a rod-like branch which assists in transferring the sperm from the paired penes on the mid-ventral surface of the last thoracic segment into the opening of the female ducts on the sixth thoracic segment. SUBCLASS: Malacostraca, CLASS: Crustacea, PHYLUM: Arthropoda.   E.E.W.

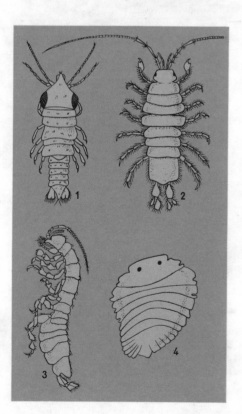

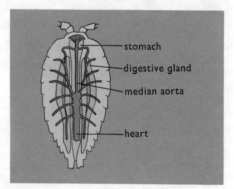

Left: representative isopods: 1. larva of *Gnathia*, an ectoparasite on fishes, 2. common freshwater *Asellus*, 3. female of *Phreatoicus*, 4. *Bopyrus*, female parasitic in the gill chamber of the prawn *Palaemon*. Above: *Ligyda exotica*, a marine isopod related to the terrestrial woodlice.

stomach

digestive gland

median aorta

heart

lie flat against the abdomen which can be raised and lowered in rapid movement to create a current of water over and between them. The surface cuticle is thin and easily permeable to oxygen and carbon dioxide. In association with abdominal respiration the heart is placed far back, where the thorax joins the abdomen. De-oxygenated blood

IVORY, the hard, white fine-grained substance obtained from the tusks of the elephant, walrus, hippopotamus and narwhal and formerly from the extinct mammoth. From very early times artists, especially of India, China and Japan, have used ivory to make many kinds of carvings and ornaments, including chessmen, charms and statuettes. Today it is still used for such things as umbrella handles, combs and billiard balls but more often substitutes such as vegetable ivory, made from the nuts of a palm tree, or plastics are used.

JACAMARS, a family, Galbulidae, of tropical American birds resembling bee-eaters. There are 14 species in five genera, ranging from southern Mexico to southeastern Brazil. They belong to the order Piciformes (woodpeckers, toucans and their allies) and are quite closely related to the puffbirds although distinctively different in appearance and habits.

Like the unrelated, but strikingly similar bee-eaters, Meropidae, of the Old World, jacamars are small to medium sized, bright-plumaged hunters of air-borne insects, which the birds await sitting patiently at favourite vantage-points in savannah woodland, farmland and at the edges of forest, often near water. Most species have an iridescent dark green head and upper-parts, rufous or green under-parts, and a contrasting white patch on throat or breast. Sexes are similar, except that any throat patch in females is buff. The bill is straight, sharp and pointed, and one to three times the length of the head. The legs are very short, with the toe arrangement (two forwards, two backwards) that characterizes the order, and the tail is moderately long and graduated. Jacamars are quiet birds, not gregarious and non-migratory.

The largest genus is *Galbula*, with eight species, and the 10 in (25 cm) long Rufous-tailed jacamar *G. ruficauda* is a typical member. A pair will perch quietly low down at the edge of gallery forest, or in the shade of a riverside shrub, and dart out after a passing insect which, despite the slender $2\frac{1}{2}$ in (7 cm) bill of this species, is deftly snapped up and brought back to the perch, where it is beaten until inactive. It is generally stated that jacamars feed principally on butterflies, dragonflies and similar large and showy insects, but in fact a recent study of *G. ruficauda* showed that their diet is almost exactly the same as that of bee-eaters in Africa, that is chiefly hard-bodied insects, with wasps and bees (Hymenoptera) comprising about 80%. Of course, in the field it is easy to identify large insects like *Morpho* butterflies caught by jacamars, but also easy to overlook the numerous small insects 3 mm long, which may even be captured and consumed unobserved.

The Paradise jacamar *G. dea* is an Amazonian species 12 in (30 cm) long, which feeds in aerial sorties from the forest canopy. It is largely shiny blue-black, with a brilliant white throat triangle, and central tail feathers elongated to 7 in (17 cm) streamers, recalling some bee-eaters. The genus *Brachygalba* contains four species of small and rather dull brownish jacamars and the remaining genera have a single species each. The White-eared jacamar *Galbalcyrhynchus leucotis* is short-tailed; the Three-toed jacamar *Jacamaralcyon tridactyla* of southeastern Brazil has its first (rear) toe vestigial (a condition found in some of its wood-

pecker relatives); and the Broad-billed jacamar *Jacamerops aurea*, at 13 in (32 cm), is the largest of its family, with a stout bill to match.

All jacamars excavate their nest cavities at the end of a tunnel 1–3 ft (1 m) long in earth banks and shelving ground. In the oval terminal chamber is laid the clutch of two or more round white eggs. For details of the nest and the rearing of the young see 'bee-eaters'. The two species are unrelated but in these respects are almost identical. FAMILY: Galbulidae, ORDER: Piciformes, CLASS: Aves.   C.H.F.

JACANAS, a small family of mainly tropical aberrant wading birds, alternatively known as lily-trotters. The name 'jaçana' is the American term for the local species. There are seven species, distributed as follows. The American jacana *Jacana spinosa* has several subspecies from Mexico through Central and most of South America. In Africa there are the lily-trotter *Actophilornis africana,* the Lesser lily-trotter *Microparra capensis*; with *Actophilornis albinucha* in Madagascar. From India through Southeast Asia to the Philippines is found the

Head of the Amazon jacamar *Urogalba amazone.*

Pheasant-tailed jacana *Hydrophasianus chirurgus,* while the Bronze-winged jacana *Metopidius indicus* has a similar but more restricted range. Lastly the lotus-bird *Irediparra gallinacea* inhabits Indonesia and Australia.

From the existence of no less than six monotypic genera for the seven species, it might be inferred that the members of the family are rather different but this is not in fact the case and the jacanas form a fairly uniform group of plover-like or crake-like birds inhabiting the fringes of lakes and only differing amongst themselves in relatively trivial points, such as the conformation of the bill and presence or absence of a horny frontal shield. In length they vary from about $6\frac{1}{2}$–12 in (17–30 cm), except for the Pheasant-tailed jacana, the name of which suggests its principle feature, an 8 in (20 cm) tail which makes the bird 21 in (53 cm) long overall. The wings are rather long but rounded, the tail short in most species, the bill about the same length as the head or rather shorter and straight, and the legs long and thin. In addition, the toes are very long

and the nails long and straight, especially the hind toenail, so that the jacana's weight is distributed widely by the foot, enabling it to walk nimbly over lily leaves.

Lily-trotters can usually be seen picking their way along the margins of sluggish rivers, water meadows, or well out in the open water of lakes with good water-lily beds, feeding on a variety of invertebrates and seeds. In foraging out over floating vegetation, they seem excellent judges of the stability of the substrate, and if they feel a lily leaf sinking beneath their weight will unconcernedly hop to another one, seldom wetting more than their feet. They are shy birds, however, and readily flee from open water to the relative safety of marginal vegetation, skittering along the surface with paddling or trailing legs or, over greater distances, flying more strongly with shallow laboured wingbeats and the long legs and feet extended out behind. A curious feature of all jacanas is that on alighting the wings are briefly stretched up above the back, before being suddenly folded. Perhaps this is a species-specific signal akin to the tail-flirting of a moorhen or the white scut of a retreating rabbit. Certainly several species of jacanas have parti-coloured or bright wings and in the American jacana the show of wings on alighting is particularly impressive because the primaries and secondaries are an unusual shade of bright lime yellow, contrasting spectacularly with the black and dark cinnamon of the rest of the plumage. Walking on firmer ground, jacanas flick the tail and have the mannerisms more of a moorhen than of a charadriine wader. In the possession of a frontal lobe of bright-coloured naked skin, soft or horny, some species of jacanas again resemble the rail family. The American jacana has a scarlet and orange forehead shield and in the *Actophilornis* species it is whitish blue.

Lily-trotters are for the most part rather solitary, although *A. africana* is so common over large areas of Africa that very many may inhabit one small lake. But after the breeding season, they are more positively gregarious and feed in family groups. Normally rather silent birds, they appear to be more vocal when assembled socially and have a wide range of chattering scolds and grating alarm calls.

Breeding takes place during the rainy season and the sexes participate equally in building the nest, a simple platform of leaves of water plants concealed in sedges at the edge of the water or built on floating vegetation, and in incubation. The four eggs are pointed and highly polished and are brown, heavily pencilled with irregular dark lines. The courtship is not elaborate, but there is a good deal of intra-specific rivalry, the birds threatening each other with upraised wings. It seems that they rarely actually fight, how-

The Pheasant-tailed jacana of Asia is one of the most handsome of the jacanas.

ever, although they could doubtless inflict damage if they did because all jacanas have a sharp spur at the bend of the wing—a rare feature in birds, and one otherwise only found in sheathbills and some plovers, screamers and some geese. Young jacanas are nidifugous, that is are hatched at a relatively advanced stage of growth, and leave the nest almost immediately to forage for themselves in waterside vegetation, in the protective company of their parents. They are concealingly striped in buffs and browns, and lie still at the approach of danger, while the parents embark on an elaborate distraction display.

Perhaps the finest species is the Oriental pheasant-tailed jacana, and it is the only one to assume a special nuptial plumage. Outside the breeding season, it is mainly dull brown, with white face, under-parts and tail and golden nape. With a pre-nuptial moult is acquired a striking pied plumage, the long tail being black, the under-parts below the breast dark brown and the shoulders white, contrasting with the dark brown back. *Irediparra gallinacea* has somewhat similar colouring throughout the year and the African species are chiefly bright cinnamon, *A. africana* with black crown and nape, and white throat, cheeks and breast. The lower breast is golden buff. Much the smallest species is the Lesser lily-trotter, throughout its range much scarcer than the larger *A. africana*. It resembles an immature *A. africana*, being like a toned-down adult, but with a golden forehead. FAMILY: Jacanidae, ORDER: Charadriiformes, CLASS: Aves.   C.H.F.

JACKALS, carnivores very similar to dogs and wolves. There are four species distributed throughout Africa and southern Asia which, although similar in habits, differ markedly in appearance. The Golden jackal *Canis aureus,* ranging through southern

Asia and North Africa, looks like a small wolf or coyote with a tawny coat and black markings on the back and tail. The much smaller Black-backed jackal *Canis mesomelas,* inhabiting the plains of central and South Africa, has a black saddle extending along the back and a black stripe along the length of the tail; its sides and legs are bright rufous

Juvenile American jacana already has long toes.

and it has large pointed ears. The Side-striped jackal *Canis adustus,* greyer in colour and with a thin black and white stripe extending along the sides of the body, a black stripe along the tail, and a white tail tip, inhabits the African tropical forest or woodland areas with dense vegetation. Finally, in a very limited area in the highlands of Ethiopia, is the little-known Simenian jackal *Canis simensis,* bright rufous in colouring and with a cream belly and black-tipped tail. Although these four species have different distributions, there are small areas of Africa where they overlap. However, the habitat preferences of each one prevents them from coming into close contact and thus interbreeding or competing for food.

Many scientists believe that the Golden jackal, with the wolf, is one of the ancestors of the domestic dog, domestication having occurred about 10,000 to 15,000 years ago in the Near East or the Middle East. Disagreement with this hypothesis has arisen because jackals tend to be less sociable than wolves and thus less amenable to taming. Also, there are many physiological and structural differences between wolves and jackals. However, the very close similarities between the South Arabian wolf *Canis lupus arabs,* and the South Asian Golden jackal

Despite their reputation for meanness, jackals are handsome dogs and the Black-backed jackal is one of the most handsome.

Canis aureus lupaster, in shape and size (especially of the skull and skeleton) and behaviour, support the theory that some jackal blood may be present in modern breeds of domestic dogs. Jackals could have been crossed with dogs by the Egyptians who held this animal in such esteem that they had a jackal-headed god, Anubis. On the other hand, jackals themselves may have been tamed and domesticated by primitive man since, as pets, they are just as affectionate and easy to handle as tame wolves and dogs. One is reported to have learned to retrieve balls for his master and would even sit on command. Finally, wolves, jackals, and dogs can interbreed and produce fertile offspring, so there is no physiological barrier to prevent the crossing of all three species either now or in the past. Given all the available evidence, however, it is probably correct to assume that the wolf was the primary ancestor of the dog, and that jackal blood is not very evident in our modern breeds.

Like most dogs and wolves, the gestation of jackals is about two months, but the timing of breeding is flexible and depends upon the area of Africa each species inhabits. Golden jackals, living north of the Equator, give birth in May or June; the Side-striped and Black-backed jackals may also give birth from May to June in central Africa, but they bear their young in September and October if located in southern Africa.

All of the jackals are extremely opportunistic, obtaining their food from whatever sources are available. Although often considered to be mainly scavengers, they will also hunt and kill birds, hares, mice, lizards, turtles and various insects. Moreover, several individuals may band together in a small pack (especially the Side-striped jackal) to prey upon larger game like sheep, goats and small antelopes. In recent years, the activities of jackals in hunting domestic livestock has caused them to be severely persecuted by farmers. Without a steady source of live prey, jackals will turn to fruits and vegetables for nourishment and will scavenge the kills of the larger African predators, like lions and hyaenas, or frequent the outskirts of towns and cities where they gather together at garbage dumps, apparently a regular activity of Israeli Golden jackals.

In hunting small prey, jackals typically stalk and then pounce suddenly, like foxes. The mouse or rat is then vigorously shaken while being held in the jaws; this sudden movement usually either kills or stuns the prey. When pairs hunt together, they may co-operate, one digging out the prey from its burrow while the second lies in wait to capture it. Larger game are overcome by sham charges which make them bolt; this is followed by a chase, and the jackal attempts to grasp either the neck or throat of its victim. Jackals are unable to bring in healthy sheep and goats so they concentrate on sick or young individuals.

On the whole, jackals are not very sociable and are either solitary or associate in pairs although occasionally small packs form for brief periods. As a result, they do not possess a complex means of communicating with one another although their visual language is quite varied and complicated. Tail, ear, and body movements express mood and status to other jackals. As in dogs and wolves, tail-wagging is an indication of friendliness, but jackals do not snarl or bare their teeth as a threat as frequently as their close relatives. Instead, they threaten with the mouth opened in a gape and the ears laid back against the head. Dominant males display their social position by bristling the fur on the back, standing erect, and raising the tail; they may also growl. During a fight, they attempt to bite the neck or hindquarters and will slam their hindquarters into the opponent's side to push him off balance. Submissive individuals being attacked often lie immobile on the back with the tail tucked between the legs, a posture which may reduce the aggression of the dominant animal. In less tense situations, subordinate jackals crouch and wag the tail. In the Side-striped jackal, the white tail tip makes this movement very conspicuous. The visual language is most important during the formation of pairs before the breeding season. Initially a male demonstrates his superior rank by threatening the female who assumes a submissive attitude. Later, the pair make hesitant approaches to one another and establish contact by touching and licking each other on the flank, muzzle, and shoulder. Once the female's fear of the male is reduced, she often invites him to play by coyly rolling over in front of him while wagging the tail. This is followed by the creation of a common territory and both sexes mark the boundaries with urine and faeces. If a long-lived pair bond is formed, the same area may be haunted by one pair for years. Pairs also keep in contact with one another and advertise their mutual possession of a territory by howling and whining together. Indeed, in the Golden jackal, the first joint howling is said to be an indication that a pair bond has formed. By contrast, in the Black-backed jackal only the male howls and the female answers with a shrill laughing cry. Before mating, the male Golden jackal has a special facial expression; he bristles the fur around the face while opening and closing his eyes. Copulation in jackals is similar to that of dogs; a 'tie' or 'lock' lasting about 15–20 minutes occurs during each mating. Females stay on heat for about a week, but usually only mate during the last three or four days. Once mating has occurred, a den is dug or a natural hole or crevice enlarged to receive the litter, usually containing between three and seven pups. Both parents rear and guard the young who are helpless at birth, being both blind and deaf. By three weeks of age, weaning begins with the parents regurgitating partly digested meat to the litter to ease the transition from a milk to meat diet. The young have special gestures used for begging for food; they whine, roll over on the ground while tail-wagging, and lick or push their snouts against the corners of the mouths of the adults. Pups begin to leave the den and play among themselves at two to three weeks of age. Some of the favourite games involve hunting and fighting movements, but pups rarely hurt one another since rough play is halted if one cub complains with a whine. After two months, the pups begin to join the parents on the hunt, but the burrow is usually not abandoned until the young are over three months of age. The break-up of the family occurs when the litter is about six months old. FAMILY: Canidae, ORDER: Carnivora, CLASS: Mammalia.   D.G.K.

A jackdaw has come to take the bait which brings it within range of the camera.

JACKASS, LAUGHING *Dacelo gigas,* or *kookaburra, an Australian kingfisher of large size and dull plumage. Its name is derived from its call like mad human laughter.

The name was probably inspired by a fancied resemblance between its call and the braying of an ass. In any event it is apt to attach to the bird some of the less desirable qualities associated with the name. This conflicts with a remark so often made about the bird, that it defends its nest and young with great courage, using its powerful bill to inflict wounds on any marauder. Observations of the nesting habits of this species were made in the Zoological Park, Smithsonian Institution, Washington, D.C., where a pair nested in 1961.

There was no opportunity to see whether the birds would defend their young because although they had previously shared the aviary with a pair of hornbills and ten bobwhite quail, these were removed before they could have done any damage. There were indications, however, of an unusual parental devotion. Both parents shared the incubation of the three white eggs laid in a nest inside a hollow tree stump, the male starting to take his share four days after the last egg was laid. The nest was never left unattended. When the female wanted to be relieved at the nest she tapped on the wood with her bill, the male immediately responding by going in and taking her place.

The young, born helpless and naked, were fed continuously in the nest for four weeks. Their eyes did not open until 21 days after hatching. If they tried to leave the nest one or other of the parents would force them back. Then, 30 days after hatching the young birds were allowed to leave the nest. The first of the three came out on its own. The other two were actually drawn out by the female standing in front of the nest entrance offering them food, then backing out with the food still in her bill when one of the youngsters moved forward to take it. She repeated this until she had succeeded in her efforts to draw them out of the nest. FAMILY: Alcedinidae, ORDER: Coraciiformes, CLASS: Aves.   M.B.

JACKDAW *Corvus monedula,* a small, gregarious crow, black with a grey hood, found through much of Europe and western Asia, nesting in colonies in holes in the ground, in rocks, in buildings or in trees. It is replaced in eastern Asia by a small pied species *Corvus dauuricus* sometimes called the Daurian jackdaw. FAMILY: Corvidae, ORDER: Passeriformes, CLASS: Aves.

JACKDAW PRETENDER. Many birds have claimed the title of king, including the eagle, wren and crane, but according to one of Aesop's fables the jackdaw made a bid for the throne by picking up feathers moulted by more brightly coloured birds and fastening them to its body. After all the birds had paraded in front of him Zeus was about to award the throne to the gaudy jackdaw when it was stripped of its borrowed feathers by the other birds.

JACK DEMPSEY *Cichlasoma biocellatum,* a small freshwater fish of the Middle Amazon. It reaches a length 7 in (18 cm). The body has a general background of mottled brown with bright blue spots anteriorly and pale spots towards the tail. In the larger males a curious bulge develops on the forehead. These fishes are often kept by aquarists but are rather unruly and are not recommended for a community tank unless very small. FAMILY: Cichlidae, ORDER: Perciformes, CLASS: Pisces.

JACK RABBITS, true hares of the genus *Lepus* (family Leporidae). The common name is derived from the resemblance of their remarkably long ears to those of the jackass. All seven species (see lagomorphs) are found in western North America and Central America.

Antelope jack rabbit *Lepus alleni:* the common name is derived from the rump flashing in frightened, running rabbits. It is produced by special muscles stretching the skin and everting the hairs. Animals not in a state of alarm do not exhibit white flashing when moving.

It has enormously large ears, 8¼ in (21 cm), with white edging but no black spot on the tip.

The distribution is principally Mexican but it also occurs in southern Arizona.

The breeding season from January to September is correlated with the average monthly rainfall. Three to four litters, averaging two young each, are produced annually. The precocial young are dropped in shallow well-concealed nests, but scatter soon after birth. It is extremely well-adapted to life in arid conditions and prefers high,

The Black-tailed jack rabbit.

dry plains with only moderate grass cover. Water is conserved as a result of behavioural and physiological adjustments. It is active at night, the day being spent in the shade. Its ability to regulate the flow of blood through the ears controls the intake or loss of heat according to environmental conditions.

When escaping, a long high 'observation' jump is performed every four to five leaps. It has been reported to clear a 5½ ft (1·7 m) obstacle, and reach a speed of over 35 mph (57 kph).

The Black-tailed jack rabbit *Lepus californicus* gets its common name from the colouring of the upper surface of the tail. The ears are 6 in (15 cm) long and are black tipped. The animal is found in southwestern North America and the tablelands of Mexico. There are 17 subspecies adapted to a range of habitats, but essentially it is an animal of the arid zone. Open plains with short, poor mixed grasses are the favoured habitat and it flourishes in drought-stricken overgrazed areas. As in the Antelope jack rabbit the ear is functional in body temperature control.

It breeds from January to April, and the gestation period is 43 days. Four to five litters are dropped annually, averaging three young each. Often no nest is prepared, and the scattered leverets are suckled for 17–20 days.

The Black-tailed jack rabbit is solitary except during the breeding season. It is sedentary, the home range of adults being about 42 acres (17 ha), and of juveniles about 35 acres (14 ha). Density is 0·3–0·5 per acre (0·5–1·0 per ha).

Frequently observed fighting, chasing and avoidance between individuals are indicative of a social hierarchy and territoriality.

Stress, induced by social behaviour and resulting in intra-uterine mortality of embryos, has been found to affect population numbers.

One of the most numerous American lagomorphs, it reached plague proportions in California at the turn of the century in response to changes in agricultural practice. Bounty was still offered in Kansas and other states until recently. It has been found that 62 Black-tailed jacks consume as much as one cow.

The Black-tailed jack rabbit has been shown to be a reservoir of diseases pathogenic to man and domestic animals, such as tularaemia, bubonic plague, brucellosis, Q-fever, and Rocky Mountain spotted fever. FAMILY: Leporidae, ORDER: Lagomorpha, CLASS: Mammalia.   R.M.

JACKS, a name often used in the United States for members of the family Carangidae, here referred to as mackerels. The name jack is also used in England for small specimens of the unrelated pike.

Jacobson's organ, the specialized region of the nasal sac, shown here in the mouth of a snake.

JACOBSON'S ORGAN, an accessory nasal organ found in tetrapods. It may take the form of an outgrowth of the main nasal cavity (Jacobson's organ or vomero-nasal organ) or may simply be a specialized area of the membrane of the nasal cavity (vomero-nasal epithelium). Jacobson's organ is well developed in land vertebrates and is especially prominent in reptiles where it becomes separated from the main nasal apparatus and has a separate opening into the mouth cavity. The organ is well supplied with sensory nerves and is used to sample fluids in the oral cavity. In many reptiles, especially snakes, airborne particles are picked up by the flicking movements of the tongue the tips of which are then placed against the opening of the Jacobson's organ. The structure is reduced or absent in aquatic reptiles and in mammals.

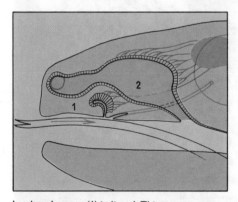

Jacobson's organ (1) in lizard. This sensory organ, discovered by the Danish anatomist Ludwig Levin Jacobson in 1809, is a specialized and more or less isolated region of the nasal sac (2), used especially in snakes and lizards as an accessory sense of smell.

JAEGER, the North American name for three of the four species of skuas of the bird family, Stercorariidae. All three have a circumpolar breeding distribution in the arctic tundra. The Pomarine jaeger *Stercorarius* *pomarinus* and the Long-tailed jaeger *S. longicaudus* breed only in the tundra, but the Parasitic jaeger, or Arctic skua, *S. parasiticus* breeds as far south as Scotland. See skua. FAMILY: Stercorariidae, ORDER: Charadriiformes, CLASS: Aves.

Female jaguar (below) and kittens (above), with the characteristic rosettes in their coat.

JAGUAR *Panthera onca,* the only living big cat of the American continent. The jaguar is sometimes confused with the leopard because both have spots in rosettes but those of the jaguar have a black spot at the centre. The yellowish buff ground colour is similar in both, but in the jaguar the rosettes tend to be concentrated along the back. The belly and chest are pale and have irregularly placed black spots, and the lower half of the tail is ringed. There is a black mark near the mouth on the lower jaw, and the backs of the ears are black. The variations in colour range from an almost white ground colour to black forms, in which the rosettes can only be seen as a variation in texture. Jaguars vary in size from 5½–9 ft (1·7–2·7 m) overall, the tail being one third of the total length. At the shoulder, they are 2¼–2½ ft (68–76 cm) high. The weight is 125–250 lb (56·7–113·4 kg), which makes it a heavier animal than the leopard or the puma. It is a good climber. It is known by a variety of names, including that of Tigre americanos.

The jaguar inhabits an area that is bounded to the north by the southwestern states of the USA, and to the south by Argentina. It lives in thick cover, in forests or swamps, but it is also found in desert and savannah areas in the north and south of its range. The species is divided into a number of geographical races, which are distinguished one from the other by size and the intensity of the colouring. Each individual has its own territory and this usually consists of an area of 2–5 sq miles (5–13 km²) although there have been records in the past of individuals that have travelled 500 miles (800 km) on their own, and more, for no apparent reason.

The jaguar is able to breed at about two years old. The individuals are solitary, only coming together at the mating time, which is probably in January in the northern part of the range, but at no fixed time elsewhere. After mating, the female has no more to do with the male and, after a gestation period of 95–105 days, the cubs are born. The usual size of a litter is two but there have been as many as four. The young are fully furred at birth and blind. They first emerge from the den at two weeks of age. From the time that the young animals leave the den, their growth and development follows a similar pattern to that of the young of other big cats.

The jaguar is one of the roaring cats, but it appears to make very little use of this ability, and in this it is similar to the leopard. The most common sound is a grunt, usually made when it is hunting. In addition to this, the male makes a mewing noise in the mating season, and a cornered animal will snarl and growl at its enemy. Like many of the other cats, the jaguar is an accomplished swimmer and has no fear of water, although it does most of its hunting on the ground or in the trees. It mainly feeds on peccaries, but the range of food taken is very wide and it will hunt deer, capybara, tapir, agouti, sloth, monkey, and a wide variety of birds. It also eats fish, which it catches by scooping them from the water, turtles and small alligators and crocodiles. Like so many of the cats it cannot resist the chance of an easy meal and will raid domestic stock whenever the opportunity arises. The jaguar demonstrates remarkable strength, and has been recorded as pulling a dead horse through 70 yd (64 m) of brush and then towing it across a river. It does not appear to have the same reputation for man-eating as many of the African and Asian cats, but this could well be because the area in which the animal lives has not yet been exploited to the same degree as have the habitats of the other cats. Jaguars will also eat carrion and they are often lured into traps by this means.

The method of killing prey is very similar to that used by the leopard, but the jaguar, if the first attempt does not succeed, will often leave the intended victim and go to seek food elsewhere. Once a kill has been made and has been dragged to a place of the animal's liking, it will usually be buried, but should the ground be too hard or rocky, no further attempt will be made to conceal the carcass. The jaguar seems unaffected by the smell of high meat and it will return several times to a kill, should it be large enough.

In common with all the big cats, the jaguar is often found in zoos, but it is generally considered to be more unreliable than its relatives and is treated with the greatest respect. Although the animal can seldom be handled after the eyes have opened, it breeds well in captivity.

Jaguars have fared better than their counterparts in the Old World and for the most part their range and numbers have not been seriously reduced since the first Europeans landed in America. FAMILY: Felidae, ORDER: Carnivora, CLASS: Mammalia.   N.J.C.

JAGUAR FISHING STORIES. There are several accounts of jaguars trailing their tails in the water, luring fish which bite the tip of the tail and are immediately flicked onto the bank with a forepaw. It seems that the jaguars wriggle the tip of the tail to attract the fishes and that their best fishing is under fruit trees where fish congregate to feed on the fruit falling into the water. Such stories have been reported from many parts of the Amazon, often in the 19th century when communication in this area was almost non-existent. Similar behaviour has been reported in foxes, raccoons, coyotes and domestic cats. In the Trobriand Islands, rats were once seen fishing for crabs with their tails.

JAGUARUNDI *Felis yagouaroundi*, jaguarondi or yaguarondi, of all the cats it is the one that shows the greatest divergence from the norm and in many ways approaches the general form of the mustelids, which include weasels and otters. The name is misleading as the jaguarundi has very little in common with the jaguar. The body is much elongated and the head is long and has a low silhouette and the ears are small. The average length of the jaguarundi is about $3\frac{1}{2}$ ft (107 cm), of which a third is tail, while the height at the shoulder is only 11 in (28 cm). A well grown individual will weigh about 20 lb (9 kg).

There are two colour phases in this species and for many years they were thought to be distinct species. They are found with either a black to brownish grey coat, or they are tawny to chestnut. Neither is spotted. The brown form is known as the eyra. The grey form becomes somewhat darker in the winter months.

The jaguarundi is found in the extreme southwest of the USA, but is far less common than it used to be, because of the thinning out of the cover along the delta of the Rio Grande. The southern limit of its range is Paraguay. It appears to be an animal of the swamp and forest and is known to be an excellent swimmer, from which it derives one of its many local names of 'otter cat'. In North America its favourite habitat is the chaparral scrub near water. This animal is never found very far away from water. In its normal habitat, it moves along clear and well defined trails, which makes it easy to trap.

Jaguarundis are thought to be mainly nocturnal, especially in the tropical region of their range, but in the other parts they have been observed to be active throughout the day. When one of these animals is cornered by dogs, and this is how they are hunted, it will take refuge in a tree. They are usually hunted at night, and they can then be picked out by the glow of their eyes in the light of a torch, and shot.

They are solitary animals for most of the year, meeting only in the mating season, which occurs either in November and December, or May and June. The young are born after a gestation period of about 70 days and the litter usually consists of two kittens, but there can be as many as four. The den is similar to that of the ocelot, in a hollow log or among rocks. The young are unmarked at birth and the one litter may well contain both the grey form and the brown.

Jaguarundis prey on a variety of small mammals and on game birds, which they

The jaguarundi, a weasel-like member of the cat family. Its name is misleading as the jaguarundi has little in common with the jaguar.

Jamoytius

appear to prefer. They often cause havoc by breaking into the pens of domestic fowl. FAMILY: Felidae, ORDER: Carnivora, CLASS: Mammalia.   N.J.C

JAMOYTIUS, a fossil fish *Jamoytius kerwoodi* from Silurian deposits near Lesmahagow, in Lanarkshire, Scotland. It has been variously considered to be either the sole representative of an order, the Euphanerida, of naked primitive, rather amphioxus-like vertebrates, or the ammocoete larva of an ostracoderm and an anaspid. Recent work by Dr A. Ritchie, while confirming both its primitive nature and its anaspid relationships has revealed unexpected lamprey-like features.

Jamoytius was elongated, up to 8 in (20 cm) or more in length. Its head was bluntly rounded and scaleless. The eyes were laterally placed and there was probably a circular mouth. The roughly cylindrical trunk was covered with unusual scales, thin and flexible, only about $\frac{1}{32}$ in (2 mm) wide, but apparently extended all the way from the belly to the back. Each was shaped like a V with the apex pointing forwards. They did not overlap but seem to have been separated from each other by a narrow gap. Dr Ritchie suggests they may have been horny, epidermal structures. Their peculiar shape suggests that they coincided with the underlying muscle blocks or myotomes. There were a number of long, low fin-folds: one along the middle of the back and one low on each flank, with a short anal fin. The tail was asymmetrical but it is not certain which was the upper and which the lower lobe. Internally there was a well developed notochord. The mouth was supported by a circular cartilage and in the branchial region on each side lay two longitudinal cartilages linked at regular intervals by seven or eight shorter, vertical cartilages, the whole forming a simple branchial support reminiscent of the branchial basket of modern lampreys.

Jamoytius was probably marine. There have been many and varied speculations as to its mode of feeding but no firm conclusions. CLASS: Pisces.

JAWFISHES, small, rather elongated marine fishes related to the weeverfishes. They derive their name from their very large mouths. Some species have a backward extension of the upper jaw like that found in some of the tropical anchovies. There is a single, long dorsal fin, the first part supported by spiny rays. The most remarkable feature of this otherwise rather undistinguished group is their habit of constructing burrows. The burrows are very elaborate, with a chamber at the end several times larger than the fish itself and lined with pieces of rock and coral. One or two of the

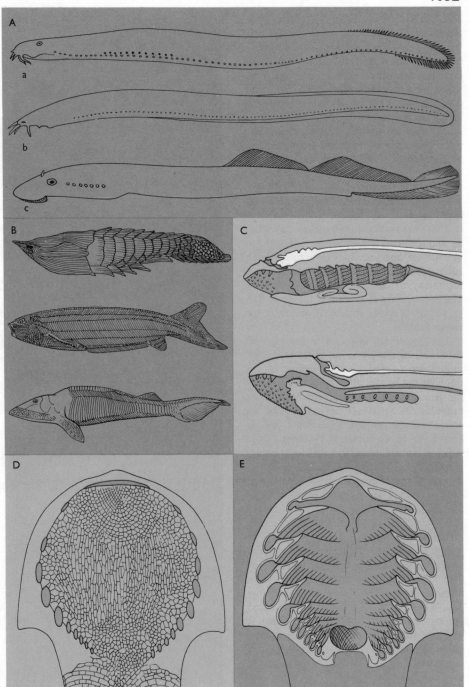

A. Three types of jawless fishes (cyclostomes). a. The slime hag *Bdellostoma*. b. the hagfish *Myxine* c. the lamprey *Petromyzon*. B. Fossil ostracoderms representing the Heterostraci (*Poraspis*), the Anaspida (*Pterolepis*) and the Osteostraci (*Hemiclaspis*). C. Sections through the head of an ammocoete larva of a lamprey and an adult, to show the division of the adult pharynx into two parts. The endostyle of the larva becomes the thyroid of the adult. D. Ventral view of the head region of a late Silarian ostracoderm of the cephalaspid type. E. Restored view of the pharyngeal region of the same viewed from below after removal of external covering of bones.

species are mouth-brooders. The Yellow-head jawfish *Opisthognathus aurifrons* from the Virgin Islands, which grows to about 4 in (10 cm), has a beautiful blue body, which becomes darker towards the tail and merges into a striking yellow on the head. It builds its burrows in sand and spends much of its time hovering obliquely over the mouth of the burrow eating small animals and larvae that float past.

Jawfishes also live in shallow waters in the Indo-Pacific region. Their burrowing and territorial habits have been studied, but as yet little is known of these fishes and there are very few specimens in collections. FAMILY: Opisthognathidae, ORDER: Perciformes, CLASS: Pisces.

JAWLESS FISHES, primitive fishes now represented solely by the lampreys and the hagfishes. When the first aquatic vertebrates evolved during the Ordovician period of 450 million years ago, they were fish-like in general shape but had poorly formed fins and lacked jaws. The absence of jaws was clearly not a complete disadvantage since two quite successful jawless groups, the lampreys and the hagfishes, have survived to the present day using an effective combination of a sucking mouth and a horny rasping tongue. The evolution of jaws was, however, one of the several major steps that led to the success of the higher fishes.

The jaws in fishes are thought to have evolved from cartilage that supported the gills. In the earliest vertebrates there was a row of perforations opening from the throat to the outside and these perforations were strengthened with rods of cartilage, the gill bars. With the passage of time the first pair of gill bars was lost. The second pair moved forward as the mouth itself developed from a simple tube to an enlarged cavity. Eventually, this second pair of gill bars came to support the sides of the mouth, which had taken over the area previously occupied by the anterior gills. From supporting the sides of the mouth it was a fairly short step to the gill bars actually forming the bones of a jaw. The third pair of gill bars changed their position and served to join the second pair to the head. In modern sharks, the hemibranch or spiracle is the remnant of the gills attached to the third gill bar. This third gill bar later became the hyomandibular, a bone which continued to change both its position and function throughout the long evolution of the vertebrates. In the reptiles it became involved in hearing and in the mammals it is represented by one of the three tiny bones of the middle ear which transmit the vibrations of the eardrum to the inner ear.

The early jawless fishes are now extinct and the modern forms appear to be somewhat degenerate representatives of what was once a flourishing group. The fossil species show considerable diversity and it is not certain whether they were evolved in marine or freshwaters. Characteristically, they had a median or pineal eye on top of the head. This is vestigial in the hagfishes but is well developed in the lampreys and under the microscope can be seen to have a pair of lenses. One lens is larger than the other and there is a possibility that the pineal eye was in fact a paired structure. This third eye is still sensitive to light in the lampreys. Just in front of the pineal eye is the nostril. In embryo lampreys it is in the normal position on the upper lip but during development it moves round to take up a position on top of the head. In the hagfishes the nostril connects with the mouth but in the lampreys the nostril ends blindly in an expanded sac. This sac, the nasopharyngeal pouch, acts as a pump and lies close to the pituitary gland.

During the course of evolution various parts of the nostrils and the sac have become involved in the pituitary gland.

The fossil jawless fishes were mostly heavily armoured and were quite unlike the modern forms (see fishes, fossil). The fossil groups are generally referred to as ostracoderms (bony-skins) in contrast to the living forms, which are loosely termed cyclostomes (round-mouths). The fossil ostracoderms are placed in two groups, those with a single nostril (Osteostraci) and those with two nostrils (Heterostraci). The lampreys and the hagfishes both have a single nostril. As yet, the fossil group which actually gave rise to the modern jawed fishes has not been determined, but the formation of jaws was a decisive step towards the evolution, not only of predators with snapping jaws armed with teeth, but of all the many jaw specializations which have enabled fishes to exploit a multitude of different foods and feeding habits.

JAYS, a diverse group of birds in the crow family, Corvidae, many of which are brightly-coloured—particularly in shades of blue—and have screeching, raucous voices. In a number of respects, both structural and behavioural, the jays are similar to the magpies and the two groups have been united by some authorities in the subfamily Garrulinae. This does not, however, seem to be a true reflection of relationships within the family.

The jays are most numerous (in the number of species as well as individuals) in America, particularly in the tropics. The original bearer of the name 'jay', however, is the European jay *Garrulus glandarius,* a shy species found in most of Europe and east through Asia to Japan. It is a strikingly beautiful bird some 13 in (33 cm) long, with a pinkish brown body, black, white and blue wings and a black tail. The rump is white and the erectile crown feathers are streaked in black and white. Like many other jays it is an omnivorous feeder and will take eggs and chicks of other birds. It is basically a bird of woodland and feeds to a large extent on acorns, of which it makes large stores in the autumn for use in the following winter and spring. The nest is a cup of twigs in which five to seven eggs are incubated for 16–17 days. There are two species closely-related to the European jay: *G. lanceolatus* of the Himalayas and *G. lidthi* of islands in the China Sea.

The other genus of Old World jay is *Perisorius* and this genus spreads also into North America. The Siberian jay *P. infaustus* reaches the Pacific coast in the east

The hen of the European jay is like the male in plumage. The sexes are distinguished by behaviour.

Jellyfish

North American Blue jay, one of the most colourful members of the crow family.

and Scandinavia in the west. The Szechwan grey jay *P. internigrans* lives in eastern Tibet and western China, particularly in coniferous forests. In similar areas of North America is found the Canada jay *P. canadensis.* These species have duller plumage than most other jays, being typically brown or grey.

There are nearly 30 other species of jays in America, 20 of them in the tropical areas. The most common species is the Blue jay *Cyanocitta cristata,* widespread in North America, mostly blue, with black and white on wings and tail. The term 'jay-bird' refers to this species more than any other. There are, however, several other species which are well-known, some of them of limited distribution. The Florida or Scrub jay *Aphelocoma caerulescens,* for example, is restricted to the scrub oak areas of the Florida peninsula. It is one of the species of jays which can be readily tamed. Another ecologically restricted species is the Piñon jay *Gymnorhinus cyanocephala* of the mountains of the western United States.

Some of the neotropical species are most strikingly coloured. The Turquoise jay *Cyanolyca turcosa,* for example, which is a bird of the Andes, is almost entirely turquoise blue. The Green jay *Cyanocorax yncas,* found from Texas southward to Peru, is green above, yellow below, with a blue crest and yellow outer tail feathers. The variety of neotropical forms is a reflection of the richness of the environment. Adaptable, omnivorous birds, such as the jays, are able to evolve to occupy a variety of available ecological niches. FAMILY: Corvidae, ORDER: Passeriformes, CLASS: Aves. P.M.D.

JELLYFISH, marine animal often seen stranded in rock pools at low tide or swimming under the surface of the sea with a pulsating bell and long trailing tentacles. They are members of the phylum *Cnidaria and are placed in the class Scyphozoa. In this class the medusa is the dominant phase, but the polyp or hydroid may be present as a small tubular animal rather like *Hydra* in external appearance and known as a scyphistoma. See alternation of generations.

Externally the jellyfish shows four-rayed symmetry. The bell varies in shape from a wide saucer to a cube and may be grooved on the upper or ex-umbrella surface. The gelatinous consistency is due to the extensive formation of a jelly-like mesogloea separating the outer ectoderm from the inner endoderm. Round the edge of the bell are a varying number of tentacles and the margin is not smooth but scalloped into lappets. From the centre of the sub-umbrella or undersurface of the bell hangs an extension or manubrium bearing a four-cornered mouth. The mouth may be drawn out at the corners into short lobes or long, frilly extensions or oral arms, which become fused together in one order, the Rhizostomae, giving rise to 'suctorial mouths'. The ectoderm of the bell and oral arms is covered with nematocysts or stinging cells enabling the capture of food organisms over a large surface area. Prey captured on the ex-umbrella surface is carried to the edge of the bell by cilia, removed by the oral arms and conveyed to the mouth.

In the typical and most familiar jellyfish the mouth leads to a central cavity, off which are four gastric pouches. Each pouch contains gastric filaments and food materials are

broken down by preliminary extra-cellular digestion. In order to transport food materials and oxygen to cells of the ex-umbrella surface an elaborate canal system has been developed. From the gastric pouches ciliated radial canals leave and travel to the margin of the bell where there may be a circular canal. From the bell margin other branched canals lead back to pores at the bases of the oral arms, thus ensuring circulation through the bell.

Round the bell margin is a strong, broad band of circular muscle, the coronal muscle, while bands of muscle fibres, radial muscles, also leave the margin and travel in the ectoderm of the sub-umbrella to the manubrium. These muscles contract simultaneously, closing the bell and ejecting water, propelling the jellyfish forwards. Relaxation is passive and brought about by the expansion of the compressed mesogloea. The nervous system, like that of all Cnidaria, consists of a diffuse nerve-net of multi-polar cells, and thus transmission is slow. To co-ordinate the swimming movements of the bell an additional 'through-conducting' system has evolved. Situated at the bell margin is a system of large, bi-polar nerve cells and it has been shown that each beat of the bell is preceded by an impulse in the through-conducting system, a single stimulus leading to the contraction of the whole bell. Associated with both nerve-nets are marginal sensory tentacles or rhopalia. Each club-shaped rhopalium is set in a pit, roofed over by a hood-like extension of the ex-umbrella and with a lappet lying underneath. At the free end of the 'club' are cells containing calcium sulphate (gypsum) and cells with long, sensory hairs making connections with the nerve-nets. These are organs of equilibrium and responsible for maintaining the jellyfish in a horizontal position.

The gonads are borne in the gastric pouches and the sexes are usually separate. Ova may be fertilized in the sea or in the central mouth region of the female. In this last, the fertilized eggs develop in the oral arms which act as brood pouches. Planula larvae leave the brood pouches of the female and the subsequent life-history is known for many, but not all, jellyfish. In most jellyfish living in shallow seas, the ciliated planula settles down and grows into a solitary, cylindrical polyp or scyphistoma, with a basal disc and an expanded oral disc with mouth and tentacles. Although it is superficially like the freshwater *Hydra,* internally its enteron is incompletely divided into four by septa or mesenteries which project from the body wall into the centre. These septa are curious in that through each runs a deep depression or peristomial pit, which is open to

Porpita, a siphonophore, often spoken of as a jellyfish, though not a true one, being eaten by a Sea slug *Glaucus.*

A fine specimen of a true jellyfish *Rhizostoma octopus* stranded on the seashore.

more oral tentacles, feeds again and may live for several years, producing ephyrae during the winter.

The class Scyphozoa can be divided into five orders: Semaeostomae, Rhizostomae, Coronatae, Cubomedusae and Stauromedusae.

The semaeostome jellyfish are the most familiar and the most typical of the class. They are usually the only order seen in temperate waters. The bell is flat, saucer or bowl-shaped with a scalloped margin of eight or more lappets and typically eight or sixteen sense tentacles or rhopalia. Numerous tentacles are found round the bell margin, either equally distributed or grouped in bunches. The oral arms are long and frilly, and leading from the gastric pouches are numerous radial canals. Members of this order are generally found in coastal waters of all seas and live mainly in the warm and temperate zones, although some species of *Cyanea* extend into the polar regions. One genus, *Pelagia,* lives in deeper waters and the scyphistoma does not occur in the life-history, planulae developing directly into small medusae. Members of this order may get very large; for example *Cyanea arctica* may be over 6 ft (2 m) across, probably the largest known cnidarian. However, the general size range is from 2–16 in (5–40 cm). Some well known genera include the Common jellyfish *Aurelia, Chrysaora, Cyanea* and *Pelagia.*

The rhizostome jellyfish are believed to be closely related to the semaeostome jellyfish and derived from them. They look very like semaeostome medusae but lack tentacles

the sea water at the oral end and closed at the base of the polyp. This pit is lined by longitudinal muscles. The projecting edges of the septa bear gastric filaments.

During the spring and summer months in temperate zones, the scyphistoma feeds and may bud off other scyphistomae, but during the late winter a process known as strobilation occurs. The polyp becomes constricted in the transverse plane either in one region or down the length of the polyp such that it resembles a pile of plates. From each plate or disc eight lobes or lappets grow out and complex internal re-arrangement occurs. Then, by contraction of the longitudinal muscles, each disc is constricted off the polyp to give a tiny medusa or ephyra larva. The ephyra is about 1 mm in diameter and swims in the plankton, feeding and growing until it reaches adult size. The scyphistoma produces

Large brown jellyfish swimming by pulsations of its bell, which expands and contracts like an umbrella being opened and closed.

Cassiopeia. a tropical jellyfish, unusual in having given up a planktonic life, lies on its back to feed, stretching out its tentacles to suck in small plankton.

round the bell margin, while the oral arms have become fused together and greatly increased in size. The arms are much branched and the original grooves close over to form canals. The main mouth also becomes fused into the system, giving rise to so-called 'suctorial mouths'. The term, however, is probably incorrect since there is no evidence of suctorial action and food materials are taken in by ciliary action. 'Shoulder ruffles', additional mouth-bearing outgrowths, occur on the outer edges of the arms in some genera, while other club-shaped appendages packed with nematocysts may be present. These are used in the capture of prey; for example, fish may be taken by some larger rhizostomes. The fused mouth leads into a central stomach region with numerous branched radial canals running out to the bell margin. Although usually living in warm shallow waters of tropical and subtropical seas, some species may extend into temperate waters, for example *Rhizostoma octopus*. The method of development is not known for all genera, but a scyphistoma which produces ephyrae is probably a common feature of the life-history. Generally reaching a large size, up to 32 in (80 cm), some better known genera are *Rhizostoma, Cotylorhiza* and *Cassiopeia*.

Jellyfish placed in the order Coronatae are all distinguished by a groove, the coronal groove, about midway between the centre and the margin on the ex-umbrella surface, dividing the bell into two parts. Above this groove the bell is often more dome-like than in other orders, while below the groove the margin is deeply scalloped bearing alternating tentacles and rhopalia. The mouth

lacks oral arms and the manubrium is relatively short. The internal arrangement of the stomach region is more complex. Since many are inhabitants of deeper waters they are relatively poorly known and are often seen only as part of a collection taken from deep water dredging expeditions. For instance, *Atolla* is not usually found above 600 ft (200 m). Some, however, are surface forms in shallow warm waters, for example, *Nausithoë* which is bowl-shaped and *Linuche* which is like a small thimble. The life-history of these medusae is not known, although in *Nausithoë* a scyphistoma does occur.

The Cubomedusae or *Sea wasps differ from the previous medusae in that the bells are cuboid with four flattened sides. There is a simple bell margin, from the four corners of which hang groups of tentacles. The mouth is deeply situated in the sub-umbrella cavity and is at the end of a short manubrium. Little is known about their life history and they are usually found in the open seas, but they do occur in shoals in shallow waters. The toxin produced by the nematocysts is very powerful and causes rashes and weals of some severity on human beings. It may even prove fatal if massive numbers of nematocysts are discharged into the victim.

Unlike other members of the Scyphozoa, the Stauromedusae or Stalked jellyfish are sedentary and live fastened to seaweeds or stones by their ex-umbrella surface. These medusae are trumpet-shaped with an expanded sub-umbrella surface and a central mouth. The short, stalk below the body is anchored by an adhesive disc, but although they cannot swim they may detach and move,

by looping movements, in a manner reminiscent of *Hydra*. The bell margin is drawn out into eight lobes each bearing small, knobbed tentacles. Halfway between each pair of lobes on the ex-umbrella surface, in some species, may be eight marginal bodies called 'anchors' which are adhesive. Between the mouth and the margin of the bell four deep, sub-umbrella funnels or peristomial pits sink into the interior of the polyp. Internally the Stauromedusae resemble Scyphistomae, the enteron being divided by four septa projecting into it, each of which is penetrated by the peristomial pit. Gastric filaments and gonads are borne on these septa. Reproduction is by planula larvae which settle down and bud off other larvae before growing into the trumpet-shaped adult. Generally these medusae live in bays and coastal waters of colder seas and may vary in colour between rose-pink, green, blue or even violet. The common genera are *Haliclystus* with eight 'anchors' and *Lucernaria*, which lacks 'anchors' and has only one peristomial pit. The evolutionary position of these jellyfish is not settled. CLASS: Scyphozoa, PHYLUM: Cnidaria.   S.E.H.

JERBOAS, rodents constituting a very distinctive family, the Dipodidae, with about 25 species in the deserts and steppes from central Asia to the Sahara. They progress by jumping on their very long hindlegs and feet in the manner of a kangaroo, a habit that they share with the Kangaroo rats of North America although the latter belong to a distinct family, the Heteromyidae. The jerboas should not be confused with the *gerbils which, although

A Hairy-footed jerboa *Jaculus jaculus* burrowing. Note extremely long hindlegs.

feeding on seeds of grass, salt-bush and other desert plants, and especially on bulbs and tubers. In southern Russia tulip bulbs are a favourite food and, where their range meets cultivated ground, crops such as water melons and germinating wheat may suffer.

Like most highly specialized rodents jerboas are less prolific and are longer-lived than most of the mouse-like rodents. Nevertheless there may be two or three litters per year, the timing depending very much on the climate and the annual cycle of rainfall. The litter size is usually about three or four and the gestation period about four or five weeks.

One of the best known of the jerboas is the Desert jerboa *Jaculus jaculus,* found in the Sahara and Arabia. It is one of the larger species and is capable of living in all but the most extreme desert conditions. The commonest of the larger jerboas in Asia belong to the genus *Allactaga. Allactaga major* for example occurs abundantly throughout the less arid steppe zone of Russia from the River Dnepr to central Siberia and extends north-

adapted to similar habitats, look more like typical rodents and are more closely related to the hamsters and voles.

Jerboas range in size (head and body) from 1½ in (4 cm) excluding tail in some of the Dwarf jerboas of central Asia (amongst the smallest of all rodents) to 6 in (15 cm) in, for example, the North African jerboa *Jaculus orientalis.* The tail is always very long, sometimes over twice the length of the head and body, and in most species has a tuft of long white hairs at the tip. It is an important organ of balance when the animal is jumping. In one group, however, the Fat-tailed jerboas, *Pygeretmus,* of Turkestan, the tail is shorter than the head and body and contains large deposits of fat, a condition parallel to that in the Fat-tailed gerbil of North Africa. The front and hindlegs are very disproportionate in size. The hindfeet are enormously elongate and in the larger species they enable the jerboa to make prodigious leaps of up to 8 ft (2·4 m). The hindfeet usually have only three toes, and these are supported by a single strong foot-bone which results from the fusion of the three central metatarsals, a condition similar to that found in the cannon bones of cloven-hoofed ungulates like cows and sheep.

Like most desert animals, jerboas have either large external ears or enormously inflated auditory chambers in the skull. An extreme example is the Long-eared jerboa *Euchoreutes naso,* of Mongolia, which is one of the most bizarre species of mammals with ears as big as a hare's, a rather pig-like snout, whiskers that reach to the base of the tail and an exceedingly long thin tail with a bold black band just before the tip. Equally bizarre are

the Dwarf jerboas, *Salpingotus,* with very short external ears but enormous tympanic chambers that dwarf the rest of the skull and make the whole head as large as the rest of the body. These Dwarf jerboas are like tiny balls of fluff with grotesquely long whiskers and tail, minute front legs, and long hindfeet on which they progress in a sequence of short hops so rapid that the legs seem to vibrate.

Most jerboas are sandy coloured, closely matching the colour of the environment in which they live, and they lack bold markings except for the contrasting black and white tail-tip. The fur is extremely soft and silky, and the ear opening is protected from sand by long hairs. The hair of the feet is also closely adapted to life on sand, with dense fringes of hairs on the toes. The teeth of jerboas are fairly normal for rodents. Most species have a pair of premolars in the upper jaw such as are found in squirrels and dormice but not in the majority of rats and mice.

Jerboas are predominantly nocturnal animals, spending the day in burrows which may be quite elaborate, with several entrances and with one or more nest chambers. These burrows provide protection, not only against predators, but against the extremes of climate that would kill even a jerboa very quickly, if it were forced to remain on the surface in the intense heat and drought of a summer day in the desert. In contrast the humidity and temperature in the underground nest are much more moderate and vary little. In most Asiatic species the burrows are also used for hibernation, the animals becoming completely dormant for up to six months of the year.

Jerboas are predominantly vegetarian,

Hairy-footed jerboa, held in the hand, its chin on a crooked finger, indicates its small size.

wards almost to Moscow. Other Asiatic species are among the least known species of mammals and some have been found only on one or two occasions, as, for example, some of the Dwarf jerboas from Mongolia. FAMILY: Dipodidae. ORDER: Rodentia, CLASS: Mammalia.   G.B.C.

JEWEL WASPS, wasps with brightly shining metallic colours. Their alternative name is Cuckoo wasps. Another name is Ruby-tailed wasps and the metallic green, red or blue are interference colours formed by the surface layers of the cuticle. Jewel wasps are related to the true wasps (Vespidae) and are included with them in the superfamily Vespoidea. They can be easily recognized by the pitted and sculptured surface of the cuticle and the plate-like structure of the abdomen which appears to be composed of three or four segments. The name Cuckoo wasp indicates the principal feature of the life-history, for these insects live semiparasitically on other insects. The adult Jewel wasp enters the nest of some other

A Jumping spider with its prey, a bluebottle.

species of solitary bee or Hunting wasp to lay its eggs and the larvae feed on the host larvae, thereby killing them. When disturbed or attacked by the adult of the host wasp the Jewel wasp can roll itself up into a ball.

Many of the solitary wasps hunt caterpillars with which they provision their nests as food for their own larvae and the Jewel wasp may be seen flying about in sunny weather searching for the entrance tunnels to the nests of such solitary caterpillar- and spider-hunting wasps. Before the host wasp finally seals its nest tunnel the Jewel wasp runs in and lays its own egg on the paralyzed caterpillar which the Hunting wasp has provided as food for its own larva. On hatching, the Jewel wasp larva devours the provisions of the rightful owner of the nest. Some Jewel wasps also devour the larvae of their host and are truly predatory as larvae, while others are internal parasites of their hosts, penetrating the body of the host, for example, a solitary bee, destroying it completely. Jewel wasps develop very quickly, taking about six days from the hatching of the egg to pupation in *Chrysis ignita* and about 20 days in *Pseudochrysis neglecta*. FAMILY: Chrysididae, ORDER: Hymenoptera, CLASS: Insecta, PHYLUM: Arthropoda.R.C.F.

JEWFISHES, large sea-perches of tropical seas otherwise known as groupers. The name is inconsistently applied to various members of the family Serranidae but some authors restrict the name jewfishes to species not belonging to the genus *Epinephelus*, the latter being termed groupers. FAMILY: Serranidae, ORDER: Perciformes, CLASS: Pisces.

JOHANNSEN, W. V., 1857–1927, Danish biologist, influential in the development of genetics. He began as a plant physiologist but soon changed to experimental genetics. He recognized that not all variations in a plant are due to hereditary factors and as a result discovered and named the phenotype and the genotype—the physical form and the hereditary structure. He achieved this by breeding isolated stocks of beans, or 'pure lines', as he was the first to call them, and subjecting them to different conditions. He showed that some, phenotypic, characters could be changed by environmental influences, while others, the genotypic characters, remained constant.

JOHN DORIES, rather grotesque fishes of temperate oceans related to the boarfish. Their name has an interesting derivation. John appears to be a nickname bestowed on the fish by fishermen. Dory is derived from the French *dorée* or golden, in turn derived from a Latin word meaning gilded, a reference to the shining yellow of the flanks. However, the John dory is also called the St Peter fish because legend has it that it was in this fish that the apostle found the tribute money, the dark blotch on the flank being St Peter's thumbprint. Yet another name given to the fish, by fishermen in northern Germany, is 'King of the herrings' since it is reputed to shepherd the herring shoals. In reality, the John dory is a fish-eater, feeding on herrings, pilchards and sand-eels.

The John dory *Zeus faber* is an almost oval, compressed fish with the rays of the anterior spiny dorsal fin greatly elongated into filaments. The pelvic fins are also long.

Head-on view of a John dory.

The jaws are protrusile and can be thrust out a surprisingly long way. This fish is found in moderate depths down to 600 ft (200 m) and it is widely distributed in the Atlantic, occurring as far north as Scandinavia and as far south as South Africa. It reaches 3 ft (100 cm) in length and although its flesh is delicious its grotesque appearance discourages would-be purchasers. Other species of dories are fishes of deeper water which are infrequently caught. FAMILY: Zeidae, ORDER: Zeiformes, CLASS: Pisces.

JUMPING SPIDERS, short-legged hunting spiders with a rectangular cephalothorax bearing eyes in three rows of four, two and two. Those of the front row face forward and are greatly enlarged. Jumping spiders have a

jerky walk except when stalking their prey when it is smooth and cat-like before a final leap is made. They leap with the hind legs and seize with the front legs.

Jumping spiders are mostly small, rarely reaching $\frac{1}{2}$ in (12 mm) in length. They hunt in sunlight and enclose themselves in silk cells at night. They are most numerous in the tropics where they attain brilliant colours. In temperate regions they are of more sombre appearance and few species reach the Arctic Circle though one species holds the altitude record for spiders at 22,000 ft (6,705 m) on Mt Everest. The Zebra spider *Salticus scenicus* is a common dark species with white stripes found on walls of buildings in Europe and North America. Some species are wonderful ant-mimics, and increase their resemblance to ants by waving their front legs like an ant's antennae.

A flickering of the front eyes is caused by internal muscular movements which may change the field of vision and/or the focus. The eyes certainly provide a clear image at a distance of many body-lengths and the males resort to visual courtship before approaching too close to the females, displaying prominently the special decorations on their bodies as they perform elaborate dances and strike attitudes. FAMILY: Salticidae, ORDER: Araneae, CLASS: Arachnida, PHYLUM: Arthropoda.   W.S.B.

Red jungle fowl, ancestor of the domestic fowl.

Cock and hen Jungle fowl drinking (below).

JUNCOS, certain North American species of finch-like birds, the most common of which is the Slate-coloured junco *Junco hyemalis*. This is a bird of coniferous woodland, about 6 in (15 cm) long, with a dark slate-grey plumage. FAMILY: Emberizidae, ORDER: Passeriformes, CLASS: Aves.

JUNGLEFOWL, the ancestors of modern domestic fowl which have been domesticated for more than 4,000 years and, as one would expect, their general appearance closely resembles that of chickens, especially leghorns. Junglefowl are found all over the warmer parts of Asia and Malaysia but are absent from Borneo. They inhabit a wide variety of country from low-altitude forest, dry scrub and bamboo groves to small woods and rough

ground near villages. They are always wild and extremely wary so that they continue to survive despite persecution by man. During the breeding season they are often found in family parties consisting of one cock and several hens and they congregate in larger flocks during the winter.

The male's courtship is similar to that of the Domestic fowl and includes circling the hen accompanied by the rasping sound produced by the movement of the lowered primary flight feathers. The crow of the male junglefowl is similar to a domestic cock's but only that of the Red junglefowl resembles it closely. The hen junglefowl makes her nest on the ground under the shelter of vegetation, the number of eggs in the clutch depending upon the species. Wild junglefowl living near villages sometimes cross with domestic chickens.

All junglefowl feed chiefly upon seeds, grain, shoots and buds, as well as insects.

There are four distinct species of junglefowl. The best known and most widespread is the Red junglefowl *Gallus gallus*. The male resembles a Brown leghorn cockerel with his fiery red and golden-brown plumage. Red junglefowl exist in the genuine wild state from northwest India through Assam and Burma, Thailand and Malaya, to Indo-China in the east and also to south China, Sumatra and Java. Males of the Red junglefowl, if of pure stock, undergo a moult into dull plumage in the summer. They have a short shrill crow which ends abruptly.

The Ceylon junglefowl *G. lafayettei*, also called La Fayette's junglefowl, is confined to Ceylon and occurs wherever there is sufficient cover from sea-level to 6,000 ft (1,800 m). It is similar in habits to the Red junglefowl but never gathers in large flocks and keeps away from cultivation and human habitation.

Sonnerat's junglefowl *G. sonnerati*, sometimes called the Grey junglefowl, is confined to western and southern India where it lives in bamboo groves and forests on mountain slopes up to 5,000 ft (1,520 m). It is usually found in pairs or family parties but appears to be monogamous and does not normally congregate in flocks. The hackles or neck feathers are much in demand for dressing flies for salmon and trout fishing and as a result of trade in its plumage Sonnerat's junglefowl has declined drastically in numbers. The Indian government has recently banned the export of the plumage.

The Green junglefowl *G. varius* is found in Java and other East Indian islands and, although small numbers inhabit inland forests, it is primarily a bird of the sea-shore and coastal valleys. It appears to be monogamous and is usually found singly, in pairs or in family parties. The cock's crow of three syllables is sharp and shrill. FAMILY: Phasianidae, ORDER: Galliformes, CLASS: Aves.   Ph.W.

KAGU *Rhynochetos jubatus,* the size of a domestic fowl, 22 in (56 cm), this bird has long legs, a strong bill and loose pale grey plumage with a long loose crest. It is the only species of the family Rhynochetidae and is found, in dangerously decreasing numbers, only in New Caledonia, where it is largely nocturnal. It lives on invertebrates and is a ground-dwelling inhabitant of the mountain forests. The sexes look similar and both participate in nesting, which is on the ground. Peculiar display antics are performed, during which the boldly-patterned wings are shown to advantage. FAMILY: Rhynochetidae, ORDER: Gruiformes, CLASS: Aves.

KAKAPO *Strigops habroptilus,* a strange nocturnal New Zealand parrot, which has presumably been isolated from other parrots for a considerable time, as it has developed unique characteristics. The kakapo is about 2 ft (60 cm) long, chiefly greenish-yellow in colour with darker barring. It is almost flightless, the rounded wings being used only for gliding. The bill is unlike that of any other parrot in having strong ridges on the lower part. The kakapo was called the 'Owl parrot' by the European colonists because of its soft plumage, 'facial disc' of feathers and nocturnal habits, but its food is almost entirely vegetable matter.

When Europeans first arrived in New Zealand the kakapo was widespread, living in the southern beech *Nothofagus* forests throughout the country, though bones found in the North Island and on the Chatham Island group indicate a previously wider distribution. The kakapo is now drastically reduced in numbers, being found in only a few remote refuges in the fiordland region and on Stewart Island in the south. We, therefore, have to rely upon early descriptions for information on its behaviour.

The kakapo runs along the paths through the forest and grassland, but occasionally climbs trees and glides for some distance. The paths are maintained by constantly trimming the surrounding vegetation and they lead from daytime forest resting places in holes among tree roots and rocks to feeding areas which are often in montane grassland above the forest or below in the valleys. Along these paths are numerous dust-bathing hollows.

Kakapos breed in natural holes or construct tunnels of their own; sometimes quite deep, one of 9 ft (2·7 m) having been recorded. The female incubates two to four white eggs in a bare nest rather late in the year, eggs having been found from January to May.

Their food consists mainly of the leaves of tussock plants, berries and nectar. Fibrous material is not swallowed, but is thoroughly chewed to extract the juices and then rejected as a ball. These balls, found attached to the plants or in the resting places and dusting hollows, provide a clue to the presence of this now rare bird.

The call is a weird bittern-like booming. It was a familiar sound to the pioneers until about 1890, when a rather rapid decline in numbers coincided with the introduction and spread of mustelid predators such as stoats. It seems likely that this, or some other result of European civilization, has been responsible for the near extinction of kakapos. Attempts to keep and breed them in captivity have so far proved unsuccessful, but this, or their introduction to predator-free off-shore islands, seems the only hope for their survival. FAMILY: Psittacidae, ORDER: Psittaciformes, CLASS: Aves. D.G.D.

KAMPTOZOA, a name unnecessarily created for the *Entoprocta and now abandoned.

KANGAROO, a marsupial animal with large hindfeet and strong hindlimbs and tail, which adopts a bipedal method of locomotion when moving quickly. The female bears a pouch, containing the teats and mammary glands, in which the young is raised. In its widest sense the name kangaroo is applied to 50 kinds of animals grouped in the family Macropodidae (big-footed marsupials). These range in size from the tiny Musky rat kangaroo *Hypsiprymnodon,* weighing a little over 1 lb (500 gm) to the largest Grey and Red kangaroos which approach 200 lb (90 kg) in weight and reach a height of 6 ft and occasionally 7 ft (2 m).

A bounding kangaroo uses only its strong hindlegs to achieve speed in escape.

Kangaroos are grouped with the phalangers, koala and wombats in the superfamily Phalangeroidea. The Musky rat kangaroo shares features in common with the phalangers, from which it (and the remaining kangaroos) is undoubtedly derived, being the only kangaroo which bears a toe on its hindfoot, has a generally quadrupedal method of locomotion and habitually bears more than one young in each litter.

The oldest known fossil kangaroos are up to about 30 million years old and probably lived in the Oligocene epoch. The phalangeroid group probably separated from the remaining marsupials much earlier—perhaps at the end of the Cretaceous period, seventy million years ago. Living kangaroos may be divided into the Rat kangaroos, commonly called Kangaroo 'rats' (subfamily Potoroinae) and the true kangaroos (Macropodinae). It is customary to call the largest of the Macropodinae 'kangaroos' while the remaining, smaller, members are called wallabies, pademelons, etc. This distinction is used here because it is in common use but there is no real criterion by which kangaroos and wallabies may be distinguished. Attempts have been made to do so on the basis of the length of hindfoot and basal length of skull but if these are rigorously applied some species fall into the kangaroo group on one criterion and the wallaby group on the other. Also the group generally called Tree kangaroos are wallaby-sized animals.

Kangaroos are heavily built in the hindquarters and lightly built in the forequarters; the forelimbs are thin, mobile and frequently used in bringing food to the mouth. Strong muscular development of the upper forelimb occurs only in the males of some species. The tail is heavily built in the largest kangaroos and serves to balance the forepart of the body, being held clear of the ground during bipedal locomotion. It is used as a prop during bipedal stance and may be the only part touching the ground during fighting when a kangaroo can kick an opponent using both hindfeet together. During quadrupedal locomotion the tail 'walks' along, behind the kangaroo, and leaves a characteristic track on soft ground. The foot is very long and bears four toes. The second and third digits are very small and bound together by skin except in their terminal regions. This condition is known as syndactyly and the fused toes as the syndactylous digits. All kangaroos, possums (phalangers), wombats, etc. (the phalangeroid marsupials) are syndactylous as also are the bandicoots. In the latter group syndactyly appears to have arisen as a parallel evolution.

The teeth of kangaroos are characteristic. There are three incisors on each side of the upper jaw separated by a long toothless gap (diastema) from the single 'permanent' upper premolar and the succeeding molars. As in other marsupials the permanent premolar replaces a deciduous (molariform) premolar, but in the kangaroos the earlier erupted premolar is usually shed at the same time. The lower jaw bears only one incisor on each side which is directed forwards (procumbent incisor) and there is a diastema separating the incisor from premolar and deciduous premolar teeth corresponding to those of the upper jaw. There are four molar teeth on each side of upper and lower jaws and these are described as being lophodont—adapted for grinding plant food. No kangaroo bears canine teeth in the lower jaw but Tree kangaroos have canine teeth in the diastema of the upper jaw.

The molar teeth erupt slowly and continuously move forwards in the jaws so the approximate age of a kangaroo is indicated by its molar-eruption stage. This may be found with the living animal under anaesthetic or on the skull of the dead animal. Red kangaroos have their first molar tooth fully erupted when one year old, two molars at two years, three molars at four years and four molars when seven to eight years old. Intermediate ages may be distinguished by the degree of eruption of a tooth. The amount of forward progression of each tooth is indicated by its position relative to the descending process of the zygoma. In seven to eight years-old Red kangaroos the zygomatic process is opposite the space between third and fourth molars whereas at about ten years the fourth molar has moved forward so that its anterior loph is opposite the process. Kangaroos may reach the age of 20 years and in very old animals the last molar tooth will be in front of the process. As the teeth move forwards in the jawline the anterior teeth become worn with use and tend to be shed. The fourth, or so-called permanent, premolars go first followed by the first molars and some very old kangaroos have only two molar teeth left in each jaw. The lower jaw of kangaroos can always be distinguished from that of phalangers by the presence of a pronounced masseteric fossa.

The alimentary canal of kangaroos is strongly adapted for herbivorous nutrition and shows remarkable parallel similarities to the stomach of the true ruminant animals. The oesophagus has a groove of unknown function along its dorsal length which greatly resembles the oesophageal groove of ruminants. The stomach is large and sac-like as in ruminants and divided into four chambers. The anterior chamber of the stomach contains Protozoa and other unicellular organisms which digest cellulose converting it to substances which are used for the nutrition of the host kangaroo. Kangaroos are thus able to convert the cellulose fibre of plant-cell walls to usable foodstuffs and are well adapted to life in the more arid regions of Australia where much of the available plant food is of a fibrous nature. Kangaroos do not chew the cud as do the true ruminants but sometimes the food is regurgitated up the oesophagus to the mouth and reswallowed without further chewing. This process is known as 'merycism' and its function is unknown.

The larger kangaroos are an Australian continental radiation and are not found in New Guinea. The Tree kangaroos presumably evolved in New Guinea forests since they are most prevalent there, but two

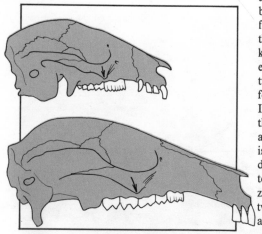

Left: Side views of the skulls of Lesueur's rat kangaroo (above) and the Yellow-footed rock wallaby (below) to show the differences between Rat kangaroos and true kangaroos. Right: The skulls of two Red kangaroos, the upper two and a half, the lower five years old. Both have three upper incisors and one lower incisor on each side separated by a long toothless gap (diastema) from premolar and molar teeth (cheek teeth).

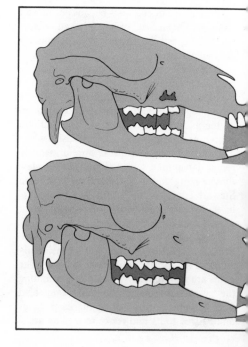

The Grey kangaroo *Macropus major*, one of the largest kangaroos, lives in forested areas and is nicknamed the forester.

species have reached the Cape York region, the nearest part of mainland Australia to New Guinea. More detailed distributions are given under the names of the various sorts of kangaroos.

Kangaroos generally produce a single young at one time although about one in each thousand Red kangaroos have twin young in the pouch. The non-lactating female kangaroo produces a single ovum each four to six weeks, depending on the species. The cyclic changes which occur in the female reproductive system between successive ovulations constitute the oestrous cycle. A succession of oestrous cycles does not, however, normally occur in wild kangaroos since the males are continuously fertile and females usually become pregnant after their first ovulation. The oestrous cycle is withheld during the period of pouch suckling which follows each pregnancy. The breeding season is defined as that part of the year at which the female kangaroo is actually or potentially capable of becoming fertilized.

The gestation period or interval between insemination and birth of young, varies between 29 and 38 days in the various large kangaroos. These gestation periods are long by marsupial standards but very much shorter than those of true mammals (Eu-

theria) of comparable size. An allantoic placenta, as is present during pregnancy in true mammals, has not been found in any kangaroo. The intra-uterine embryo breathes, and is nourished throughout gestation, by means of a simple but voluminous placenta derived from a vascularized part of the yolk sac. The yolk sac is a diverticulum of the hind gut of the developing embryo. It is also found in the embryos of true mammals where it forms a placenta which is transitory, and functional before the full development of the allantoic placenta.

The female kangaroo about to give birth cleans the inside of her pouch by licking it, and then assumes a resting position with her back supported, hind legs extended forwards and tail passed forwards between them. Birth is preceded by the appearance of a little straw coloured fluid and the embryonic allantoic sac containing waste products accumulated during pregnancy. The young is born enclosed in a fluid filled amnion which bursts allowing the young to grasp the mother's fur up which it climbs to enter the pouch between one and five minutes later. The mother pays no attention to the young during its climb to the pouch but remains in the birth position licking the blood and embryonic membranes, expelled after birth,

Not all kangaroos live in wide open spaces. The Tree kangaroo has returned to the habitat of its ancestors and become treeborne. Its capacity to jump has been lost on the way. Like the true kangaroo it feeds exclusively on plants.

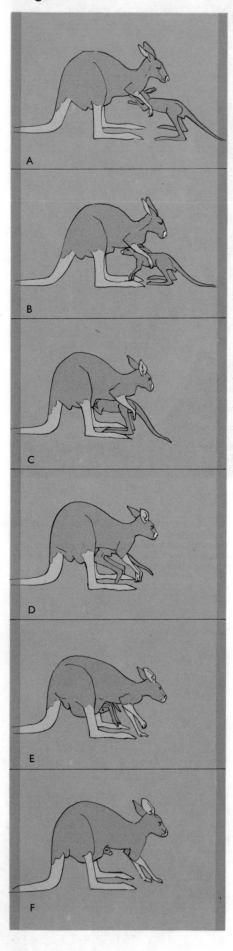

from her fur. Once in the pouch the young attaches to one of the four teats from which it draws nourishment throughout pouch life.

The newborn kangaroo is blind and hairless and the ears lack developed semicircular canals. Lungs, brain, some sense organs, kidneys and reproductive organs are incompletely developed at birth but in other respects the newborn kangaroo shows precocious development. The forelimb musculature is well developed and the digits are equipped with sharp recurved claws for gripping the mother's fur. The tongue is large and muscular and capable of a suction pump-like action. The nostrils are open and those centres of the brain concerned with sense of smell are well developed. It is probable that the young is guided to the pouch by its sense of smell since it has no sight and is not aided by its mother. Earlier observers thought the infant had an instinctive urge to climb upwards to the pouch and could not, in fact, do other than climb upwards. However, the young does sometimes miss the pouch on ascent and afterwards descends to the opening. The structure of the epiglottis is such that breathing and swallowing of milk could occur simultaneously but the mother kangaroo does not, as has been asserted, pump milk down the throat of the young. The development of the tongue and mouth musculature is sufficient to cause milk to be drawn into the throat during the sucking movements made by the young while attached to the teat.

Rates of development of young in the pouch vary from species to species. Red kangaroo young leave the pouch when seven to eight months old but Grey kangaroo young occupy the pouch for almost a year and have a rather slower rate of growth than in the Red kangaroo. The following description is based on the Red kangaroo. The average weight of the newborn is 23 grains (1·5 gm) and the birthweight is doubled during the first five post-natal days. This is a remarkably rapid rate of growth which continues through much of pouch life. At 29 days the young weighs about twelve times its birth weight and the weight doubles again during the next nine days. During the succeeding 11 or 12 days the weight is doubled again being 1½ oz (42 gm) at 50 days. The growth rate slows somewhat in the terminal stages of pouch life but by the time the young kangaroo is ready to vacate the pouch it has increased in weight some

Young Red kangaroo aged 210 days entering the pouch: A. feeling for pouch opening, B. moving farther under mother's body; C. grasping sides of pouch and inserting head; D. pushing into pouch with hind feet on the ground; E. turned over with head protruding and hindlimbs still out of pouch; F. feet drawn in and head turned over.

five thousand-fold to between 9–11 lb (4–5 kg).

Claws develop on the hindfeet of the young in the pouch when it is 7–11 days old and the male young may be distinguished from the opposite sex when 9–16 days old. The mouth opening of the newborn is circular and terminal and the teat is sucked into the mouth when attachment is made. The mouth begins to open along the sides when the young is a little older than 40 days and it is completely open along the sides at about 160 days. The first readily visible hairs are found at 90 days and hair spreads over the body during the next 75 days; the young being completely furred at about 164 days of age. The eyes do not open until the young is 120 days old.

The mother kangaroo cleans the interior of the pouch and the young by licking during its growth. Young first protrude their heads from the pouch when about 150 days old

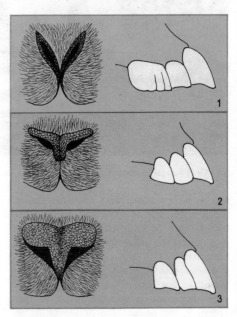

The muzzle, as seen from the front, and right upper incisor teeth of kangaroos. In the Grey kangaroo (1) the nose is largely hairy and the third incisor is broad with two deep grooves in the forward part. Red kangaroos (2) are partly hairy between the nostrils and the third incisor is small and roughly triangular. Hill kangaroos (3) have no hair between the nostrils and the third incisor is broader than that of red kangaroos.

and leave the pouch for short periods when about 190 days old. During the terminal part of pouch life they spend increasingly long periods out of the pouch. When they return to the pouch the mother bends her body downwards so that the forepaws are close to, or actually touching the ground, and the young approaches between them. It feels for the pouch opening with its forepaws and inserts its head when it finds the pouch. Entry is always made head first and the young turns over inside the pouch bringing its head up so that it lies close to, and can be protruded from, the pouch opening. The mother aids the entry of small young to the pouch by relaxing the pouch opening and bending her hindlegs backwards so as to bring the entire pouch area close to the ground.

The composition of kangaroo milk changes continuously throughout the period of lactation. A clear fluid can be expressed from the teats at the time the newborn young becomes attached. As lactation proceeds the clear fluid gradually changes to a milk of more normal appearance. The early milk contains very little fat but its fat content increases throughout lactation. Kangaroos frequently give birth to a second young while a large young is suckling from the exterior, using the greatly elongated teat and enlarged mammary gland it used while in the pouch. The second young attaches to another of the four teats and it is a remarkable feature of kangaroo lactation that the mother concurrently produces two milks of vastly different chemical composition. The newborn young is nourished on the clear fluid while the young out of the pouch is suckled on milk rich in fat.

Kangaroos exhibit embryonic diapause—the prolonged storage in the female reproductive tract of a dormant but viable embryo which consists of a total of about 80 cells. The cells are arranged in a hollow sphere, $\frac{1}{100}$ in (0·25 mm) in diameter, surrounded by a shell-like structure called the shell membrane. The dormant embryo arises as a result of fertilization while a young is being suckled in the pouch and it remains dormant until about a month before the young is about to vacate the pouch permanently. Newborn young which appear in the pouch within a day or two of it being permanently vacated by a large young are derived from a hitherto dormant embryo as are young born to female kangaroos long isolated from males of the same species. Development of the dormant embryo is initiated if the pouch young is lost due to misadventure when birth of the derived young will occur about a month after loss of the pouch young. Suckling of a young in the pouch keeps the embryo dormant. Occasionally pouch suckling fails to inhibit development of the uterine embryo and the pouch is then occupied by two young about a month different in age. The smaller is, however, invariably unable to complete pouch development in competition with the larger young.

Kangaroos have responded to the increased amounts of grass and herbage available since the adoption of grazing practices in outback Australia. No census of kangaroos was taken at the time of the first European settlement and it is extremely difficult, even today, to get an accurate assessment of the numbers of any one species. The widespread destruction of forest and brush

Grey kangaroos at a waterhole, with typical treed habitat in the background.

vegetation, the encouragement of grasslands and the installation of unattended watering points have, however, benefited the kangaroos which increased in numbers after European colonization. Since the latter part of the nineteenth century great fluctuations in numbers have occurred, probably reflecting increased breeding during series of good seasons and lack of breeding during periods of drought.

A build up of kangaroo numbers occurred in most inland areas of Australia during a series of years of generally above average rainfall from 1948 to 1963. During the years 1960 to 1967 about 7 million lb (3 million kg) of kangaroo meat was exported each year from Australia. About 300,000 kangaroos were killed annually to provide this

meat. Many more were killed to supply the Australian pet food market, for skins and as pests making an annual average slaughter of about 2 million kangaroos. Some reduction in numbers was evident in 1967 and considerably less animals were killed in the state of New South Wales in 1968 and 1969 than in earlier years. However, the reduction in numbers, evident in 1967, followed a severe two year drought in 1964 and 1965 which was accompanied by complete failure of breeding in many areas.

The Grey kangaroos have 16 chromosomes as do the larger wallabies to which they are closely related. They are distinguished from the Hill kangaroos and Red kangaroo by characters of the rhinarium (muzzle) and third upper incisor tooth. Like

The potoroo or Long-nosed rat-kangaroo *Potorous tridactylus*, marsupial equivalent of a rodent.

other kangaroos, the Grey kangaroos have a long period of growth and may not reach adult size until six or seven years old when females weigh up to 50 lb (22·5 kg) and males up to 150 lb (70 kg). The Eastern grey kangaroo *Macropus giganteus* has a range extending from 14°S latitude, on Cape York, to the most southerly parts of continental Australia and into the northeast of Tasmania. Although primarily a coastal animal it is found, towards the southern end of its range, 600 miles (950 km) from the east coast at Wilcannia in New South Wales. Here, and elsewhere over a north-south belt 150 miles (250 km) long and 50 miles (80 km) or more wide it overlaps in distribution with the Western grey kangaroo *Macropus fuliginosus*. The two species do not interbreed in the wild, where they occur in mixed populations, but limited interbreeding may occur in captivity. The Western grey kangaroo occurs to the west of the zone of overlap, along a narrow coastal belt of mallee scrub north of the Great Australian Bight and into South-western Australia.

The Eastern grey kangaroo does not have post-partum ovulation. Mating, and ovulation, may occur when the developing pouch young has completed about 100 days of its greater than 300 day pouch life. Embryonic diapause of the fertilized egg then occurs and its development to a newborn young is only completed at the end of the pouch life of the earlier young. Embryonic diapause is not known to occur in the Western grey kangaroo.

The Hill kangaroos, often called wallaroos or euros, consist of one or more species usually grouped under the name *Osphranter*

Female Red kangaroo *Macropus rufa*.

An athlete jumps 26 ft (8 m) with great effort, the average being much less. A large kangaroo can progress by leaps of the same length effortlessly.

robustus. They are distinguished from the remaining kangaroos by having a large area of the rhinarium free of hair and a single groove in the lateral aspect of the third incisor tooth. The Antilopine hill kangaroo has a greatly swollen rostrum (anterior part of skull bounding the nasal cavities). It occurs in Arnhem Land, Cape York and the Kimberly district, all in the more northern parts of Australia, where it is sometimes found in hilly country but more often in flatter wooded country. The Eastern hill kangaroo has an enormous range, in suitable areas, thoughout continental Australia except for the most northerly parts of the tropics and the southeastern and southwestern corners. Female Eastern hill kangaroos reach full size when five to six years old at a weight of about 42 lb (19 kg). Males continue to grow until seven, or more, years old and reach weights of up to 100 lb (45 kg). All four molar teeth of both sexes are fully erupted when they are seven years old. The pouch life of the young lasts about seven months and breeding may be continuous throughout the year, although it is profoundly influenced by drought which may cause both premature loss of pouch young and failure to breed. Embryonic diapause occurs in females fertilized at post-partum oestrus.

There is but one species of Red Kangaroo *Megaleia rufa* which inhabits plains country with scattered mulga, and other, trees anywhere within the 20 in (51 cm) rainfall isohyet of continental Australia—a total area of about 2 million sq miles (5½ million sq km). The Red kangaroo is distinguished by having a smaller bare area on the rhinarium and a smaller third incisor tooth than either Grey or Hill kangaroos. The male Red kangaroo is usually, as the name suggests, red in colour and may reach a weight of 175 lb (80 kg). Females are usually bluish-grey in colour with a maximum weight of 77 lb (35 kg). However, blue males and red, or sandy-red, females may occur in almost any locality and in central Australia the majority of animals of both sexes are the same reddish colour.

The Tree kangaroos *Dendrolagus* consist of six species of animals of stocky build which retain the non-prehensile tail and general hindlimb structure of their terrestrial kangaroo ancestors. In returning to the trees they have redeveloped the ability to move their hindfeet independently; terrestrial kangaroos are able only to move them together. Tree kangaroos weigh up to about 25 lb (11 kg) and have a head and body length of 27 in (70 cm), the tail being about as long as the head and body. Lumholtz's tree kangaroo *Dendrolagus lumholtzi* and Bennett's tree kangaroo *D. bennettianus* occur on the Cape York Peninsula and are the only Australian continental representatives of a group otherwise confined to New Guinea. The Tree kangaroos apparently have a litter

size of one but otherwise their breeding habits are virtually unknown. FAMILY: Macropodidae, ORDER: Marsupialia, CLASS: Mammalia.   G.B.S.

KANGAROO RATS, small members of the kangaroo family grouped in the subfamily Potoroinae and often called Rat kangaroos to distinguish them from other Kangaroo rats which are jerboa-like true mammals. The Rat kangaroos have typical kangaroo features, such as a long tail and a generally bipedal locomotion, but are distinguished from the true kangaroos (subfamily Macropodinae) by their small size, ranging from about ½ lb (1 kg) for the Musky rat kangaroo to about 6½ lb (3 kg) for the largest Rufous rat kangaroos. Rat kangaroos have well-developed canine teeth in the upper jaws and are distinguished from the true kangaroos by the arrangement of the bones on the side of the brain case. The urethra is long and the urogenital sinus short compared to that of most true kangaroos. A Pleistocene Rat kangaroo *Propleopus* was much larger than any of the living forms.

The Brush-tailed rat kangaroo *Bettongia penicillata* occurred, at the time of the first European occupation of Australia, over the entire eastern half of the continent and into the southernmost portion of Western Australia. Today it occurs only in the extreme southwest of Western Australia, in northeast coastal Queensland and in a small area to the east of the Great Sandy Desert or in about 10% of its former range. It runs with the head low, the back arched and the tail fluent; its black 'brush' of hairs being prominently displayed. It is a nest-building animal throughout its range from hot rain-forests, with a rainfall exceeding 50 in (125 cm) per year, to sand-ridge spinifex desert. It used also to occur on mountains at about 5,000 ft (1,500 m) altitude. The nest is round and largely made of woven grass stems although sticks and twigs may be included.

The Desert rat kangaroo *Caloprymnus campestris* is also a nest-builder and is known only from sparsely grassed desert country east of Lake Eyre. The tail of this, and all other Rat kangaroos, lacks the brush of the Brush-tailed rat kangaroo.

Lesueur's rat kangaroo *Bettongia lesueuri* formerly had a range exceeding that of the Brush-tailed rat kangaroo but it is today known only from Bernier and Dorre—two small islands off the west coast of Western Australia. It is a burrowing animal which constructed large communal warrens, characteristically depressed towards the centre, throughout the drier inland parts of Australia. Nesting material is gathered in the mouth and then pushed backwards under the body by the fore- and hindfeet to be gathered in the tail. The tail is curled under to hold the material while it is carried down the burrow.

The gestation period is 21 days and pouch life of the single young lasts 115 days. The young is sexually mature and of adult weight, 2½ lb (1·1 kg), when less than a year old. Embryonic diapause occurs during suckling of a young in the pouch (see kangaroo). Lesueur's rat kangaroo has the fastest rate of reproduction of any known kangaroo.

The Long-nosed rat kangaroo *Potorous tridactylus* is abundant in Tasmania and parts of Victoria and New South Wales. A related animal, only doubtfully specifically distinct, was once known from southwestern Australia. Unlike Lesueur's rat kangaroo, the Long-nosed rat kangaroo has a comparatively long gestation period (38 days) and carries its young in the pouch for four and a half months. Embryonic diapause occurs during pouch suckling.

The Rufous rat kangaroo *Aepyprymnus rufescens* lives in open forest and woodland in northeastern New South Wales and in Queensland. It constructs a nest, apparently occupied by only one animal, in clumps of grass or tussocks. The nest rests in a basin-shaped depression 8–9 in (20–23 cm) in diameter and 2–9 in (5–23 cm) deep, dug in the ground, and is a domed structure 12–18 in (30–45 cm) in diameter. Nesting material is carried to the nest held in the distal part of the tail, which is curled under to hold the material. FAMILY: Macropodidae, ORDER: Marsupialia, CLASS: Mammalia.   G.B.S.

KATYDID, see bush-crickets.

KEA *Nestor notabilis*, a New Zealand mountain parrot, placed with its close relative the kaka or New Zealand forest parrot *Nestor meridionalis*, in a suborder which is considered primitive and not closely related to other parrots. The bill of both species is rather long and little curved. The tongue has a hair-like fringe at its tip and the tail feathers have projecting shafts. The kea is not as gaudy as some parrots, being largely olive-green with dark edges to the feathers. The wing and tail quills are bluish-green, and it is only in flight that the scarlet underwing comes into view. The male is distinguished by a longer and stronger bill, while that of immature birds has a yellow base.

Keas are now found only in the South Island of New Zealand, though there are sub-fossil remains in both the North Island and the Chatham Island group, 500 miles (800 km) east of New Zealand. This wider distribution possibly occurred during the 'Ice Ages'.

The nest is usually placed in a rock crevice or in a hollow log in the forest, and is often near a rock vantage point. The two to four white eggs are usually laid between July and January, although they have been found throughout the year. They are incubated mainly by the female for three to four weeks. The young take about 14 weeks to fledge. Males may be polygamous, but adult females do not necessarily lay every year and on average each female raises one young bird every second year. A life expectancy of at least six years is thus needed to maintain the population.

The kea is responsible for much controversy in New Zealand. To the hiker or mountaineer keas are a romantic sight as they fly overhead with their loud 'keee-aaaa' ringing in the mountain valleys. On the ground a small flock of keas is a most humorous sight as they move with a clown-like clumsiness, poking into and tearing at any objects that take their interest and conversing with a variety of mewing calls. But keas are not popular with sheep farmers, because around 1870 a new feeding habit was noticed. As well as their natural food of berries, young shoots and small animals keas were found to be feeding on the copious quantities of carrion associated with high country sheep farming. It was soon suspected that keas were attacking weak as well as dead sheep and they rapidly acquired a reputation as killers. Since then thousands of keas have been shot on high country farms for the bounty offered by the run holders or local bodies. However, a recent analysis of this habit by J. R. Jackson showed that the keas' bad reputation was ill founded. Accounts of the mode of attack on sheep varied greatly and first hand observations were difficult to find. Geographic variation in the accounts suggested that the accounts were based on local tradition and many details were obviously false. While there is little doubt that there is some factual basis for the kea's reputation as a sheep killer it seems that the

'problem' has been grossly exaggerated.

In spite of the heavy human predation and the keas' own rather low breeding rate they are still plentiful in the less accessible parts of the New Zealand mountains. Indeed it is claimed they have become more widespread since about 1870 and they are a welcome addition to the attractions of many a mountain village and hiker's hut. FAMILY: Psittacidae, ORDER: Psittaciformes, CLASS: Aves.

D.G.D.

KELP CRABS, live in the surface layers of the sea usually far away from the shore. They are small crabs, up to 1 in (25 mm) across. Their legs are flattened and fringed with bristles, so that they can swim. *Planes minutus* and *P. marinus* are more particularly associated with the floating Sargassum weed of the tropical Atlantic. Sometimes they drift to the southwestern shores of Britain with the North Atlantic Drift. As well as attaching themselves to seaweed Kelp crabs may also be found on large jellyfish, pieces of wood and turtles. SUBORDER: Brachyura, ORDER: Decapoda, CLASS: Crustacea, PHYLUM: Arthropoda.

KELPFISHES or Scaled blennies, members of a large family of shorefishes otherwise referred to as the klipfishes and discussed under blennies. FAMILY: Clinidae, ORDER: Perciformes, CLASS: Pisces.

KESTRELS, a distinctive group of falcons, contrasting with most other falcons by persistently hovering for ground prey, rather than taking birds or insects in flight. They form the biggest subdivision of the large genus *Falco*. There are about ten species of true kestrel, together with four others re-

garded as aberrant kestrels and usually included with them. The average size is $11\frac{1}{2}$ in (29 cm), the largest being the Fox kestrel *F. alopex* of Africa reaching 15 in (38 cm) and the smallest the Seychelles kestrel *F. araea* of 8–9 in (20–23 cm). Females are usually larger than males. The colouration of the upper-parts is typically reddish-brown spotted black; underneath they are more buff, streaked and barred black. Males are often distinguished by the inclusion of grey on the upper-parts.

They are world-wide in their distribution. The Common kestrel *F. tinnunculus* has many races and occurs throughout Europe, Asia and Africa, being replaced in the New World by the similar American kestrel *F. sparverius,* commonly known as the sparrowhawk in America. Other species occupy the islands in the Indian and Pacific oceans: the Madagascar or Aldabra kestrel *F. newtoni,* the Seychelles kestrel, the Mauritius kestrel *F. punctatus* and the Moluccan kestrel *F. moluccensis* of the East Indian islands. The Australian or Nankeen kestrel *F. cenchroides* is the kestrel of Australia and New Guinea. Most kestrels are resident, the exceptions being the Common kestrel, the Lesser kestrel *F. naumanni,* the Australian kestrel and the Red-footed falcon *F. vespertinus* which migrate. The Lesser kestrel and Red-footed falcon are often gregarious during migration. Throughout their range kestrels occupy rather open habitat, but this can be desert, savannah, cultivated, partially wooded or mountainous. They also now occur commonly in cities and suburbs.

Kestrels do not build nests, but lay their eggs on ledges, in holes and in the old nests of other species. The Lesser kestrel and Red-footed falcon are unusual in being colonial nesters. Incubation is usually by the female alone, the male hunting and bringing food to the vicinity of the nest. The principal food is small mammals, but in certain areas or at certain times of the year their diet may be largely insectivorous; small reptiles, frogs, worms and birds are also taken. Because of their ground feeding habit, kestrels are unsuitable for falconry. FAMILY: Falconidae, ORDER: Falconiformes, CLASS: Aves.   I.P.

KIANG *Equus hemionus kiang,* the Tibetan subspecies of the Asiatic wild ass. For further details see the entry on ass. FAMILY: Equidae, ORDER: Perissodactyla, CLASS: Mammalia.

KIDNEYS, paired organs in vertebrates lying in the dorsal wall of the abdominal cavity and projecting into it. They are concerned with maintaining the composition of the blood by excreting unwanted harmful or surplus substances, and in addition they are involved to some extent in the male

Kea. New Zealand mountain parrot. Its long, little curved beak, distinguishes it from other parrots.

Parent Common kestrel bringing food, a small mammal, to the young at the nest, which is the abandoned nest of some other large bird, such as a crow.

reproductive system in all vertebrate species. Each kidney consists of a very large number of tubules, several million in man, each ending in a double walled funnel (Bowman's capsule) which encloses a knot of small blood vessels (the glomerulus). Basically the mechanism consists of the filtration under pressure of water and many substances of low molecular size, but not the blood proteins, through the thin walls of Bowman's capsule followed farther down the kidney tubule by the selective reabsorption of water and substances required by the animal, and the active secretion of other substances into the tubule. The resulting fluid is urine which drains down the ureter and so to the bladder or cloaca. An unusual function for kidneys is the production of a sticky substance used by stickle-backs in nest-building.

Kidneys develop from a part of the mesoderm known as the nephrotome. The first part to develop in the embryo is known as the pronephros and its tubules may have funnels opening into the coelomic cavity, a very primitive arrangement. The pronephros usually degenerates rapidly and is only functional in a few lower vertebrates. The remainder of the nephrotome can develop into one organ, on each side, known as the opisthonephros; this is the arrangement in most fishes and all amphibians. In the male the anterior part of the opisthonephros passes sperm from the testis through into the kidney duct which serves to carry both urine and

sperm; the anterior part may be reduced in the female. Alternatively, the nephrotome behind the pronephros can develop into two structures on each side: an anterior mesonephros, which loses its excretory function and becomes vestigial or absent in the female or the epididymis closely associated with the testis and conveying sperm in the male; and a posterior metanephros, which is the excretory kidney of both sexes, with its own duct carrying only urine. This second arrangement is found in reptiles, birds and mammals. See excretion and excretory organs.   Jo.G.

KILLDEER *Charadrius vociferus,* a noisy North American plover of farmland. It is about 10 in (25 cm) long, brown above, white beneath with two black breast bands and a rufous rump. Its common name is derived from the sound of its frequently repeated call. FAMILY: Charadriidae, ORDER: Charadriiformes, CLASS: Aves.

KILLER WHALE *Orcinus orca,* or grampus, an example of a true dolphin without a beak. The males reach truly whale proportions of 30 ft (10 m) and it has always been said that the females are only about half this size, rarely reaching 20 ft (7 m). So it is always quoted as one of the few species of Cetacea in which females are smaller than the male, the Sperm whale being the only other species to show this. During 1948–1957, however, Nishiwaki measured 600 Killer whales

caught in Japanese coastal waters and found the average adult lengths to be 21 ft (6·4 m) for males and 20 ft (6 m) for females, a difference which is negligible.

The head of a Killer whale flows straight back onto the trunk but the powerful stream-lined appearance is offset by very large rounded foreflippers, a large dorsal fin and large tail flukes. In the males the flippers and dorsal fin continue to grow throughout life until they become very large. In a young male or a female the flipper is about a ninth of the body length but has increased to a fifth in an old male. The dorsal fin grows to about 2–6 ft (0·6–1·8 m) in height and for this reason, and because of the shape, the Killer is sometimes called a 'swordfish'. Killer whales have a black back and white belly. There is a large white patch behind the eye and a large white invasion of the flank from the belly as well as a pale coloured saddle behind the dorsal fin.

The Killer whale is a fast and voracious feeder. It eats dolphins and porpoises, seals and sealions, penguins, fish and squid. Even the largest Whalebone whales may be attacked and killed by a hunting pack of Killer whales. They may hunt in small groups or in packs of up to 40 or more. A reported attack on sealions illustrates their hunting method. A collection of 10–15 sealions were swimming some way offshore when a school of five to seven Killer whales approached. The sealions dashed for the shore with the killers apparently herding and playing with them. As they approached the shore the killers suddenly attacked as if at a signal and all the sealions disappeared; none appeared to have escaped. Seals and penguins are swallowed whole where possible, but larger animals such as the larger whales are seized by the tongue, mouth and flukes first and then the helpless animal is eaten in large pieces bitten off by the killers' powerful teeth and jaws. Records such as that of the Killer whale with remnants of 27 porpoises and seals in its stomach are not uncommon.

Killer whales are found throughout the world but most frequently in arctic and antarctic waters. They commonly appear around British coasts and there is little in the dates of sightings to suggest any particular migrations.

The False killer whale *Pseudorca crassidens,* although closely related to the Killer whale, has external differences which make it closer in appearance to the Pilot whale. There is little difference in size between the sexes and each may reach up to 16 ft (5 m). The False killer is black almost all over though there may be white scar marks. It is slimmer than the Killer whale with a narrower flipper and smaller dorsal fin whilst the snout is rather rounded over the lower jaw. It is a deep water animal of world-wide distribution, except for the polar regions, and is found in large schools of up to several hundred individuals. It feeds on squid, cod and other fish which move in the oceanic currents. FAMILY: Delphinidae, ORDER: Cetacea, CLASS: Mammalia. K.M.B.

KINESIS, a term used to describe an animal's random movement made in response to a stimulus. The animal wanders about in an undirected manner and the path it follows is not either towards the source of the stimulus or away from it; it is, in fact, not orientated in any way. Kineses are of two kinds: *orthokinesis* and *klinokinesis*. An animal shows orthokinesis when its speed of movement alters with changes in levels of stimulation, for example, when the light intensity is increased. When its rate of turning (or rate of change of direction) alters with similar stimulus changes it shows a klinokinesis. If these responses are made to light, the prefix photo- is added to make photoklinokinesis, when to amount of contact, thigmo-, thus thigmo-orthokinesis, and so forth.

This type of behaviour has adaptive value for the changes in speed tend to make animals congregate where there are optimum conditions. Woodlice come to rest where humidity is high and loss of moisture from the body is reduced to a minimum. Earwigs tuck themselves into cracks where their bodies are in maximum contact with the ground; this is thigmokinesis. Their speed of movement is then nil when there is maxi-

mum stimulation. The ammocoete larvae of the Brook lamprey *Lampetra planeri* respond to light by becoming active. They are usually to be found buried head downwards in the mud of streams or of lake bottoms. If they are swimming free in the light, they wriggle actively with their heads pointing downwards. The more intense the light, the more vigorous the movement, the result is that in a tank divided into a dark and a light half the larvae congregate in the darker part. When their heads make contact with mud, movement continues, so that what was previously a swimming movement now causes them to burrow deeply into the mud. They continue to do this until the tip of their tails, on which a light receptor is borne, is shaded from the light.

Animals which respond to adverse conditions by an increased rate of turning (klinokinesis) will tend to avoid them. On moving from the dark into the light, a Planarian worm *Dendrocoelum lacteum* turns violently on crossing the border. This is likely to turn it back into the dark where the path straightens out once more. If the worm fails to reach the dark, the initially increased rate of change of direction declines with time (adaptation). In this way the worm follows a straight path for long periods, so moving over greater distances and probably encountering darkness once again. Equally, however, a high rate of turning in a favourable area will lead to this result. A number of parasites and commensals show a kinesis in responce to stimuli from their hosts. A louse changes direction more frequently in that part of a temperature gradient which is equivalent to the body heat of a mammal; this would tend to make the louse spend more time where temperature conditions indicate that a host is near. The commensal crab (*Pinnixa*) behaves similarly where the highest concentration of chemical stimulation from its polychaete host is found.

If the rates of movement or of change of direction increase with increasing intensity of stimulation, the kinesis is described as *direct* (i.e. directly correlated). If the rates increase with decreasing intensity it is an *inverse* kinesis (i.e. inversely correlated). Thus, woodlice which are more active in atmospheres of low relative humidities, come to rest in high humidities, showing inverse hygro-kinesis. The Coat-of-mail shell *Lepidochitona cinerea* moves faster as the intensity of illumination increases, showing a direct photo-orthokinesis. J.D.C.

KINESIS, CRANIAL, the mechanism by which certain vertebrates can move the upper as well as the lower jaw. It is found in sharks, some dinosaurs, lizards, snakes and birds. The bones of the upper jaw and snout are not as rigidly fused to the braincase as in other vertebrates, so that there are hinges and the

front part of the skull can be raised. In reptiles, at least, cranial kinesis increases the gape allowing large prey to be swallowed and probably assists with the hauling in of the prey in a series of gulps. In snakes, where the bones of the skull are less firmly attached to each other, cranial kinesis allows the teeth to slant forwards to bring them into use. This is most marked in the vipers where the gape is nearly 180° and the poison fangs are rotated forwards.

KINGBIRDS, certain species of the genus *Tyrannus* of the North American family of tyrant-flycatchers. The plumage is dark, usually black, grey or brown above and white, grey or yellow beneath. Kingbirds are aggressive and show the typical flycatcher behaviour of perching rather upright in an exposed position and darting out from time to time to catch passing insects. A common species is the Eastern kingbird *Tyrannus tyrannus,* some 9 in (23 cm) long, black above and white beneath with a white tail tip and red crown mark. It breeds in rural country through much of the eastern half of North America. FAMILY: Tyrannidae, ORDER: Passeriformes, CLASS: Aves.

KING COBRA *Ophiophagus hannah,* the largest species of *cobra, reaching a length of 18 ft ($5\frac{1}{2}$ m) and remarkable for its diet, which consists entirely of other snakes. The female builds a nest of leaves and coils herself above the incubating eggs. FAMILY: Elapidae, ORDER: Squamata, CLASS: Reptilia.

KING CRAB *Paralithodes camtschatica,* one of the Stone crabs which are not true crabs but are related to the Hermit crabs. This is a large bright red species, with legs spanning up to 3 ft (90 cm). It forms the basis of a large commercial fishery in the North Pacific, where American, Japanese and Russian fleets operate. The fishery is on such a large scale that the Russians operate canning factory ships which preserve the crab meat while still at sea. SUBORDER: Anomura, ORDER: Decapoda, CLASS: Crustacea, PHYLUM: Arthropoda.

KING CRAB, alternative name for *Horseshoe crab, used especially in the United States, not to be confused with the King crab *Paralithodes camtschatica*.

KINGFISHERS, a family of birds related to the bee-eaters, hornbills, motmots and others and sharing with them a syndactyl foot, the three front toes being joined for part of their length. They also share the structure of the palate bone, the form of the leg muscles and the way the tendons are joined to them, and

Common kingfisher flies to its nest in a river bank.

the feather distribution and arrangement of the feather tracts.

There are 87 members of the kingfisher family in two subfamilies: Alcedininae and Daceloninae, the former being the familiar fishing kingfishers with long narrow, sharp-pointed bills, and the latter the Forest kingfishers which often live far from water and whose bills are broader, flatter and sometimes hooked at the tip.

Europe has only one species, the Common kingfisher *Alcedo atthis* which is also found in Africa and the Far East, eastward to the Solomon Islands.

The Common kingfisher is a dumpy bird only 6½ in (16.5 cm) long. The azure feathers of its back can also look emerald green depending upon the angle of the light. The tail feathers are a darker cobalt, as are those of the head and wings where the striae glow with rows of azure speckles. In contrast the underparts are a warm chestnut orange. It has a white throat or bib, white neck patches and orange cheek patches behind the eye. The 1½ in (3.8 cm) dagger shaped bill is the only external indication of the sex. In an adult male it is wholly black, but the female usually has a partially or completely rose-coloured lower mandible. The small feet and legs are sealing wax red. Juveniles are duller than their parents, slightly smaller with shorter black bills and black feet.

Kingfishers live mainly on unpolluted rivers, lakes and streams, canals and fen drains. They also inhabit tidal estuaries, salt marshes, gutters and rocky sea shores, especially in the winter when driven to the coast because fresh water has frozen over.

The chief prey is fish, which the kingfisher secures underwater by grasping the fish between its mandibles, not by stabbing as is the popular misconception. The bird will watch from a perch, usually overhanging the water, until it sights its prey, and then, having aimed, it tenses and dives headlong into the water straight as an arrow, beak open and the opaque nictitating membrane or third eyelid closed. On grasping the fish it pivots and, using the buoyancy of its body, flaps its way back to the surface, propelling itself out of the water on the downstroke of the wings. The whole action takes about ⅓ sec. Once back on the perch the kingfisher prepares to kill the fish, the treatment varying for each type of fish. Minnows, its most common prey, are quickly nipped behind the gills and swallowed headfirst. Sticklebacks are beaten furiously against the perch to flatten their sharp spines and scutes. The Miller's thumb or bullhead has its outsize head almost pulped to soften it and the large fins which could choke the bird if erected are flattened to the sides.

A kingfisher may also hover prior to diving for a fish. This is usually because of the absence of a perch and it has been known to catch dragonflies and spiders in this manner.

The diet also includes tadpoles, small molluscs and Crustacea, and kingfishers will try for fish in trout hatcheries if they are not protected by netting. For this offence the kingfisher was once persecuted mercilessly.

Kingfishers pair for life and share a common territory throughout the year, defending it by chasing off aggressors. An encounter starts with a series of aggressive stances, on opposite perches, and when one kingfisher judges he has caught the other off guard he dashes towards his opponent in an attempt to knock him off his perch and duck him in the water.

Early in the year the pair of kingfishers fly high in a courtship flight, after which they look for a suitable place to nest, in a chamber at the end of a tunnel in a bank of the stream. They may return to the nest of the previous year; usually they excavate a new one. If the banks of the streams are not high enough they may choose the earthy roots of an up-rooted tree, a hole in a stone wall or bridge, or they may travel some distance overland to a sand, gravel or chalk pit where they excavate in the layer of topsoil.

To excavate they fly at the bank in quick succession, at a point well above high water level, driving in their bills to loosen the soil, until they have made enough of a depression to cling and from there continue to peck their way in. Once in the tunnel they shovel the earth back with their feet, pushing it out

backwards with their tails. Whilst one bird is in the tunnel the other remains on watch, uttering a low reassuring 'cheep'. The tunnel may measure up to 3 ft (0.9 m) long and slope slightly upwards. At the end a spherical chamber is formed where the eggs are laid in a depression on the bare soil. Once the chamber is formed, the digging bird will reappear head first instead of tail first as it can then turn around inside. The excavation may take up to a week, depending upon the looseness of the soil.

Once the nest is complete the ritual of courtship feeding takes place. The female sits bolt upright, beak in the air, wings drooped and juddering, and utters a pleading, bleating call. The male bird catches a fish and returns with it presented head first. The female takes it and eats it, coition usually following.

The eggs are a delicate translucent pink about ¾ in (1.9 cm) long, and are laid upon the bare soil. The normal clutch is seven eggs and incubation starts once the clutch is complete. Again the work is shared, each bird spending 1¼–3 hours on the eggs. Whilst on the eggs the parents throw up pellets, of clean fishbones, which accumulate around the eggs, until it looks as though the eggs may have been laid upon a bed of fishbones, so giving rise to the old fallacy that the kingfisher makes a nest of fishbones.

After 19–21 days the eggs hatch, and the parent takes the broken eggshell in its beak

A Pied kingfisher, of southern Africa, looks out from its nest burrow.

The Pygmy kingfisher *Ispidina pictus* of Africa, recognizable by its violet collar.

and drops it well away from the nest. It will then return with a very small fish not more than 1 in (2·5 cm) long. It will remain in the nest until its mate returns and calls it out. The squabs are ugly, a pink mass of tangled heads, naked and blind, but they grow fast and within a week are taking fish as big as those their parents eat. Their quills show as dark spikes under their skin and, after 14 days, the feathers completely enclosed in these waxy sheaths have broken through their skin.

The young kingfishers queue for their food, the hungriest ones at the front of the chamber, facing the tunnel, and the others asleep at the back. From the first days they call incessantly for food, especially when they hear the parent approach, croaking in the tunnel to attract their attention. All excreta is aimed down the tunnel which soon becomes filthy and slippery, and the parents need to bathe on leaving the nest. This may be two or three quick dips in the stream whilst still in flight or a full bathe if the parents have finished feeding for a while. At three weeks old the young are full feathered and spend much of their time preening and stretching their wings. They are duller than their parents with shorter black bills and black feet. Between 24 and 26 days they leave the nest of their own accord scattering up and down the streams and sometimes joining up in twos and threes. They will attempt to fish for themselves on the day they leave the nest though their parents will continue to feed them until they are good at fishing. There is, however, a high mortality rate through drowning.

There is a second brood if the first brood has failed, sometimes a third. In late summer and early autumn the parents drive the youngsters out of their territory to seek a territory of their own, some even going down to the estuaries to winter.

The North American Belted kingfisher *Megaceryle alcyon*, 13 in (33 cm) has habits similar to those of the Common kingfisher. This blue-grey bird has a belt across its white chest and has a slight crest. A common sight is to see the Belted kingfisher perched high upon telegraph posts and wires along the roadside ditches. The Texas kingfisher *Chloroceryle americana* ranges southwards from Mexico and is very similar to the crested Amazon kingfisher *C. amazona*, 11 in (28 cm) whose brilliant green upperparts contrast with its white underparts. The male is distinguished by his chestnut breast. These birds live along the tropical jungle streams.

The largest kingfisher is the Giant African kingfisher *M. maxima*, 18 in (45 cm). It is grey speckled with a chestnut breast. The Pied kingfisher *C. rudis* is common south of the Sahara. It hovers at a great height and drops like a stone on its prey, a favourite food being crayfish which it batters before swallowing. Its plumage is black and white. Among the Forest kingfishers are the inland kingfishers of the genus *Halcyon*. The Grey hooded kingfisher *H. lemocephala*, 7 in (18 cm), with a striking red beak, has a brilliant cobalt and turquoise back and chestnut underparts, and lives on beetles, grasshoppers and small reptiles. Another inland kingfisher is the Striped kingfisher *H. chelicuti* which nests in ready-made holes and will often evict swallows from their nests under the eaves. Some of these Forest kingfishers never go near the water but feed in the forests and on the savannahs catching insects, small mammals, amphibians, and reptiles. The Malachite crested kingfisher *Corythornis cristatus*, a very common African species, is also one of the smallest, being 4½ in (11·5 cm) long. It lives on flies, water invertebrates and small fish.

New Zealand has only one kingfisher, the yellow Sacred kingfisher *H. sancta*, which also occurs in Australia. Also in Australia, the Forest kingfisher *H. macleyi*, an insect eater, nests in termite nests on the sides of eucalyptus trees. Best known in Australia is the kookaburra *Dacelo gigas*, 17 in (43 cm), whose diet of snakes and lizards makes it popular amongst the bushmen, though it loses its good name by robbing farmyards of chicks and ducklings. Besides the name of 'Laughing jackass', from its human-like laughing voice, it is also called the 'Bushman's clock', as its weird laughing notes can be heard regularly as it goes to its tree-top roost at dusk and again at dawn. Picture on page 1059. Widely distributed with about 50 known local races is one of the noisiest species, the White collared kingfisher (*H. chloris*), 8 in. (20 cm). It has brilliant turquoise upperparts and white underparts. It ranges from the Red Sea to Samoa, where it frequents the mangrove swamps and coastlines. It is often mistaken for the smaller Sacred kingfisher which fishes the coral beaches and mangrove inlets in the winter, but goes south to Australia to nest inland.

The greatest numbers of kingfishers are to be found in Southeast Asia, the most elegant being the Racquet-tailed kingfisher *Tanysiptera galatae*, found from the Moluccas to northeast Australia. It hunts the forest floors amongst the decayed leaves for centipedes and lizards. Living on the dry uplands of India is the White-throated kingfisher *H. smynensis*, 11 in (28 cm), which has a scarlet bill, as has the Stork-billed kingfisher *Pelargopsis capensis*, 14 in (35 cm), a fish-eating bird which also catches frogs, crabs, lizards, and insects, as well as robbing other birds' nests of the young. Another inland kingfisher is the Ruddy kingfisher, of whom the Japanese say that it is so astonished by its own reflection in the water that it cannot drink, so it is always thirsty and on sunny days it is continually calling for rain. There are little gems among the smaller kingfishers of the genus *Ceyx* which have only two toes in front and one behind. One of them is the Indian three-toed kingfisher *C. erithacus* 5 in (13 cm). They eat small fish, amphibians, Crustacea and insects. The Shoe-billed kingfisher *Clytoceyx rex* of the New Guinea forests differs from all the others, having a flattened bill with which it digs for earthworms. FAMILY: Alcedinidae, ORDER: Coraciiformes, CLASS: Aves.   R.E.

KINGLET, a small warbler-like bird of North America related to the European *goldcrest. There are two species, the Golden-crowned kinglet *Regulus sapatra* and the Ruby-crowned kinglet *R. calendula*.

KING SNAKES, North American nonvenomous snakes of the genus *Lampropeltis*, that range from a little over 2 ft (60 cm) to 6 ft (180 cm). The Eastern king snake *Lampropeltis getulus* is one of the largest and has a wide distribution over much of the eastern

King snakes owe their name to their habit of eating other snakes, killing them by constriction.

United States. It occurs in several races or subspecies which may be recognized by minor differences in the colour pattern and the numbers of scales on the underside. It is strikingly coloured, usually black with numerous small yellow spots. King snakes are constrictors and their food includes a wide variety of small mammals and lizards, but it is commonly smaller snakes, including rattlesnakes, to whose venom they are immune. FAMILY: Colubridae, ORDER: Squamata, CLASS: Reptilia.

KINKAJOU, or 'Honey bear' *Potos flavus,* South American member of the raccoon family Procyonidae which is almost exclusively arboreal. Living in forests from Mexico to Brazil, this agile climber is a long, low-bodied animal the forelegs of which are shorter than the hind ones. The most outstanding feature is the prehensile tail which serves as a fifth grip, when moving cautiously through the tree tops. The only other carnivore to share this trait is the binturong, an East Asian relation of the civets, genets and mongooses. Cat-sized, kinkajous measure $31\frac{1}{2}$–$44\frac{1}{2}$ in (81–113 cm) overall, the tail being at least as long as the body, and weigh from 3–6 lb (1·4–2·7 kg). The ears are small, placed low on either side of the round head in line with the dark,

sparkling eyes. General coat colour varies from golden yellow to brown and the fur's texture is soft and woolly. Kinkajous are sometimes confused with olingos (*Bassaricyon*) but can be distinguished as the olingo's tail is ringed and bushy whereas that of the kinkajou is short-haired and uniformly

An agile climber, the kinkajou uses its prehensile tail to advantage.

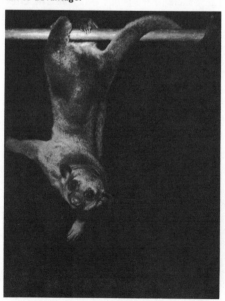

coloured. Further, the kinkajou is stocky with a broad head while the slender olingo has a pointed snout. Finally, unlike this other South American procyonid, kinkajous are not gregarious. During their nocturnal forays, they travel singly or, during the breeding season, in pairs. They sleep in elevated tree crevices and, when disturbed during the day, hiss and spit loudly. When cornered they will inflict painful stab wounds with their grooved canines and scratch with their powerful claws.

Favourite food items include fruit, such as bananas and pulpy citrous fruits, but a variety of insects and even bird nestlings are also eaten. Kinkajou 'troops' have been observed, on occasion, congregating in ripe fruit trees until the supply is depleted but, at dawn, each one returns to its nest separately. A particular adaptation to the frugivorous diet is a very long tongue, used to lick sticky tropical fruits which are held between the forepaws. It is possible that insects under bark are also retrieved in this way.

Although very little is known about the breeding habits in the wild, kinkajous have been born in zoos between May and September after a three month gestation period. Usually only one cub, very rarely two, can be found in the leaf-lined nest until the eyes open ten days after birth. The mother may carry the offspring cross-wise under her abdomen, a method common to many arboreal animals, which is perhaps an explanation of the low litter size. Two months later the cub can follow the female up and down trees and use its prehensile tail. Kinkajous are reputed to make endearing pets when obtained young but, because of their strictly nocturnal habits, may become irascible with age when awakened during the day. Adapting well to captive conditions in zoos, several individuals have lived over 20 years but the more usual life-span is 14–15 years. FAMILY: Procyonidae, ORDER: Carnivora, CLASS: Mammalia. N.D.

KINORHYNCHA, a class of small worm-like creatures related to the nematodes or roundworms, but differing from these in having the body divided into segments or zonites. These zonites are not equivalent to the segments of annelids and arthropods, but are restricted to the superficial layers of the body. The head is retractile and bears girdles of spines. When the head is retracted the spines are also hidden. The mouth opens at the end of the protruded head and sometimes projects forwards as a small cone bearing a girdle of spines, the oral styles. Behind the head is a flexible zonite called the neck. This allows retraction of the head, and in some kinorhynchs it bears a circle of small plates which seal off the retracted head from the outside world. Behind the neck are the trunk zonites, which vary in number up to 12.

Brahminy kite *Haliastur indus* frequents rubbish heaps in India to feed on mice, lizards and insects gathering there.

These zonites often bear spines, particularly at the sides. The hind end of the trunk may also bear spines, often at the sides, but some forms also have a single long spine originating from the middle of the last zonite.

There are no cilia in the kinorhynchs. They do not swim, but creep about using the spines of the head to pull themselves along. The head is protruded and the spines dig into the surface over which the animal is moving. The trunk muscles then contract and shorten the body, pulling the hind end forwards. This also results in partial retraction of the head. The cycle begins again with a full protrusion of the head.

The internal anatomy shows some resemblances to that of the nematodes. The digestive tract has a muscular pharynx and a simple tubular intestine. The excretory system consists of a pair of flame bulbs (see excretion), each with its own duct opening to the outside on the 11th zonite. The nervous system is surprisingly complex for such a small animal. The main mass of nervous tissue forms a ring around the front of the pharynx. From this ring a chain of ganglia extends backwards underneath the gut. In addition there are two lines of nervous tissue at the sides of the body and one down the mid-dorsal line. A few kinorhynchs have simple eyes, but apart from these the only known sense organs are the bristles and spines extending from the sides of the trunk zonites. These projections contain extensions from nerve cells and are presumed to be sensitive to contact.

The sexes of the kinorhynchs are separate but the details of fertilization and egg laying are not known. The earliest known larva has an undivided body and no head spines, although there are three or four large spines at the hind end of the body. The gut of the early larva is also simple, without the muscular pharynx of the adult, and lacking an anus. The further development of this simple larva involves the gradual segmentation of the body and an elaboration of the gut. A remarkable feature of this development is that the larva moults several times, casting off the old cuticle after a new one has formed underneath.

All the known kinorhynchs live in the sea, usually in the surface layers of mud. None of them exceeds 1 mm in length. They appear to feed on fine detritus and algae which are sucked in through the mouth by the muscular pharynx. In contrast to the rotifers and the gastrotrichs the kinorhynchs appear to be relatively long-lived, some individuals having lived in laboratory cultures for a year. PHYLUM: Aschelminthes.   Ja.G.

KITES, a supposedly primitive but very varied, successful and beautiful group of birds of prey, world-wide, but especially developed in America and Australia. The name 'kite' is properly applied to the Old World Fork-tailed kites *Milvus* spp and near relatives (*Lophoictinia, Hamirostra* and *Haliastur*), but is extended to include 25 other species in 13 genera. These vary from the large insectivorous Honey buzzards (*Pernis* and *Henicopernis*) to the tiny insectivorous Pearl kite *Gampsonyx swainsoni,* and include such specialized birds as the Bat hawk *Machaerhamphus alcinus* and the American

Swallow-tailed kite *Elanoides forficatus.* Two thirds of all kites are mainly or entirely insectivorous or feed on invertebrates such as snails. Only a few eat animals larger than mice.

Kites are classified in three groups: 1 the pernine kites including the Honey buzzards, Cuckoo falcons (*Aviceda*), Grey-headed kites (*Leptodon*), Hook-billed kite (*Chondrohierax*), American Swallow-tailed kite and Bat hawk. 2 Elanine kites including Black-shouldered, White-tailed and Letter-winged kites (*Elanus*), African Swallow-tailed kite *Chelictinia riocourii* and Pearl kite. 3 Milvine kites, including Snail kites *Rostrhamus,* Double-toothed kites *Harpagus,* Plumbeous and Mississippi kites *Ictinia,* the Square-tailed kite *Lophoictinia,* the Australian Black-breasted buzzard-kite *Hamirostra melanosternon,* the Old World Fork-tailed kites *Milvus* and the Brahminy kite and Whistling eagle *Haliastur.* The pernine group is separated from the rest by the lack of a bony eye-shield, and milvine kites have the basal and second joint of the middle toe fused, a character which allies them to Sea eagles *Haliaetus* spp. Between these groups there are examples of parallel specialization. For instance the Snail and Hook-billed kites both feed on snails and the Plumbeous kite is much more like *Elanus* spp and its hunting habits than it is like *Milvus* spp.

The Old World Fork-tailed kites include the Red kite *M. milvus* and the Black kite *M. migrans.* The latter is widespread in the warmer parts of the Old World and is probably the most abundant and successful medium-sized raptor in the world, being omnivorous, aggressive and largely commensal with man. It is migratory, both within and from beyond the tropics. The Red kite is larger, somewhat more specialized, less adaptable and aggressive, but was the species that formerly scavenged the London streets.

The largest and most powerful kite is the Australian Buzzard-kite *Hamirostra*. It resembles in general habits buzzards *Buteo* spp, but is also reported to be a tool-user (one of four known examples among birds) breaking emu's eggs by dropping stones upon them (*cf* Egyptian vulture). Large kites are most common in Australia and the East, other large species include the Whistling eagle *Haliastur sphenurus* and the Brahminy kite *H. indus,* sacred in Indian mythology.

The elanine kites (*Elanus, Chelictinia*) and the Plumbeous and Mississippi kites *Ictinia* hunt insects and rodents in open grassy country or over forest. *Elanus* and *Chelictinia* hover very gracefully like kestrels (*Falco* spp). *Elanus* is not large, but for its size is a more powerful predator than most kites, feeding on Grass rats.

More specialized kites include the Hook-billed and Snail kites and the Honey buzzards, which dig out nests of wasps and bees with their feet, often disappearing underground in the process. The European Honey buzzard *Pernis apivorus* migrates to Africa in winter, and is secretive and difficult to watch both in its summer nesting woods and African winter quarters. The Cuckoo falcons *Aviceda* spp, so called because they have a tooth on the mandible, are not closely related to falcons but are small, inoffensive, insectivorous species of tropical woodland and forest. The South American Double-toothed

kites *Harpagus* also possess the mandibular tooth, the purpose of which is obscure. The Bat hawk *Machaerhamphus* is one of the few really predatory kites, hunting bats and swifts with rapid falcon-like flight. It catches all its prey in half an hour or so at dusk, and is reluctant to fly by day, but is not truly nocturnal. The American Swallow-tailed kite *Elanoides* is perhaps the most beautiful of the world's birds of prey, the ultimate perfection of graceful sustained flight, with the forked tail opening and closing like scissors as it courses over the country. In fact kites as a group, although supposedly primitive, include some of the most remarkable of all raptor species. FAMILY: Accipitridae, ORDER: Falconiformes, CLASS: Aves.   L.B.

KITE'S VOICE. According to one of Aesop's fables kites once had beautiful voices but that, on hearing horses neighing, they were filled with envy and tried to imitate them. As a result they lost their ability to sing yet were unable to learn to neigh. Both Red and Black kites have a drawn-out squealing or whinnying call that is heard particularly in spring, and it is presumably this horse-like call that gave rise to the fable.

KITTIWAKE *Rissa tridactyla,* a medium-sized, lightly-built gull of the open sea, differing from the more typical gulls in a number of respects. The kittiwake is more oceanic than the other gulls, being found over the open sea outside the breeding season rather than near the coasts. During the nesting period it frequents rocky coasts where it nests on precarious cliff ledges. The average length is 16 in (40 cm) and the adult looks like a rather dainty version of the more

common gull species. The wing tips, however, are entirely black, not having the white 'mirrors' seen in many other species, and the legs also are black. The bill is yellow. The plumage is basically grey above and white beneath. Juveniles, however, have a striking plumage-pattern with a black neck band and tail tip and a long, black shallow 'V' stretching the length of each wing.

The kittiwake is widely distributed around coasts in the northern hemisphere including those of Britain, Scandinavia, Iceland, Greenland, Labrador, Alaska and eastern Asia, but with very large gaps in the distribution. Their oceanic habit results in considerable wanderings and birds ringed in Britain have been recovered in Labrador.

Kittiwakes feed on marine organisms, principally invertebrates, which they usually take by dropping to the surface of the water. Sometimes, however, they will dive like terns from the air and at other times from the surface. They commonly follow ships.

Except during the breeding season kittiwakes tend to be solitary birds but like other gulls they breed in colonies. The species is unusual amongst gulls in nesting on very small projections and ledges on steep cliffs. This is probably an anti-predator device, kittiwake broods apparently being less subject to predation than those of other gulls because many predators are unable to reach the cliff ledges. E. Cullen has listed 25 characteristics of the kittiwake which are adaptations to cliff-nesting and in which it differs from other gulls. Some of these peculiarities involve relaxations of the anti-predator behaviour found in other gulls. For example kittiwakes rarely utter an alarm call, predators are not attacked, the chicks are not camouflaged and the easily seen egg shells are not carried away. Precautions against falling off the cliff include the development of strong claws, a deep nest-cup, two eggs only and the chicks' habit of staying relatively immobile, facing the wall. Even in fighting and mating there are departures from more typical gull behaviour, connected with the lack of space on the cliff ledges. The nesting is unusual in that mud is trampled to make a nest platform, the nest is guarded even when empty, to prevent other kittiwakes usurping it and nest sanitation is improved by incomplete regurgitation of food when feeding young. In complete regurgitation the food is dropped into the nest for the chicks to pick up. In incomplete regurgitation the parent holds it in the mouth for the chick to extract. Furthermore the parents do not seem to recognize chicks individually and do not have a special food call. Through a study of its peculiarities, the kittiwake has enabled us to see the nature of other gulls more clearly. FAMILY: Laridae, ORDER: Charadriiformes, CLASS: Aves.
P.M.D.

Red kites at nest with young. Kites formerly scavenged the streets of European towns.